FROM LANGUAGE TO COMMUNICATION

COMMUNICATION
TEXTBOOK SERIES

Jennings Bryant—Editor

Language and Discourse Processes
Donald Ellis—Advisor

TRACY • Understanding Face-to-Face
Interaction: Issues Linking
Goals and Discourse

ELLIS • From Language to Communication

FROM LANGUAGE TO COMMUNICATION

Donald G. Ellis
University of Hartford

LEA LAWRENCE ERLBAUM ASSOCIATES, PUBLISHERS
1992   Hillsdale, New Jersey   Hove and London

Lawrence Erlbaum Associates, Inc., Publishers
365 Broadway
Hillsdale, New Jersey 07642

Library of Congress Cataloging-in-Publication Data

Ellis, Donald G.
From language to communication / by Donald G. Ellis.
p.   cm. — (Communication textbook series. Language and
discourse processes)
Includes bibliographical references and index.
ISBN 0-8058-0022-0. — ISBN 0-8058-1071-4 (pbk.)
1. Communication.   2. Language and languages.   I. Title.
II. Series.
P91.E38   1992
302.2—dc20

91–27645
CIP

Printed in the United States of America
10 9 8 7 6 5 4 3 2 1

For

Florence and David Ellis

and

Karen, David, and Alexandra

Contents

Chapter 6   Coherence and Global Organization   105

Chapter 7   Coherence and Local Organization   139

Chapter 8   Communication Codes   179

Introduction

Donald G. Ellis
University of Hartford

There is a story in Judges 12:1–7 about the Gileadites who held the fords of the Jordan river against the Ephraimites. Whenever someone from Ephraim tried to cross the river the Gileadites would say, "Pronounce the word *Shibboleth*." If the person said "*sibboleth*," not being able to pronounce the word correctly, he was seized and slain by the fords of the Jordan. Forty-two thousand Ephraimites fell. If nothing else, the story certainly demonstrates the practical importance of language. People draw conclusions about how others use language to communicate, and they act on those conclusions! But language is more than a social indicator. Language is the toolbox of communication.

This book is about language and its relationship to human communication. It is preoccupied with essential principles of language and the subtle ways that language is responsible for creating and sustaining social interaction and meaning. The book is designed for advanced undergraduate and beginning graduate students who are interested in learning more about the relationship between language and communication. Yet the volume should be useful to anyone who is pursuing an introduction to these matters, or as a companion text to others that might be used to study communication, psychology, sociology, or linguistics.

I am concerned in this volume with issues in language of many kinds, but not all kinds. It is my fervent conviction that language is the fundamental tool of communication; that language and a linguistic system are definitionally a part of the communication process. This book offers a current sample of the significant issues in language and communication. Writing a book such as this requires the author to assume that his vision is an acceptable lens through which many others can see a field. As such, I should say something more about my own vision of communication, and how that vision influences what follows.

Communication is a very misunderstood discipline. The term *communication* can conjure up images of such diversity as telephones, computers, television, radio, public speeches, therapy sessions, and intimate relations. And all of these are in one fundamental way or another communicative. But each has something else in common. Because each is communicative in nature *it is concerned with using language to constitute and interpret reality.* The technology of computers, television, and telephones makes it possible for language to reach larger numbers of us more quickly. New communication technology means we can now store and retrieve the mountains of information that is packaged in language. But whether a message is fashioned from the grunts of two cave men arguing over a bone, or finds its way into your living room after passing through computers and a short voyage in space, that message uses some symbolic form to establish meaning.

My view of language in general and communication in particular is that segmenting it is the best way to understand it. This motivated my decision to define and organize the chapters the way I have. It is possible to draw some sharp distinctions between some issues of language and language use, more specifically between language use and grammar, and form and strategy. There is on the one hand a clear need for people to communicate and express thoughts and perceptions of the world. But on the other hand principles of grammar and language structure are only remotely concerned with communication. Many sections of chapters 1 through 4 describe issues in language structure. And chapters 5, 6, 7, and particularly 8 are more shaped by concerns for accomplishing the act of communication.

Another way to say this is that language is form and strategy. The *form* of language is of patterns, rules, and structures that are the scaffolding on which we build messages. These structures range from phonological, morphological, and syntactic rules (chapters 2 and 3), to sequence structures and rules of initiating and terminating a conversation (chapter 7), to larger structures that allow entire discourses to cohere such as propositional analysis and story structures. A good portion of this book (chapters 5, 6, and 7) is devoted to these principles.

The *strategic* aspect of language use, on the other hand, assumes that communicators use language for a purpose or to achieve a goal. All language is pragmatic and strategic in that it is used to accomplish something; language directs people to some selected reality. There are also rules, principles, and patterns of strategic language use. These rules are not inviolate but they act as tools and resources that language users can draw on. Strategic rules can be adhered to or violated and in either case there is some interesting communicative consequence. Sections of

Chapters 4, 5, 6, and 7 pertain to strategic language. But Chapter 8 is most completely devoted to a theory of language use. It outlines a concept of practical codes that communicators use to express individuated meaning.

Unfortunately there is no unified theory of language and communication and I am afraid I make little progress toward that goal in this volume. Instead, I present language and communication as a series of topics that have some connections. I have organized the entire text as a movement from specific issues in language (linguistic traditions) to topics more generally concerned with coherence and orderliness of communicative texts. Hence, the title *From Language to Communication*. In one sense the title is misleading because I do not mean to imply that language is logically prior to communication or can be separated from it. On the contrary, I believe that communication is the *only* function of language and even abstract linguistic structures serve the communicative nature of language (see chapter 8). Nevertheless, the title reflects the organization and presentation of topics in the book and is consistent with my decisions about how to segment the subject matter.

Textuality is an important concept in this book because it is achieved when language is alive and performing some function or doing a job in a context; that is, when language is being truly communicative. I do not focus in this book at all on social psychological issues in language. My concern is not to examine attitudes and perceptions that accompany particular language that is used by certain social groups or within certain institutions; I do not discuss the relationship between language and social categories such as sex, class, demographics, or regional variations. Rather, I focus on discourse and the structure of texts. A text can be an object in its own right and an instance of meaning. It is a product of the resources and choices we make during the communication process. I try to provide some flavor for the work in these areas with particular emphasis on issues in coherence.

I believe that a book of this nature should present the current important and interesting thinking on a subject even if the author is less interested in some topics. I have tried to summarize and organize the ideas in many areas as accurately and as interestingly as possible. I use data illustratively in many places and have gone to considerable effort in some instances to clarify issues.

Some of my colleagues will disagree with a few of the choices I have made. Chapter 1, for example, is an essay on the history of thinking about language and somewhat tangential to principles of communication. Moreover, chapters 2, 3, and 4 are an overview of issues in linguistics, cognition, and semantics and they too are a step removed from the primary communicative experience. But each of these subjects comprise the tools of communication; they are the carpentry on which texts are built. *From Language to Communication* is not a complete treatment of either language or communication. Nor is it a highly specified analysis of a limited topic. Rather, it emphasizes the recent tradition of language and discourse studies. The book represents my desire for students to have an understanding of the relationship between language and communication. I will have satisfied my own goals if a reader, on completion of this book, feels as if he or she has a sense of key issues in the history and nature of language, and how language works to stitch together a coherent text that is an instance of social meaning.

For me, this book represents various paths along the intellectual route I have been traveling. I have encountered many helpful people and institutions along the way. My colleagues in the Department of Communication at the University of Hartford are always a source of discussion and pleasure. I would also like to thank the university for a sabbatical in the Spring of 1990 which allowed me to complete the book. Jennings Bryant and all of the people at Lawrence Erlbaum Associates have been helpful, supportive, and tolerant. Bill Villaume of Auburn University read a draft of the manuscript and offered valuable insights and suggestions. And the Stockbridge Group (you know who you are) has been a pleasant source of discussion and criticism all of which has found its way into various places in this book.

Above all, my family deserves special attention, especially my wife Karen who is the most talented communicator I know, and David and Alexandra who simply communicate.

The Nature of Language: From Magic to Semantics

This book is essentially an argument that language is the primary mechanism of experience. Moreover, language is assumed to be in the first instance communicative. Traditional approaches to the study of language, and formal linguistics in particular, have separated the language system from the communicative experience. I suppose it is possible to call this book a functional approach to language. Although the perspective is conceptually akin to functionalism, I avoid discussion of *functionalism* as a philosophical position in the social sciences. When scholars such as Ernst Cassirer and Kenneth Burke ruminate about the nature of human knowledge and intelligence they find it impossible to avoid associating human action with purposeful (i.e., functional) human behavior. Chomsky's contributions to linguistics notwithstanding, the foundations of language are in social life.

The study of language straddles the line between logic and sociologic; it relies on, to borrow a classical metaphor, both the closed fist of logic and the open hand of culture. Natural language—that is, the meaningful sounds uttered by humans as opposed to artificial or specially created symbol systems—is both a rigorous system that is susceptible to mathematical modeling, and a delicate system that demands intimate knowledge of language users and their communities. Although it is somewhat simplistic, the approaches to language in the past 50 years have generally agreed to this distinction—functional versus structural. The structuralist has been concerned with language as an autonomous system of sounds that have clear referents for their meaning. A structural linguist, epitomized by Noam Chomsky (1965) and others, is concerned with language universals and those aspects of language that can be shown to be invariant and not associated with individual or social idiosyncrasies. The functionalist, perhaps most represented by sociolinguists such as Dell Hymes (1974), recoil at the thought of language separated from social use. Sociolinguists maintain that language cannot be separated from a community of users, and that "organized diversity" is more important than the search for linguistic universals.

The title "From Language to Communication" is intended to imply the mutuality of both "language" and "communication." Neither has the more vital role in studying social interaction. In fact, the definitions of each imply the other; that is, any definition of language must include a communicative function, and it is equally impossible to define communication without reference to a linguistic component. But it is communication that provides the more general frame of reference. It is language that serves communication. Language is only useful or practical to the extent that it ministers to communicative goals. The aim of understanding a communicative system in any culture or species is to clarify and keep in view the relationships between messages and contexts, and not divorce them. Studies of social life make little sense if they are separated from the communicative systems that establish them, just as examining language and communication is futile if they are separated from the contexts and situations that drive them. Let us begin with some orientation toward the historical treatment of language.

ORIGINS OF LANGUAGE

Early theories of language were preoccupied with its origins. Before the 18th century, theories attributed the origins of language to divine intervention. Language was considered a gift from God. Most cultures have a story or myth about the creation of language and the nature of the first language. In the Judeo-Christian tradition Hebrew was the language of the Garden of Eden. Andreas Kemke, a 17th-century Swedish philologist, boldly claimed that Swedish was spoken in the Garden of Eden. Other cultures have creation stories that include the origin of language. The Egyptians are the oldest race and maintain that Egyptian was the original language. One of their ancient stories is about a ruler who removed children from their home at birth and placed them with shepherds who were ordered not to speak to babies. The story has it that the children spontaneously uttered Egyptian words at about the age of 2. This presumably proved that Egyptian was the original language.

All cultures have a language origin story. Although the facts of the story are irrelevant and certainly apocryphal, the existence of the stories and the elements they share are interesting. The sun goddess, Amaterasu, was the creator of language in Japan. In China the Son of Heaven was T'ien-tzu and he gave language and the power of words to man. Creation myths almost invariably have a god from the heavens or the god of light both creating man and giving him speech powers. These tendencies are recurring in the creation myths of the American Indians. Michabo was the god of light in Algonquian mythology, and the culture god of the Iroquois was the god of the dawn. From these collections of stories and myths come reports of similar experiences and behaviors. It is possible to interpret the myths as saying that language accompanied reason. The metaphor of light is typically associated with "knowledge" and "understanding" and it seems to be no accident that theories of the origin of language would accompany beliefs about when intelligent human behavior began. It must have been impossible for the ancients to conceive of human life without language so language must have coincided with the birth of human beings.

Plato marks the beginning of the serious considerations about language. Early myths, including the Genesis narrative, simply stated the fact that language existed and a god gave it to man. In Genesis it was the power to name things that God bestowed upon us. The author of the Genesis narrative provided no analysis or exposition of the history and nature of language. Plato, on the other hand, accepted the facts of language as given and then asked: "How did language come about?" or "What was the principle that guided the making of the first words?" Plato's approach was radical for its time and his analysis in the *Cratylus* is a combination of philosophy and science. Although Plato and the Greeks were somewhat vague about the origin of language, at least they were not mystical about it. Socrates, who does the talking about language in the *Cratylus*, reports that some words were not of Greek origin and must have been borrowed from their barbarian neighbors. The word *barbaros* in Greek implies "babbler" and certainly suggests what the Greeks must have thought about their own language compared to others. Socrates reasons that because barbarians were an older race that came before the Greeks (more primitive of course), it would be necessary to trace these original forms in order to do a complete analysis and account of the language. Socrates was on the right track!

The *Cratylus* is an intriguing work by Plato and became the foundation for future arguments about the nature and origin of language. In the play, Cratylus is the character who argues tenaciously that the names for things are naturally correct. That there is a natural and fundamental relationship between a thing and the name for it. Cratylus continues by insisting that knowledge of things is the same as knowledge of names and "lying" is impossible. Socrates plays devil's advocate by maintaining that "naming" is a special art and responsive to human desires. Socrates points to the great variation in languages and asks how the

differences could have come about. But Cratylus is unimpressed and insists that
these differences are due to unimportant variations in societies and these have
nothing to do with the truth function of language. Socrates skewers Cratylus by
asking: If knowledge of things is through names, how could the first name giver
have known anything? Cratylus resorts to the same answer given by many before
him and after. He claims that the first names for things were given by a power
greater than ours.

The *Cratylus* was important because it posed a question worth asking at the
time. It marked the first time that the conventional nature of language was
treated as a serious possibility. In many ways the question of "nature" versus
"convention" is immature. Some, as did Cratylus and Hermogenes, make the
illogical leap that we know truth if we know names; or, if names are arbitrary, there
is no truth. Such is simply not the case and even Socrates warns Cratylus and
Hermogenes that there are bigger and more important questions. Interestingly,
Aristotle reports later that Cratylus grew old and became convinced of the
naturalness of change and abandoned the use of language altogether. When asked
a question he would only point to things.

Later Theories

Rousseau's essay on the *Origin of Languages* can be considered a marker that
separates ancients theories from more modern ones. Until Rousseau, most
theories of language were still under the control of Christian Europe and divine
origin was the prevailing account. But although Rousseau identified a number of
themes and issues pertaining to language, he struggled with the ultimate question. He wrote that he was "frightened" by the problems one encounters when
attempting to show that language was born of human means. Rousseau was more
interested in the practical needs of man than in language itself. He wanted to
know how language changed as a function of societies and governments. His
essay is on the origins of languages, not language. But even though his observations are sometimes inconsistent he offered a number of important insights.

Language, according to Rousseau, was born out of passion. He did not maintain
that God "gave" language to man, rather that language emerged from the cries
and vocalizations of primitive man. Primitive language was more expressive and
emotional than instrumental. It utilized all of the senses including gesture and
movement; it was rhythmic, sensuous, and figurative. Rousseau believed that
man had a natural state, which could be associated with primitive man, but
that this natural state was prior to social and conventional man. It was language
that had become man's first social institution. Language followed the natural state
and must, therefore, have been derived from our native passions. Rousseau was
continually frustrated by what he thought was an unsolvable problem. How could

we discover truth when man was constantly changing and trying to better himself. If man changed then there were no permanent truths. Language was an accomplice in this dilemma because language was changing. Rousseau worked to strip away the artificial in man in an effort to discover his nature. Language posed a particular problem because of its complexity. It had lost its original coherence and beauty as the generations passed and language became more conventional, syntactic, and rule bound. History, law, and art, according to Rousseau, were originally sung and announced publicly in instinctive and spontaneous ritual. Now that the law and history were codified there was a loss of innocence and public unity. Even written language fell under Rousseau's critical stance. Writing, according to Rousseau, caused true expression to be sacrificed for precision and language that was commonplace and undistinctive. He agreed with Plato who wrote in the *Cratylus* that language was dangerous because it drew attention away from seeking the truth of things.

Herder. Rousseau clarified issues confronting the nature and origins of language, but he erected more obstacles than bridges. In the end Rousseau, as did Socrates, warned that the question of the origin of language may not be the most useful question to ask. A German scholar named Johann Gottfried Herder deserves very special attention when considering the history of language. Herder offered the classic statement on the question and it has permanent scientific value. A mere 22 years after Rousseau's *Origin of Languages*, Herder won a prize for an essay called "*Treatise on the Origin of Language*." In the treatise Herder responded to issues raised by numerous others in the decade before its publication. Herder's essay answers the questions posed by the Berlin Academy when they announced the contest: Could men have invented language? If so, how did they do it?

It is important to remember that the scientific work of Darwin and Lamarck, and the German philosophy and science of Kant and Geothe establish the historical context for Herder's classic essay on language. Kant in 1755 explained that the present world was the result of a long and gradual evolution through natural causation. Herder was a student of Kant's and carried forward his ideas of evolution and unity. Language was examined as a natural evolutionary process and the question of divine origin was not worth asking because it was not an answer—on the contrary, it required an explanation itself. Herder's essay presented the arguments that follow.

His first argument is quite elegant and, more importantly, established communication as the basis for language development. Men in their animal states expressed themselves by cries and howls that were physiological responses. Yet these were acts of self-expression and had no communicative value beyond the individual making the sounds. But this self-expression preceded language because it gave some form or structure to inward feelings. This form was represented in sound and presumably developed into a cognitive component. When this external form (sound representing feeling) was directed outward it became communication. Language developed as an evolutionary process where simplicity gave way to complexity through adaptation, change, and natural selection. Language and reason were born when man isolated an object and held a conception of that object in his mind. The next step was to associate sounds with the object and concept.

The second aspect of Herder's argument begins with the presumption that because only man possesses language, theories of language should include something about the differences between man and other animals. Man, wrote Herder, does not have the same instinctive nature as animals. Animals have more highly developed and sophisticated instincts, but they are focused on a very narrow range of experience. So a bee is quite skilled at extracting honey from a flower and building a hive but that is all it can do. It has no *use* for language. An animal such as man can engage in a greater variety of activities; his senses take in everything around him. Man is inferior to other animals with respect to instinctual capacity but can direct activity toward multiple points in his environment.

Herder identified the specific nature of man as reflectiveness. Man is capable of thinking and cognition to such a degree that he can "think about thinking." Language was not invented it was discovered. Humans confront a sea of chaotic sensations and impressions and their reflectiveness allows them to identify objects and to describe characteristics of that object. Where natural cries and howls were the internal becoming external, language is taking the external and making it internal. The outer world is mapped onto the human psyche. A child learning language has his or her attention drawn to objects but a parent does not "supply" reflectiveness or linguistic ability. Herder placed the origins and purposes of language squarely in the realm of communication. Language is the ordering principle of the mind and becomes the medium of communication. Herder wrote:

> Yet I cannot imagine the first human thought nor the first reflective judgement without at least trying to create a dialogue within my soul. And so the first human thought by its very nature prepares the way for the possibility of a dialogue with others. The first distinguishing mark (*Merkmal*) that I apprehend is a distinguishing word (*Merkwort*) for me and a communicating word (*Mitteilungswort*) for others. (cited in Stam, 1976, p. 124)

In the final part of the treatise Herder stated four principles of human nature, all of which pertain to the centrality of language. These principles also help explain differences and changes in language and how these differences and changes are natural. The first principle, briefly, is that man has freedom of thought and is thus dependent on language. Language is crucial because man has reflectiveness and not instincts. The second principle places man in the center of society; he needs the associations of others for physical and emotional sustenance and for these reasons language must always change and develop. The third principle is an extension of the second because it states that because all men cannot be in a single society there cannot be a single language. Languages must be flexible enough to accommodate the communication needs of a variety of social organizations. The final principle holds that because the human race developed from a single origin, all language and social groups are tied to a single stream of culture. Language and culture were invented progressively and, therefore, have historical and genetic commonalities.

Darwin and Muller. Herder's work stimulated critical response from all corners of philosophy and science. But the next significant turn in thinking about the history and origin of language came from Darwin. The essence of Herder's thinking about language was that it was a unique human capability derived from our advanced and sophisticated reasoning and abstractive abilities. But in 1871, Darwin published *The Descent of Man* and expanded the boundaries of arguments about language. Darwin challenged the notion that linguistic abilities were a special human gift and wrote that the distinctions between the human world and the animal world with respect to language were artificial and arbitrary. Darwin thought the difference between the language of man and the cries of animals was one of degree only. Humans had more distinct connotative meaning and precise articulation, but these were the extent of the differences. A dog, according to Darwin, who recognized his owner was employing symbolic capabilities, and a parrot was ample proof that animals could have articulatory virtuosity.

Darwin did acknowledge important differences between human speech and other forms of expression, but he did not see a distinct break in the evolutionary branches. He made the very wise and important distinction between the essential impulse of language and the varieties of articulation and conventionality. So linguistic ability was a native predisposition distinctive of human beings, but particular sounds and communicative uses were not part of this native predisposition. One question Darwin had to answer was that of the "original cause" of language. Where earlier theorists evoked divine agency or inherent nature, Darwin turned to the biological nature of humans. He thought it possible that the speech organs used for cries of emotion were capable of improving. But did improved speech organs influence intellectual development or did the brain improve speech organs? In the end, Darwin figured the influence was reciprocal and thereby placed the development of language in the evolutionary process. Darwin wrote that the evolutionary process endowed man with the capacity and inclination for language. Evolution, not God, gave birth to language.

It was not long before various extensions of Darwinian theory began to appear. Just as there were social Darwinists there were linguistic Darwinists who espoused the rule of the strong in matters of grammar and vocabulary. The fittest of the species and the language were bound to survive. Even Darwin wrote that some languages were dominant and would flourish, whereas others were doomed to extinction. "The survival or preservation of certain favored words in the struggle for existence," wrote Darwin, "is natural selection" (Darwin, 1899, p. 92).

Max Muller advanced most of the objections against Darwin. But he did it more from the mountain of authority than from the trail of logic. Muller was a professor of philology at Oxford and was simply enraptured with the unique linguistic capabilities of humans. He simply could not imagine that human language was anything but special. Muller's arguments were similar to Socrates' in that he proposed a special harmony between sound and meaning. But Muller was a fine stylist with a sarcastic wit to which he turned for most of his objections. He never really addresses issues raised by Darwin except by way of sarcasm and humorous examples that were entertaining but not very illuminating. Muller, however, was a strong proponent of linguistics as a physical science and not as a historical science. He thought that language should be the study of natural human processes such as sound production. This is an important perspective that begins to develop seriously in the 19th century. There was a growing interest in comparative phonology and more "sound laws" were discovered. Near the end of the 19th century there was a significant loss of interest in abstract and often mystical speculation about the origin and nature of language. Scholars were turning their attention to the technical work of studying language systems and making comparisons among languages.

Modern Theories: The Rise of Linguistics

If it is possible to identify a single year that marks the beginning of contemporary linguistic science, it is the year 1786. This is the year that Sir William Jones of the East India Company presented his famous paper establishing beyond a doubt that classical Indian Sanskrit was related to Greek, Latin, and Germanic languages. Although it was Muller who popularized the new scientific study of linguistics it was this earlier work with Sanskrit that formed the first stage in the systematic growth of historical and comparative linguistics. Moreover, European scholars now came into contact with Indian scholars who had a well-established tradition of linguistic scholarship. Near the end of the 18th century we have the new "comparative philology," as opposed to "classical philology," where the concern is with comparing one language with another. Classical philology was preoccupied with the origins of words. Although Sir William Jones wrote the definitive paper establishing the relationship between Sanskrit and European languages, others before him had noted relationships. The Italian merchant Filippo Sassetti reported similarities between Italian and Sanskrit as early as the 16th century. The word "snake," for example, was *serpe* in Italian and *sarpa* in

Sanskrit; seven was *sette* in Italian and *sapta* in Sanskrit; god was *dio* in Italian and *deva* in Sanskrit. But it was Jones who wrote the often quoted paragraph that asserted:

> The Sanskrit language, whatever be its antiquity, is of a wonderful structure; more perfect than the Greek, more copious than the Latin, and more exquisitely refined than either, yet bearing to both of them a stronger affinity, both in roots of verbs and in the forms of grammar, than could possibly have been produced by accident; so strong indeed, that no philologer could examine them all three, without believing them to have sprung from some common source, which, perhaps, no longer exists. (cited in Robbins, 1967, p. 134)

The early part of the 19th century was devoted to comparative linguistics. This was a turning point in the history of linguistics as a science because the scholarship increased in both sophistication and systematization. Much of the earlier work was fragmented and isolated. The new science of language was stimulated by the Indo-European hypothesis that predicted correspondences between European languages and those of India and Persia. There was the new science of *comparative grammar*, a term used by Friedrich Schlegel, and it was meant to be analogous to *comparative anatomy*. Biologists in the 18th century had met with success by going beyond simple descriptive classification into comparisons of more central dynamics of an organism. Biology had achieved deductive powers where a whole could be deduced from parts. Comparative linguists became more interested in the inner structure of a language and how a particular feature of a language functioned in terms of the whole. There was a transition from philology to linguistics and languages were studied in order to determine their own structure and place in historical development. Many thought the methods of comparative linguistics would result in the discovery of original language. But even in the face of tremendous successes reconstructing the roots of extant languages, the goal of discovering the origin of language was unreachable.

In 1808 Friedrich Schlegel published *On the Language and Wisdom of the Indians*—a significant work that not only introduced and expanded on the methods of comparative grammar, but stressed the importance of the "inner structure" of language; the genetic structure that could account for the historical development of the language. Previous linguistic classifications had compared words to note similarities and differences. But Schlegel warned that corresponding words in two languages only prove that there has been contact between speakers of the language, not that the two languages have an essential relationship. It was only grammatical structure and internal form that could lead to "deep" insights about language that would shed some light on genetic origins and historical developments. Schlegel wrote that some languages were *organic* in that they were natural. They sprang forth from pure native intelligence and their grammar and structure was complex and complete. They were flexional languages that developed specialized mechanisms for indicating tense and grammatical form. Changes in these languages represented growth and accommodation to the need for specific idiom but they were always clearly related to the prototype. These languages held the purity of ancient wisdom. *Mechanical* languages were thought to result from the barbaric cries of animals and Schlegel postulated that change in these languages was simply the result of annexing words. He thought that organic languages held the wisdom of primordial man. Interestingly, some scholars in the 19th century argued that the development of language was from simple to complex and sophisticated. But the ancient language of Sanskrit was as "complex" and complete as any 19th-century European language. Perhaps the history of language signifies a fall from original clarity and purity.

German scholarship dominated the 19th century. There was a flurry of activity in which historical linguistics met with many successes that formed the foundation of contemporary linguistics. Many believe that Rask, Grimm, and Bop are the founders of contemporary historical linguistics. Rasmus Rask was a Dane who concentrated on phonetics and formulated laws of sound change that allowed him to compare Germanic languages. He proved the similarity of many languages and fulfilled Schlegel's hopes for a systematic historical linguistics. Franz Bopp was a very rigorous scientist and a precursor of many contemporary linguists who eschew any cultural or philosophical presuppositions about language. Bopp's rigorous objectivism led to many successes in showing that Sanskrit was not the parent language of Greek and Latin; rather all three languages developed from a more original tongue, but Sanskrit was the nearest in structure to the protolanguage. Jakob Grimm, and his brother Wilhelm, were not only compilers of fairytales but the first to apply linguistic analyses to German folklore and tales. They were influenced by Rask's discovery of sound shifts and posited what is known as Grimm's law. Grimm built on the techniques of comparative phonetics and posited laws of sound change in various languages. The chart in Table 1.1 reproduces the methods used by Grimm and the comparativists. As words were added to the list it was possible to note the differences and similarities. Grimm noted, for example, that "father" was similar in Sanskrit, Latin, and Greek but that the initial consonant had changed from a /p/ to a /f/. The same thing was true for "fish" and "foot." A /p/ is an /f/ in the Germanic languages but no such initial

TABLE 1.1
Word Comparisons in Languages

English	Sanskrit	Latin	Greek	German	Old Eng
foot	pada	pedis	podos	fuss	fot
mother	matar	mater	mitir	mutter	modor
father	pitar	pater	patir	vater	faeder
fish	piska	piscis	ikhthis	fisch	fisc

consonant change was found for sounds such as /m/ in "mother." After much detailed work and exhaustive data, it is possible to posit a law such as: /p/ > /f/, or voiceless stops become voiceless fricatives. This means that sounds that did not use vocal cord vibrations and had an abrupt stoppage of air became sounds that did not use vocal cord vibration and created a vibrating sound by forcing the air stream through a small closure, thereby creating friction. These changes were presumed to have taken place sometime during the first millennium B.C. when the Germanic tribes split from Roman and Greek tribes and other descendants of Indo-European languages. There are many more sound changes that are part of Grimm's law and the law worked perfectly in most cases.

It was Muller, whom we met earlier, who was the dominant figure near the end of the 19th century and he heralded the work of the comparativists of the preceding years. Many scholars were beginning to seriously question the utility of searching for an original language, a protolanguage. The successes of the comparativists led to increased attacks on earlier thinkers who were often so preoccupied with the mystical or natural origins of language that they posited outlandish theories. Serious linguists were doing comparative phonology or morphology; speculations about the origins of language were left to clergymen, amateur ethnologists, and professors of philosophy. Muller's whimsical terminology for the various theories of language origin is still popular today. He termed the onomatopoeic or imitative theories, which he associated with Herder, the "bow-wow theory"; those who assumed that language originated in expressive or emotive sounds were considered adherents of the "pooh-pooh theory"; some suggested that linguistic beginnings emerged from the natural vibrating resonance of voices. They subscribed to the "ding-dong theory"; and one author, who was obviously influenced by Darwin, wrote that just as humans developed from a primeval mass of gelatinous matter, so too did language. This was the "jelly-fish theory."

In 1871, ten years after Muller's lectures at Oxford, came a group called the "young grammarians." This was a group of young German scholars who boisterously and boldly announced that they were the future and their elders were reactionaries. The young grammarians charged that sound changes took place according to laws that admitted no exceptions. Earlier scholars including Grimm had no trouble with various phonetic exceptions to their rules of sound. But the young grammarians felt that if sound changes were not regular and law governed then linguistics was not a true science. The young grammarians argued that even the exceptions to phonetic laws must be governed by laws, and the recent work of Verner clarifying some of Grimm's exceptions gave impetus to the thesis that sound laws had no exceptions. Nineteenth-century scientists were strong believers in the uniformity of nature. Young grammarians such as Osthoff, Brugmann, and Leskien believed that language changed according to blind laws independent of individuals. They turned the uniformity of nature into dogma.

The young grammarians were heavily data based. They rejected any form of theorizing and speculation about language. Even though the young grammarians were the intellectual fathers of contemporary descriptive linguistics, and their work clearly belongs in the modern age, their work prompted Jespersen (1922) to write:

> These phonological studies were not, as a rule, based on real, penetrating insight into the nature of speech-sounds, the work of the etymologist tended more and more to be purely mechanical, and the science of language was to a great extent deprived of those elements which are more intimately connected with the human 'soul.' Isolated vowels and consonants were compared, isolated flexional forms and isolated words were treated more and more in detail and explained by other isolated forms and words in other languages, all of them being like dead leaves shaken off a tree rather than parts of a living and moving whole. (pp. 86–87)

Jespersen's opinions notwithstanding, the young grammarians stimulated many productive lines of research. Their tenets have been modified but not superceded. The movement's complete preoccupation with linguistic data officially ended the question of language origin. In fact, in 1865 the Linguistic Society of Paris literally forbade the study of language origin in one of their articles of constitution. A number of respected linguists such as Jespersen continued to speculate and encourage the study of language origins, but the stage was set for contemporary linguistics. Classifying developments in language and communication by centuries is certainly arbitrary but in this case can still provide a workable category system. De Saussure is usually considered the founder of contemporary linguistics and he is the key figure in the transition from 19th-century to 20th-century work. Although he was a classmate of Brugmann and the young grammarians, he influenced Brugmann to moderate his conservative ways. de Saussure represents a revolution in the study of language for he is responsible for the final marriage of language data and theory. But we save discussion of de Saussure for chapter 2.

LANGUAGE AND HUMAN NATURE

It is easy enough to understand humans as biological entities. What I mean is that we are in a very real way composed and physiologically governed by chemical and physical properties. Much of early philosophy was devoted to discovering a human "essence" or "nature"; that is, a universal substance or truth about human beings that was thought to be at our definitional core. Scientists and philosophers assumed that this nature was "substantial." In other words, a crucial substance or inherent principle that constituted our essence, an innate instinct or faculty that could be empirically observed and amounted to our most outstanding characteristic. When such an essence could not be observed or agreed upon it was presupposed. Platonic categories and idea types are examples of such presuppositions.

As the problems associated with attempts to identify and clearly define a human nature became thorny, certain philosophers turned their attention to human development. A human essence, some argued, was not an a priorily established reality but existed in evolution and social development. Comte adopted a sociological perspective and wrote, "To know yourself, know history." Such thinking was a radical and fundamental departure from most of early philosophical inquiry. Human nature was not to be understood in terms of physics, metaphysics, or biology but as the result of historical and generational influences. It is also true that descriptions of human "nature" are very difficult, if not impossible. Attempts to identify a singularly defining human quality— whether it be an ideal type, a vitalistic element, an instinct or nature, or a metaphysical substance—are always disappointing. The terms are nebulous and provide little more than a descriptive label for something we do not understand very well.

Even after Comte and others began to argue that laws of human behavior owed much to social and historical principles, there were others who resisted this new direction. They argued that even the social world of humans had its roots in physiology. The goal was to authenticate a purely natural and logical relationship between the biological world and the social one. Some scientists and philosophers worked to establish the unique biological nature of humans and show how our cultural world was a function of this nature. The strongest case could be made for human intelligence. It seemed so obvious that humans were intellectually superior to other species that it simply had to be true that we were biologically and psychologically exclusive.

The question remains whether or not there is a useful and defensible way to understand humans that does not rely on biological or psychological essences, or on historical investigations alone. It is best to understand humankind from a cultural perspective. We should not diminish the important biological differences between humans and other species, especially with respect to the evolution of the brain, but for the most part we will accept Darwin as having solved the problem of anatomical and evolutionary differences between species. And if there is anything about humans that we want to claim for exclusivity, it is our symbol using capacity and the influence of culture on symbolic behavior. This is certainly not a new or innovative position. Such an argument is most completely and elegantly stated in Cassirer (1944). "The philosophy of symbolic forms," wrote Cassirer, "starts from the presupposition that, if there is any definition of the nature or 'essence' of man, this definition can only be understood as a functional one, not a substantial one" (1944, pp. 67–68). This means that the essential

structures and categories of human nature are born out of the practical requirements of culture. Our nature is existential and there lies the essence. Cassirer
continued: "Man's outstanding characteristic, his distinguishing mark, is not his
metaphysical or physical nature—but his work" (p. 68).

Human culture, argued Cassirer, is a constellation of activities that culminate
in art, language, and science and determine humanity. An understanding of
humans requires an understanding of human activity not human biology. A true
science of humanity is an examination of the common threads that weave cultural
activities into a coherent fabric, and these threads are functional rather than
substantial. One does not eschew the older methods of logical observation and
quantitative analysis but they are understood as part of the cultural fabric. Even
more important is how structural principles become central to understanding
functional principles. In the study of language, linguistics, and communication
the central concern is with meaning and how it is achieved. It is impossible to
fully understand "meaning" without recognizing the importance of basic descriptive work, which lead to general structural principles that are responsible for
frameworks of order and classification. In linguistics there had been much emphasis on historical work but little emphasis on *principles* of language, at least until
recently. Historical linguistics was preoccupied with raw descriptions of languages and language change with little or no concern for the structural properties
that might underlie these languages and their change processes. Chomsky
changed all this. He began the search for generative principles of language and
linguistic universals. And Chomsky was interested in the human mind as much
as he was language. He wrote that "language was the mirror of the mind," and the
best way to understand fundamental human structures was to understand language. The important feature of Chomsky's work was his concern for the creative
and generative process of language rather than the end result of language. And
this must be the focal point of a functional perspective on human culture,
language, and communication. For the products of art, and language, and communication are surely less interesting and fundamental than the search and
ultimate verification of the principles that *generate* these products. We must begin
with the assumption that human culture is driven by functional prerequisites and
that language, or symbolic form, is the fundamental requirement for culture.

Language and Function

All language is metaphor. It does not describe or refer to anything directly, but
rather it represents various aspects of reality. Even the most concrete reality relies
on the representational nature of language. The word "table" is not a table but a
metaphoric reference to an object that serves some function we typically ascribe
to tableness. It seems logical that if the world must be described in this meta-

phoric entity called language then functionalism must be the primary nature of this entity. Language functions to refer and characterize the world. Moreover, although the capacity for language is biologically determined, an individual's particular language and how it serves him or her is socially determined. A child learning language is mapping the external world onto his or her own cognitive one. Many individual and cultural differences emerge from this mapping process. It is no accident that language and myth were two sides of the same coin for the primitive mind because the external world of nature and society were so bonded. This is also true of the child's world. The relationship between the linguistic system and the world it represented was so intimate that primitive man could not tell the difference between language and what it was supposed to represent. The "words" were presumed to be equally as powerful as the reality. The result was magic and myth. The primitive mind could not tell the difference between language and the external world. But, interestingly enough, magic and myth have something fundamental in common with contemporary science: reality. Early magic and myth was an attempt to describe and understand reality in much the same way that modern social science does. Magic is concerned with causal relations and how one event leads to another, and it is language that is responsible for these relationships. Language and myth are real in the same way: ceremonies, rituals, secret words, and incantations are the stuff of the mythical world. We talk about people who are "possessed" and "transformed" by supernatural influences that travel in language. In short, the first functions of language were an attempt to harness and control the world's recalcitrant ways. Language was psychological nutriment. But soon the limitations of language became apparent and magic gave way to semantics.

At some point in the dawn of Greek society, language lost its immediate and transmundane powers. It could no longer solve problems and summon the supernatural quite as easily as once believed. But language remained important. One difference was that language itself became the object of study. Philosophers began to examine the meaning of meaning and how language worked. Language was an important dimension of human existence but it no longer was considered transcendental. This point in the history of thinking about language was crucial. First, it was the beginning of serious inquiry into the nature and function of language and, second, it placed language at the center of knowledge and truth.

The Greeks always held that there had to be some identity between a person and an object that he was trying to understand. If there were no such identity then it would be impossible to have knowledge of something. Being and thought could not be separated. And if language was at the center of being then it was inextricably related to thought. At this point the Greeks were lead astray because they reasoned that if language were at the center of being there had to be some natural relationship between a word and what it meant. If a word were to "mean" something it had to have some relationship with its referent and this relationship must be natural or inherent in the language–object relationship. Although the assumption of an identity between a subject and an object might be a sensible theory of knowledge, it is a misguided theory of language. The capacity to "make" a connection between a word and an object or idea is necessary for a theory of language, but it is unnecessary and incorrect to assume that such a connection is natural. If this natural relationship were the case, it would seem, at a minimum, as though there should be many more phonetic and semantic similarities between the vast array of different languages.

There were attempts to overcome criticisms such as those cited here. Some argued that it seemed futile to search for similarities between sounds and objects because our language was subject to so much change; that if we went back to original linguistic forms we would discover the natural relationship. Such thinking generated etiological searches as if the patterns of change for a current word could be discovered and lead to the first sound that ever represented each object or idea, and these sounds would reveal the natural relationship between the sound and the object. These approaches were interesting but, of course, futile.

In the mean time the Sophists were arguing that language had no objective nature and the purpose of language was to express emotions and move men to action. The Sophists maintained that language was practical and rhetoric, the first theory of communication, was born. The spoken word was very important in Greek society. It is probably difficult for contemporary man to fully realize just how important and potent the spoken word was to citizens of Greece. Sillars (1964) showed how rhetoric was an "act" with all the emotional, legal, and practical realities that the word implies. Skilled use of the language was valuable to a Greek citizen and he was responsible for the consequences of his words. Schools of rhetoric were designed to teach people how to be effective with words; how to speak and act in the world. Rhetoric was part of a theory of knowledge that discounted the objective and supposed natural relationship between language and the world. We were still a long way from truly understanding language but, interestingly enough, theories of rhetoric were the beginning.

After the early philosophizing about language theorists turned their attention to linguistic history and psychology. The Sophists were responsible for establishing a line of theorizing and thinking called *rhetoric*. But rhetoric was always considered a practical art; it taught people techniques—"tricks" according to some—of argument, invention, and delivery. Rhetoricians were considered skilled orators who could make their listeners believe or act in any way they desired. The "effect" of a message or speech was more important than its beauty or truth value. To this day, rhetoric is considered by many to be a pejorative term. It was called a "phantom art" by Plato and typically associated with artificial and empty discourse. But it is important to understand early Greek and Roman culture. Success in the culture was in the province of oral competence. In contemporary society we have many more avenues of information (radio, television, computers, etc.), and we devote more time to teaching writing rather than speaking. Writing eclipsed speaking as the primary mode of communication. And contemporary society relies on, and will continue to emphasize, new technological modes of communication. But the rhetorical tradition, in some altered form, will become important for the study of language. The rhetorical tradition fell into disrepute because of its insistence on practical skills and teaching people how to win arguments, when scholars of the time were more interested in discovering absolute truth rather than temporary effect. But as we move along in this chapter and the next we see that the relationship between language and communication is naturally rhetorical.

Although the Sophists were teaching how to make effective speeches, the philosophers and linguists were studying the history of languages. They argued that language had to have passed through various stages and probably developed from an amorphous and confused state into the current level of order. In the 19th century, history was still considered to be the key to understanding language. During this time many languages were catalogued and compared. It was a time of great descriptive activity with linguists identifying phonetic and syntactic features of many languages. There was still the presumption that historical description would inevitably lead to philosophical understanding of the relationship between humans and language.

Language as Social Process

Sociolinguistics is the appropriate contemporary term for the issues and problems that face language and a social community. Although the term has become over associated with dialects and regional variations of language, it should be used in accordance with its original definition, which referred to any correlation between language use and the social occasion that prompted it. This would include face-to-face encounters, speech acts, speech episodes, and the like.

A *speech community* is at the core of sociolinguistics and has attracted much attention, but its sense remains ambiguous. The concept of speech community is fundamental because it establishes the unit of understanding as social rather than linguistic. One begins with the problems of a social unit (e.g., family, decision-making group, couple, organization) and then considers the entire communication system that constitutes the social unit. Language problems are defined as problems of communication and social functioning. Some theorists, such as Bloomfield (1933), use the term to refer to people who use the same speech signals and thereby emphasize large-scale groups who share a language. The structural linguists have used the term in this way to describe the ideal speaker in the ideal speech community. They are concerned with identifying a language and discovering the universal features of that language. The term is used in this case to outline a group of speakers who share a tongue. A second use of the term *speech community* draws on a sociological or anthropological perspective in which a "group of people" is defined according to any of the various cultural or social conditions that occasion their organization. Hymes (1974) defined speech community tautologically and quite generally as "a community sharing knowledge of rules for the conduct and interpretation of speech" (p. 51). This definition allows for any social unit, which shares at least one rule for the production and interpretation of language, to be considered a speech community.

But language is more than a social group's mechanism for making meaning. Language, or symbol using ability, is the defining characteristic of humans. Much philosophical inquiry has been devoted to a definition of humankind and I do not attempt to extend that literature here. However if, as I argue, language was born to serve communication and is, therefore, a social process, some continued understanding of how that argument evolved is necessary.

2

Contemporary Theories of Language and Linguistics

The 19th century was dominated by historical studies. As we examine the current status of linguistics and language study we return to some of the foundational issues established in the 19th and preceding centuries. The study of language was coming of age. There had been great advances in the discovery of phonetic principles and scholars were making rigorous and accurate assertions about the nature of human language. The early part of the 20th century was still dominated by historical linguistics and the work of groups like the young grammarians. But there were other strands of influence. Two of these lines of influence are particularly important to current work in language and linguistics. In the first place, linguistic science, especially phonetics and morphology, began to be assimilated into general assumptions about science, especially the positivism of natural sciences. Linguistics was experiencing a new rigor. And although some were critical of this cold and analytical approach to languages, with its attendant loss in poetic and aesthetic concerns, there is little doubt that this work established the status and credibility of language study. The 20th century would continue this tradition. Unfortunately, the separation of formal language study and communication was also a by-product of this tradition. Although the linguistic system was receiving systematic attention, the communication system was relegated to haphazard speculation that could not stand the new tests of scientific validity. The success of historical linguistics is the second important influence of the 19th century because these successes were necessary for the current work in descriptive linguistics. The difference between descriptive and historical linguistics is the disparity that most characterizes the differences between the 19th and 20th centuries.

de SAUSSURE AND STRUCTURALISM

The Swiss linguist Ferdinand de Saussure was the pivotal figure in the transition from the 19th to 20th century, and is generally considered the founder of modern linguistics. He was a classmate of Brugmann and Leskien and an important figure in the young grammarians. He published a few highly respected papers but his more influential work was published after his death. His students at the University of Geneva were so impressed by his lectures that they collated and edited their notes and published his *Cours de Linguistique Generale* in 1916. The *Cours* has been described as a revolution in linguistics.

De Saussure was responsible for three key directions in the study of language. First, he broke with the young grammarians by positing the distinction between historical linguistics and the state of a language at any point in time. He was determined to delimit and define the boundaries of language study. To this end he began by distinguishing between historical linguistics and descriptive linguistics, or diachronic and synchronic analyses respectively. *Diachronic* linguistics is the study of language history and change. This was the type of work that characterized most of de Saussure's predecessors because the crucial question about language, at least until the 19th century, revolved around discovering the origin of language. Moreover, scholars believed that the "truths" of language lay in the earlier tongues that were closer to protolanguages. *Synchronic* linguistics, on the other hand, is descriptive linguistics and concerned with the state of a language at any point in time, especially the present. This distinction is significant because synchronic analyses were either ignored or overlooked in the past. But most importantly, the distinction drew attention to the current structural properties of language as well as historical dimensions. A language system is complete and operates as a logical system at any point in time regardless of influences from the past. A language has an existence separate from its history. The language is constituted at any point in time by the people who speak it and, of course, these people are typically ignorant of its history. This may seem like a relatively insignificant distinction but it served to direct attention away from historical studies and toward contemporary issues in linguistics such as psycholinguistics, semiotics, and related matters.

This led to de Saussure's second contribution: the distinction between *langue* and *parole*. Language is such a complex and varied phenomenon that it would be impossible to study it with any scientific rigor without assuming some basic operating principles. Moreover, it is the ability to produce language and the distinct ideas and meanings of people that are most characteristic of human nature. Vocalization is simply the instrument for actualizing the world of the mind and social relations. *Langue*, then, is an abstract system that all of us have in common and enables us to speak. It is the cognitive apparatus that members of a community share that allows them to use a vocabulary, grammar, and phonology in order to actualize speech. *Parole* is the actualization of *langue*. It is the way we actually speak—the vocabulary, accent, and syntactic forms. De Saussure used the game of chess as an analogy. The game is constituted by a system of rules and conventions that exist beyond actual games played. There are an infinite number of possible games of chess that can be played, and these are generated by the finite set of rules and conventions. So it is with language. There are untold numbers of accents, words, syntactical forms (i.e., languages and dialects in the world), and they are all manifestations of *langue* or superordinate set of rules.

A third contribution of de Saussure's completes his tenets of structuralism. He showed that the principles of *langue* must be described synchronically as a system of elements composed of lexical grammatical, and phonological components. The terminology of linguistics was to be defined relative to each other. In other words, an element of the linguistic system is meaningful only in relation to other elements. So the difference between the /p/ sound in *pin* and the /t/ sound in *tin* is established by contrasting articulatory responses necessary to produce the sounds. Moreover, it is this difference that accounts for the difference in meaning between the two words. The difference in meaning between the two words is accounted for by the structural relationship between the two initial sounds. The English language recognizes this difference.

This structural contrast perspective on language and meaning is a radical departure from historical traditions. According to Charles Fries (1964, p. 64), it meant the abandonment of a "word-centered" thinking about language for a "relational" or "structural" view of language. Language was now assumed to be a conventional system of symbols that had an arbitrary relationship to reality. The notion that a word had a natural relationship with what it stood for was no longer taken very seriously. It was now clear that what made a word "meaningful" was not its particular individual elements, but the *difference* between these elements and others. "Dad" is differentiated in sound from "bad" and "mad," for example; it is conceptually different from "mom," "son," "cousin," and so on. The most immediate and significant impact of de Saussure's structural theory was in the area of phonology. It led to the concept of the *phoneme* as a distinct and indivisible sound of a language. It is the speaker's perception of the differences between the initial consonants in "dad" and "bad" that pose a meaningful contrast and allows us to hear and understand the two words as different. The concept of the phoneme is now a linguistic universal.

Sign Relationships

The science of signs is certainly one of the most significant and exciting contributions of de Saussure. He called this science *semiology* (from the Greek *semeion* "sign") and the developments in this science have been extensive in the past decades. Although de Saussure's structuralism was crucial to the development of phonology, he was really interested in the larger and more abstract "system of signs." Linguistics was really the study of signs and their relationships.

De Sausurre characterized signs as a relationship between "concept" and "sound"; to use de Saussure's words—*signified* and *signifier*. The linguistic sign is constituted by the structural relationship between a concept (e.g., "house"—the *signified*) and the sound of the word "house" (*signifier*). A language is essentially composed of such structural relationships, and the study of language is the study of the system of signs that express ideas. As we have discovered before, the relationship between sound and concept is arbitrary. The word "house" has no necessary and natural links to the concept of house or to actual "houseness." The noun "house" refers to a structure where people live because the language makes it mean that, and the meaning of the word "house" can only be confirmed within the structure of the language. Language, then, is a shaper of the world and a conservative one at that because we are forced to apprehend the world through the structures of language. "Language," said de Saussure, "is a system of interdependent terms in which the value of each term results solely from the simultaneous presence of the others" (de Saussure, 1959, p. 114).

Two types of structural relationships in a language system presented by de Saussure are syntagmatic and associative. *Syntagmatic* relationships of a word are those relationships that can obtain with neighboring words in a sentence. For example, there is a syntagmatic relationship between the words "Roger" and "threw" such that the words can appear in the sentence "Roger threw the ball." This is true of any two words where one performs a subject function and the other a verb function. This is not true for two proper nouns such as "Roger Don" or two verbs as in "thrown threw." If a word changes its relationship to a neighboring word then it changes its identity. So if there were a person whose name was "Thrown" then a particular sequence of sounds that results in the sound of "Thrown" would be a different word. The sentence "Thrown threw the ball to me" would be perfectly sensible. The meaning of the sentence is unfolded as you read along and is not complete until you finish the sentence. *Associative* structural relations pertain to the ways in which words can replace one another, and the ways in which they do not. Part of the meaning of a sentence such as "Bob's wife threw a plate at Bill" is derived by what words and sounds were *not* chosen. We know it is a "plate" and not a "skate" or a "date," and throwing a plate "at" someone is, of course, different than throwing at plate "to" someone. These relationships are about how words and sounds are associated with each other and form part of the synchronic relationship within the language structure.

The influence de Saussure had on language was revolutionary. His work had a profound influence on many aspects of linguistics but synchronic analysis is one of the most radical because it turned language on itself. He argued that language was a closed and self-defining system, and his work caused linguists and scholars of language to look "inward" toward the internal mechanisms of language rather than "outward" to an empirical world. Language was structure not function; it was form not substance. The rewards of structuralism are significant. His theorizing led to the phonology of Jakobson (1962) and the generative syntax of Chomsky (1957). And his semiotics or "science of signs" had made great headway in understanding verbal and nonverbal modes of communication: images, musical sounds, rituals, and social conventions all constitute fascinating systems of meaning. But human communication is concerned with function not structure; its essences lies in use not form. In many ways de Saussure's work, and the work of those who followed, directed attention *away* from human communication. The role of language in the history of communication in the last decades is almost absent. We develop this argument more fully later, but for now we can see that de Saussure was the intellectual impetus for relegating language to the realm of internal logic and structural mechanisms that had little concern for the vicissitudes of language in context, or how people actually use language to accomplish social goals.

OTHER SCHOOLS OF THOUGHT

Since de Saussure there have been other developments in structuralism and theorizing about language in general. Although the structuralists were popular and stimulated many to develop structural principles, some became concerned with more pragmatic matters about language. They began to consider more functional issues, but now had the tools of diachronic and synchronic analysis to guide them. Structural linguistics began to blossom on both sides of the Atlantic. The American school is most represented by Boas, Sapir, and Bloomfield; the European traditions resulted in what is known as the Prague (or "functional") school, and the Copenhagen (or "glossematic") school. We consider each briefly.

Copenhagen School and Glossematics

Louis Hjelmslev (1961) is the chief proponent of what is called *glossematics*. Glossematics is a de Saussurean emphasis on form or structure in the "content plane." The content plane is the area of linguistics that deals with semantics and meaning. Hjelmslev wanted to apply structural principles to content by arguing that analysis of content of language must be independent. Identifying the elements of the content of language and establishing relationships among these elements was the only way to fulfill the de Saussurean goal of an independent linguistic science. For example, the word "father" could be analyzed into phonetic constituents, but also into content constituents such as "male," "human," "singular," and so on. The phonological plane and the content plane are separate because the phonological sequence and structure is unrelated to the content structure; but both planes are to be analyzed in the same way and are equivalent in the language system. Hjelmslev tried to work out a "calculus" capable of describing the linguistic structure of any given text. The major weakness of the theory is the claim of equivalence for the phonetic and content planes because semantic content is limitless and only knowable through differences in the phonetic plane.

Prague School and Roman Jakobson

Proponents of the Prague school maintained that language was a coherent structure and all of the functions of language could be governed by structural principles. It is called a "*functional*" school because they identified key functions of language in a society. The group was formed by a group of Czech and other scholars under the direction of Prince Nikolai Trubetzkoy. The Prague phonologists elaborated the concept of the phoneme by relegating the phoneme to *langue* and actualized speech sounds to *parole*. The phoneme was a theoretical entity that was a fundamental structural principle of the linguistic system. A phoneme can be realized in actual speech sounds in a finite number of ways based on distinctive features that are present or absent. A sound might be voiced or voiceless at a particular articulatory position. Prague phonology was not noted for establishing distinctive phonological features, but analyzing unitary phonemes that are realized in speech as ordered sets of specific contrasts between smaller distinctive features was a true advance in phonological and descriptive methods. So the sounds /p/ and /b/ are produced at the same articulatory position but one is voiced and the other is not. The same is true for /s/ and /z/, /k/ and /g/, and others. In English the sound "p" and "b" are in contrast and thereby make for different meaning. The word "pat" is semantically separated from "bat." But the contrast does not occur in all languages and becomes a feature that helps distinguish among languages. So where an American would say "I have pink pants," an Arab would say, "I have bink bants."

In addition to advances in phonology, the Prague school also recognized more sociological functions of language. Thus, one function of language was to transmit information and this function was termed the *referential* function; communicating mood or attitude of a speaker was an *expressive* or *emotive* function; the *injunctive* function was used when trying to influence someone, and they also referred to various *phatic* functions of language. Trying to apply structuralist principles to these more functional domains pushed structural formalism into more general issues in signification. It was now possible to think about works of art and everyday communications as part of the general science of signs. We return to the "science of signs" later, but it is important to note that the question now is how these functions become integrated into the fundamental principles of structural linguistics. This strand of structuralism has become very important in contemporary philosophy and communication theory and finds it most complete and elegant expression in authors such as Barthes (1967, 1973), Eco (1976), Greimas (1970), Morris (1971), and Sebeok (1969). But Roman Jakobson was the key figure in this sphere in the Prague school and his work laid the intellectual foundation for the later efforts to incorporate the aesthetic, poetic, referential, and general communicative functions of language into the field of linguistics.

One aspect of Jakobson's contributions to contemporary linguistics is especially unique and important because he successfully pursued an account of the *functions* of language, but did it within the framework of a comprehensive linguistic theory. Jakobson was a member of the original Prague circle and largely responsible for advances in distinctive feature analysis where phonological systems were set out on a matrix of feature oppositions. His work led to significant modifications of the neogrammarian school because attention was directed toward systems of contrasts and away from individual sounds that were assumed to be unrelated to other sounds. But Jakobson did not stop here because he extended this structural thinking into the realm of the functional use of language and the ways in which messages were created. He was, therefore, interested in communication. He was concerned with the entire *communicative* act and, true to the Prague school, with the *functions* of the language involved in the communicative event. We examine this aspect of Jakobson's work in more detail in chapter 5.

American Linguistics

The seminal figure in American descriptive linguistics was Franz Boas (1858–1942). Boas was a German and a contemporary of de Saussure. He moved to the United States in the late 1880s and began to work on culture and language. Boas is significant because he was not trained as a linguist; rather, he was trained as an anthropologist and this perspective equipped Boas to face the challenge of American Indian languages. Indians were moving off reservations and into predominantly English-speaking communities where their children were learning English as their native tongue. Boas directed a research project designed to capture and preserve Indian languages, many of which were unwritten. Furthermore, Boas brought a fresh perspective to linguistic analyses for three reasons. First, he emphasized collecting data in the field while he was learning the language. Second, he refused to impose the categories of traditional European languages on to Indian languages. And third, Boas worked to generalize about culture and philosophy from the data he collected in the field rather than adopting established European thinking.

Before Boas, scholars would typically work with written documents and established languages. Written documents are an interesting source of linguistic information but they are divorced from the context of the actual language user. Boas was able to identify and become immersed in the culture he was studying. This allowed him insights that would not otherwise be possible. By working in the field and studying a language while he learned it, Boas was able to devise new categories of grammar and function. He did not assume, for example, that the cases in Latin apply to Indian languages. Indian languages prompted the new polysynthetic linguistic classification because in Indian and Eskimo languages it is possible to begin with a root morpheme and affix additional morphemes. Boas' speculations about the relationship between language and mind are some of his most enduring contributions to language and communication. Where most English speakers would assume that some linguistic device for distinguishing past (I washed the car), present (I am washing the car), and future (I shall wash the car) is eminently logical, such an assumption turns out to be false. The Hopi Indians have no such distinction, although they do have a grammatical device for representing timeless truths (Clouds are high), reports of presumably known happenings (The rain fell yesterday), and events that are uncertain (I shall pay you tomorrow). The Kwakiutl Indians also do not mark time of action but they do have word endings (inflections) for indicating whether a speaker actually witnessed an event or had it reported to him.

These striking differences excited another individual who was to become very influential in American linguistics and communication theory. Boas was a great teacher and produced one very influential work (1911) that was essentially the result of de Saussurean synchronic analysis applied to Indian languages. But another German named Edward Sapir was excited by Boas' work and began to devote himself to the full-time study of cultures and the relationship between thought and language. Sapir was also a superior teacher who influenced many students. One of those students at Yale was Benjamen Lee Whorf, and they developed what has become known as the Sapir–Whorf hypothesis, or the principle of *linguistic relativity*. The principle of linguistic relativity is very controversial. Some consider it little more than mystical speculation, whereas others believe it fully. In either case, it remains of great interest to many and is discussed in university courses around the world.

Briefly, the linguistic relativity hypothesis holds that the structure of a language is determinate of thought and culture. Whorf reasoned that languages were a system of classification and categorization, and that the labels people placed on objects and activities were determinate of how members of that speech community "perceived and understood" those objects and activities. The Sapir–Whorf hypothesis attempts to link linguistic differences with behavioral differences in cultures. The Hopi concepts of time and space are the most cited evidence for the Sapir–Whorf hypothesis. Whorf compared Hopi language to what he called Standard Average European language (Whorf, 1956) and noticed differences in structure and perception. English speakers objectify the world so they have nouns for seasons of the year or times of the day: summer, winter, spring; morning, night. These nouns are count nouns, which means they can take plurals and we can talk about "summers" or "mornings." By objectifying time we take what is a continuous process and put beginnings and endings on it. We treat it as an objective entity that exists on its own, and we can manipulate it in many ways. There are no nouns for temporal terms in the Hopi language. Only adverb-like mechanisms that indicate the experience of "getting late." The day or the year "moves along" or "gets later" but it cannot be broken up into units. Whorf hypothesized that such differences in language were responsible for different perceptual experiences for the Hopi. They experienced the world in "subjective real time" because even though the seasons were repetitive—and the Hopi recognize this repetition—time was a matter of accumulating valuable experience, and not beginning and ending the same cycle. When a Hopi communicates something about the future he adds a subjective set of verbs that indicate expectation and hope, and he includes nature and the Great Spirit in this hope. The Hopi concept of time, according to Whorf, was incomprehensible to the standard average European.

There have been a few attempts to test the linguistic relativity hypothesis. Some linguists worked on color codability tests where they reasoned that cultures with languages that only had a few color terms would have trouble recognizing and perceiving colors they had no term for (see Brown, 1979). The premise was that a color would be recognized if there were a term for it. Some evidence was supportive when researchers found that the Zuñis, who had no color terms to distinguish between yellow and orange, could not tell the two colors apart. But despite some of these results the evidence for the linguistic relativity hypothesis is scant. It is still difficult to know whether or not language influences thought or the other way around. And although language users who do not have terms for certain objects or activities certainly have increased trouble understanding and recognizing such objects, it is not impossible for them to do so. Experiments like the color studies say more about the cognitive influences on concept formation than anything else. In any case, the linguistic relativity hypothesis remains controversial and intriguing, and scholars of many persuasions still toy with its premises. Bloom's (1981) interesting work with the differences between Chinese and English is somewhat supportive of the hypothesis, but he prefers to argue that language is a product of culture and not the other way around.

Leonard Bloomfield is probably more known to linguists than either Sapir or Whorf. His book, *Language* (1933), is a superbly written classic in linguistics. It is considered the standard reference for the science of linguistics. Bloomfield did field work on Indian languages and applied principles developed by de Saussure. He was a structuralist and rigorously scientific. Bloomfield can be contrasted sharply with Sapir, Whorf, and Boas, especially Sapir. By contrast, Sapir was interested in all aspects of language and life. He explored relations with music, literature, art, and was Humboldtian in nature because he insisted on the centrality of language to thought and mind. But Bloomfield's attitudes were most characteristic of linguists in the 1930s and 1940s. The ensuing "Bloomfield era" (1933–1957; or, from the publication of his book to Chomsky), was the period when linguistics became well established in American universities. Bloomfield concentrated on the formal analysis of phonological and morphological phenomena, and he argued that it must be possible to describe the allophones and allomorphs of a language. Most of the vocabulary of linguistics in the next section was developed further in the Bloomfield tradition. It was intended to be an objective scientific language that was free of mentalistic intuitions.

THE LANGUAGE OF LINGUISTICS

Linguistics is the scientific and rigorous study of the formal nature of language. To that end, the study of linguistics has provided us with a vocabulary for talking about language. This vocabulary has been specified and has become widely accepted in the 20th century. And it is important that scholars and laymen alike be comfortable with this vocabulary and use it in a consistent manner. Any area of expertise is composed of a basic vocabulary and terms that must be mastered. A skilled auto mechanic has mastered words that refer to the basic parts of the internal combustion engine (e.g., "distributor," "intake valve," "head gasket") and understands how these parts work together (e.g., "the fuel system," "carburation"). Part of becoming knowledgeable in any field of endeavor (law, medicine, science, communication) is learning the vocabulary of that field. The terms and concepts given here are the building blocks of the study of language and are indispensable for understanding language. We refer to the concepts described here many times throughout this book. In some cases (e.g., discourse), we devote entire chapters to the subject matter. We consider the vocabulary of linguistics in hierarchical order from the smallest unit of linguistic analysis to the largest.

Phonology

When linguists speak of language they are talking about *spoken* language. Spoken language is essentially a sound system. The phoneme is the fundamental theoretical component of the sound system. One branch of phonetics is called *acoustical phonetics* and it is primarily concerned with the physical properties of sounds. This aspect of sounds can be measured by sophisticated technological instruments. One could measure events in the upper respiratory tract, vibrations of the vocal cords, force of the aspiration of breath from the lungs, muscle movements in the oral cavity, sound duration, tonal composition and intensity, and a variety of other physical properties of sound production and hearing. On the whole, however, linguists have ignored the physical parameters of speaking and listening and have argued that the really important facts of sound systems are something other than such observations can produce. These observations are physical manifestations of abstractions such as phonemes. Phonemes cannot be measured but are the theoretical standard by which minimal units of sound can be measured against one another. Linguists are interested in sounds that result in a difference in meaning, that is, sounds as phonemes rather than sounds as breath groups or respiratory movements.

There are about 40 phonemes in English (depending on an individual's accent) but there are a great variety of ways that individual phonemes can be expressed. It is an oversimplification to say that a phoneme is a minimal sound unit because the pronunciation of a particular phoneme can vary. The phoneme /p/, for example, is pronounced differently in "pity" than it is in "sport." In the first case you can feel what is called aspiration, or a slight puff of air following the /p/. What is important is that this distinction (aspirated, not aspirated) is not used in English to distinguish between the meaning of two words. This is not true of Thai language. In Thai these two p's are separate phonemes because they distinguish between word meanings. A phoneme is a mental construct. When we say that the first sound in "pity" is the phoneme /p/, we are making a claim about how the minds of speakers of English work.

Linguists are mostly interested in how sounds are articulated and this branch of linguistics is known as *articulatory phonetics*. The articulation of sounds are described by the events that occur in the throat, mouth, and nose. One event is the vibration of the vocal cords. When they are vibrating the sound is called *voiced*. The "b" in "bet" is voiced where the "p" in "pin" is not. Another way to describe sounds is whether or not air exists partially or fully through the nose. If it does then the sound is called *nasal*; if it does not then the sound is oral. So the "N" in "Nancy" is nasal, but all of the sounds in "pat" are oral because no air exists through the nose. A third event during sound production is whether or not the flow of air is interrupted or not. Interrupted sounds are *consonants* and noninterrupted sounds are *vowels*. The type of interruption is still another issue: The "t" in "tip" is pronounced by abruptly stopping the air and this type of interruption is called a *stop*. The "f" sound in "fish" is called a *fricative* because the interruption is of a frictional nature.

In the preceding paragraph we have been talking about the manner in which sounds are articulated. There are other manners of articulation, but sounds are also classified according to the place of articulation in the oral cavity. The "p" sound in "pin" is produced by placing the two lips together. This is called *bilabial*. The "t" in "tip" is produced by placing the tip of the tongue underneath the ridge above the top row of the teeth. This is called the *alveolar* ridge. The "p" in "pin," then, is articulated by putting the two lips together and abruptly stopping the flow of air. By stating the place of articulation (bilabial) and the manner of articulation (stop) we have identified what is called a *bilabial stop*. The "t" in "tip" is an *alveolar stop*. The "f" in "fish" is pronounced by placing the top row of teeth behind the bottom lip. This is the labiodental position so the "f" sound is called a labiodental fricative. The "s" sound in "sip" is an alveolar frictive.

Phoneticians can make fine distinctions between sounds and the various parts of the vocal apparatus used to make sounds. Most people do not hear the slight differences in sounds that result from the location of a sound within the sound sequence of a word. What precedes and follows a particular sound is called the sound environment. These environments influence the articulation of particular sounds. The "p" in "peace" is aspirated because it is in the initial sound position in the word. If you put your hand in front of your mouth you can feel a puff of air after making the sound. But the "p" in "speech" is in a medial position and is not aspirated. This aspiration is one factor that contributes to the differences in accents. If you practice pronouncing the initial "p" without aspirating it you will be approximating a French accent. Variations on phones are called *allophones*. A phoneme is not a single sound but a family of sounds with slight differences among them. The "i" in "milk" can be pronounced in the front of the mouth or in the back of the mouth and produce a slightly different expression of the same phoneme. These variations are called *allophones*.

It should be clear by now that what are phonemes in some languages are not present in others. And in some languages the manner of articulation creates a different phoneme and different meanings. Nasalization has phonemic value in some American Indian languages. In Towa the nasalized *kwi* means "wind" but the nonnasalized *kwi* means "a light." In Chinese the unaspirated To means "many" and the aspirated t'o means "to take off." Tonality also has phonemic value in Chinese and this is what gives Chinese its sing-song quality. The various tone patterns create different meaning.

It is almost impossible to distinguish phonemes in normal speech patterns. Although phonemic theory and principles of articulation are invaluable for describing and classifying sounds, they do not capture the essence of "real" speech. During actual speech the vocal organs are constantly moving and do not stop such that one could isolate phonemes. The sounds flow together and form a continuum that is sometimes difficult to decipher. Beginners in a new language usually think that the native speakers are speaking too fast for precisely this reason. And the sign sold in joke shops that reads "kwicherbellyakin" is a humorous (I suppose) attempt to capitalize on this fact. All of this underscores the theoretical nature of phonemes. When we say the middle sound in "pin" is the phoneme /I/ we are making a statement about a family of sounds in the minds of English speakers.

It is also important to understand the differences between spelling (orthography) and sounds. There is not a one-to-one correspondence between spelling and sounds and that is why the International Phonetic Alphabet (IPA) was developed. When we spell it is possible for the same letters to represent different sounds such as the "th" in *th*in versus *th*en, or the "t" in *t*oe compared to the second "t" in sta*t*ion; or different letters can stand for the same sound such as *J*oe and bri*dge*. Although the IPA has been modified over the years to accommodate new sounds it is a useful notation system for representing the variety of actual sounds that are present in normal speech. One reason for the discrepancy between spelling and speech is that spoken language changes faster than writing. Writing is a conservative influence on a language and changes at a slower rate than speaking. Grammar books and precise rules for writing and spelling are relatively recent in the history of language. When languages were first being written down there was more correspondence between how people actually spoke and how words were spelled. But as time passes old sounds drop out of the language and new ones enter. Moreover, people begin to speak differently on the basis of geography, education, work, and so forth and spelling rules cannot keep up with phonetic changes. In Chaucer's day the "gh" in "light" and "night" was pronounced; in time the sound of these words changed but the spelling did not. Men such as Benjamin Franklin, Noah Webster, and George Bernard Shaw have all advocated spelling reform but change is very slow. Spelling phonetically would certainly be easier for school children and foreigners learning English but it would probably be impossible for spelling rules to keep up with sound changes. And, more importantly, if we did spell phonetically whose pronunciation would we use. When someone from New York City says "idear" for "idea" should we spell it with the added "r." Should we spell the word "four" the way someone from Brooklyn pronounces it—"foa." Needless to say, there probably will not be much pressure to spell phonetically in the near future.

Suprasegmentals. Natural language is digital in that it can be decomposed into discrete units. These discrete sound units are called *segmentals*. As we have seen, it is possible to decompose words into sound segments or segmental

phonemes. In addition to these structural properties there are other oral characteristics that signal meaning during speech. These are called suprasegmentals
because they are vocal qualities that are superimposed over a string of phonetical
segments. These qualities are juncture, pitch, and stress and are quite central to
communication, even though most structural linguists pay little attention to
suprasegmentals.

Juncture is the slight pause between elements—syllables, words, sentences—
and can apply to the time spent articulating a sound (the length of the sound), or
the amount of vocal pause between segments of a utterance. The differences
between the two utterances below are subtle but distinct:

It's a nice house.
It's an ice house.

Juncture is indicated in writing by commas, periods, and punctuation in general.
Punctuation is a sort of stage direction about how to group words and where to
pause. The spacing between words in writing is also a visual expression of
juncture. But in spoken language we listen for meaning, not mechanics. So if I
mean to ask, "Where did you go?" and I utter it as, "Wherja go?" I am able to
eliminate the pauses between the first three words because I expect my listener
to understand the meaning of the utterance.

Pitch results from the vibration of the vocal cords. The pitch is higher when the
vocal cores are vibrating more rapidly. Pitch frequency results in a change of tone
which, as we have seen, is very important in some languages. But unlike Chinese,
pitch in an individual English word does not affect its meaning. The word "book"
has the same meaning whether it is pronounced in a high, medium, or low pitch.
How a listener is to interpret the function of an utterance is also determined by
pitch. If the final syllables in "He asked Mary" are a falling low pitch then the
utterance is a statement. A high rising pitch would make the utterance be heard
as a question: "He asked Mary?"

The final suprasegmental is *stress* or loudness or softness of an utterance. It is
the amount of intensity given the vowel of a syllable. Stress can affect the
meaning of a word or a sentence but it is mostly responsible for noun–verb
contrasts in English. The word "permit," for example, with the accent on the first
vowel (e) is a noun. It is a thing you have. If the stress is on the second vowel (I)
the word is a verb. "I will not permit it." The same is true for words like contract
(noun) and contract (verb) or subject (noun) and subject (verb). Some languages
are called fixed stress languages because they do not shift stress from vowel to
vowel. In French the stress is always on the last syllable; Polish always stresses
the penultimate or next to last syllable. English, Spanish, Russian, and others are
free stress languages where the stress can shift from syllable to syllable and
significantly affect the meaning of a word.

Morphology

It is possible to consider the basic structures of language to be hierarchically arranged. Phonemes are the smallest units of sound and when they are strung together they make *morphemes,* or the smallest group of sounds that have meaning. A morpheme is a meaning unit. The word "house" is a morpheme because as a noun it is an indivisible meaning unit that refers to a structure where we live; or, when it is a verb, the word refers to the act of providing accommodations for someone. But if we were to add an "s" to the word house and make it "houses" we would change the meaning of the word, albeit slightly. Anytime a sound functions as a grammatical unit to influence the meaning of a word it, too, is a morpheme. So the "s" added to "house" is also a morpheme because it makes the word plural and makes the word mean "more than one house."

A word like "house" or "dog" is called a *free morpheme* because it can occur in isolation and cannot be divided into smaller meaning units. The "s" that was added above is called a *bound morpheme* because it must be attached to another meaning unit. The word "quickest," for example, is composed of two morphemes, one bound and one free. The word "quick" is the free morpheme and carries the basic meaning of the word. The "est" makes the word a superlative and is a bound morpheme because it cannot stand alone and be meaningful. The morpheme that comprises the essential meaning of a word is called the *base;* the bound morpheme that attaches to the base is called an *affix.*

Linguistics recognize two classes of bound morphemes. The first are called *inflectional morphemes* and their influence on a base word is predictable. Inflectional morphemes modify the grammatical class of words by signaling a change in number, person, gender, tense, and so on, but they do not shift the base word into another form class. When "house" becomes "houses" it is still a noun even though you have added the plural morpheme "s." These inflections actually make our language easier to use. In English anytime you want to make something plural you simply add the plural morpheme "s." There are some irregular forms (e.g., man:men or child:children) but for the most part it is easy to form the plural in English. This consistency in inflections makes forming the comparative and superlative easy also. The "er" morpheme compares one thing to another, and the "est" morpheme is the superlative. I can say, "Bob is quick," "Jim is quicker," and "Mary is quickest."

Derivational morphemes are the second class of morphemes and they modify a word according to its lexical and grammatical class. They result in more profound changes on base words. The word "style" is a noun but if I make it "stylish" then it is an adjective. In English derivational morphemes include suffixes (e.g., ish, ous, er, ly, ate, and able) and prefixes (e.g., un, im, re, and ex). Some derivational morphemes do not radically change the meaning of a base word. Adding the "er" morpheme to make a noun an agentive noun (the person who does something) does not radically alter the base word. Someone who "runs" is a "runner" and someone who "throws" is a "thrower." All words that end in "er" are not composed of the "er" morpheme. Words like "anger," "butcher," and "mother" utilize the same phonetic ending to the word, but these are not agentive noun morphemes. A mother does not "moth!" These odd cases are often confusing to the foreigner or second language learner.

Just as there are phonetic variations called allophones, there are morphemic variations called *allomorphs*. These are typically phonetic variations within a morphological class. The most common example of this is the plural morpheme "s." When writing a plural word we simply add the letter "s." But pronouncing a plural depends on the phonetic environment. The "s" sound in "cats" is a /s/ because it follows a voiceless stop. But the "s" sound in "kids" is a /z/ (kidz) because it follows a voiced stop. The plural of bushes is an /iz/ sound. These are all the plural morpheme but pronounced differently. Other allomorphs are the irregular plurals such as "oxen" as the plural of "ox" and "children" as the plural of "child." And finally there are what are called zero classes where the singular and plural forms of a word are identical. The plural of "sheep" is "sheep" and "deer" is "deer."

Some languages are highly inflected. Latin is perhaps the most highly inflected language. In Latin an inflectional affix is used to grammatically modify a word to signal a change in gender, person, number, and so on. Following is a comparison of Latin to English.

porto	I carry
portas	you carry
portat	he, she, it carries
portabo	I will carry

It is easy enough to see that although Latin is highly inflected, English is less so. English depends much more on separate auxiliary elements, especially pronouns.

Morphological Classification of Languages. Finally, the languages of the world have been classified according to morphological similarities. Some languages, such as Chinese, have isolated morphemes for each lexical item. These languages are called *analytic* because they can be broken down into individual morphological units. Analytic languages are composed of morphemes with separate meaning or grammatical standing. The morphemes do not affix to one another. English is also quite analytic but not nearly as much as Chinese. In the English sentence, "This is my house" the Chinese version would be translated literally as "This + is + I + possessive + house." The English pronoun "my" is a possessive pronoun in that it indicates person and possession. In Chinese the fact that the house was owned by the speaker would be communicated with a separate word (morpheme). Synthetic languages are at the other end of the continuum from analytical ones. *Synthetic* languages are highly inflected such as Latin, English, French, Spanish, and German. But extremely synthetic languages are called *polysynthetic* because instead of separate morphemes in a sentence with a few inflections, polysynthetic languages begin with one base morpheme and affix morphemes to it until it becomes the entire sentence. This category was created for American Indian and Eskimo languages. The following is the Eskimo word for house and an example of how this base word can be developed into variations.

igdlo	a house
igdlorssuaq	a large house
igdluliorpoq	he builds a house
igdlorssualiorpoq	he builds a large house

The final morphological classification is *agglutinative* and is most descriptive of non-Indo-European languages such as Turkish and Japanese. Agglutinative languages are similar to inflected languages but there is more regularity in the affixes and bases. Agglutinative languages have morphemes that have attached to roots and become fused with them. The important differences between agglutinative languages and inflected languages is the stability of the roots. In English we say, "to love" and in Turkish it would be sev-mek; "to be loved" would be "sev-il-mek" in Turkish. The English word "love" becomes "loved" but the Turkish roots remain constant.

As we see throughout this book language is often used as a mirror to the mind. The study of language offers insights into how the mind works because it is the filtering system for reality. Classifying languages according to morphological structures is useful in this endeavor because it is possible to compare various languages and to try to correlate the structure of a language with the knowledge and sophistication of the culture that it serves. Some earlier theorists (e.g., Jesperson, 1922) who speculated about the origins of language on the basis of morphological structure, suggested that language is changing in a reasonably consistent manner. They proposed that human language developed through three stages beginning with analytic languages that were irregular and happenstance. There was one morphemic utterance (usually a simple syllable) representing one idea or concept and no logical or grammatical harmony. From here some roots attached to others (agglutinated) and lost their independence so as to be fused with the other root and form a logical relationship. The third stage was flexional such that grammatical information (e.g., tense, plurality, etc.) became coded into the root.

Jespersen (1922) was critical of this theory but still maintained that a "law of development" is possible. Jespersen asserted that evolution of language was from inseparable irregular conglomerations to freely and regularly combinable short elements. Even vocabulary, according to Jespersen, develops in a manner parallel to grammar. He stated that advanced cultures have more information, especially abstract information, coded into a word. The Zulus can talk about a "red cow" or a "white cow" but no word for the general concept "cow." Some languages can refer to "elder brother" or "younger brother" but have no word for "brother." The Melanesians have a distinct morphological unit (word) for the different numbers of the same class of objects. A "buru" is 10 coconuts, a "koro" is a 100 coconuts, and "selavo" is a 1,000 coconuts. Much has been made of the languages of various peoples of the world but it is always difficult to generalize. The languages of primitive tribes are not necessarily "simpler" than the language of more advanced cultures. Detailed study of these languages reveals the intricacies and complications of the grammar and usage. Words are functional and if a culture develops separate words for different numbers of the same class of objects then this simply reflects the importance of these different groups. Languages do reflect the "reality" of a culture and although it is tempting to assume that some languages and cultures are inherently better than others, it is typically an error to make such an assumption.

Syntax and Grammar

Ordered arrangements of phonemes make morphemes. Strings of morphemes make sentences and sentences are the concern of syntax. *Syntax* is that aspect of grammar that is devoted to the order or arrangement of words and morphemes in a sentence. The sentence "The ashtray is ugly" is composed of sounds, morphemes, and these are ordered according to rules of sentences. A sentence, in the formal sense, is really a unit of discourse in written communication. We do not really speak in sentences; we speak in word groups and phrases with numerous beginnings and endings but they are not neat and orderly sentences. The structure of a sentence, however, is related to the structure of natural (oral) human communication because all sentences are composed of subjects and predicates, and this is little more than a grammatical coding of the fact that any utterance is structurally composed of a topic and a comment on that topic. Grammar has become associated with syntax because its popular usage refers to "correctness" of language use such as subject–verb agreement. Technically, a *grammar* is a set of principles governing a body of knowledge and often concerned with the rules that guide sequential ordering. There is such a thing as a grammar of mathematics or a grammar of music. In linguistics grammar typically refers to the scientific study of the phonological, morphological, and syntactic structure rules that explain how language works. Grammar does not usually concern itself with meaning (semantics) and rules of communication, but we see later that much of this is changing.

Syntax is especially important in English because word order determines meaning in English. All languages adhere to syntactical rules of one sort or another, but the rigidity of these rules is greater in some languages. It is very important to distinguish between the syntactical rules that govern a language, and the rules that a culture imposes on its language. This is the distinction between descriptive grammar and prescriptive grammar. *Descriptive grammars* are essentially scientific theories that attempt to explain how language works. The goal of the descriptivist is to simply state how language actually works. People spoke long before there were linguists around to uncover the rules of speaking. The intent of descriptive grammar is to posit explanations for the facts of language use, and there is no assumption of correctness or appropriateness. *Prescriptive grammars*, on the other hand, are the stuff of high school English teachers. They "prescribe," like medicine for what ails you, how you "ought" to speak. Newspaper columnists and pundits who continually decry the state of the language are arguing for the concept of "correct" usage. If someone asks me how much money I have and I respond with, "I don't have none" I am using a sentence that, according to contemporary teaching, is ungrammatical and is poor usage. From a purely communicative perspective the sentence is just fine. You would know exactly what I meant if I said "I don't have none." People use constructions such as these all the time. But grammar books caution against using double negatives and say that one should utter: "I don't have any." The first sentence is not "wrong," it is prescriptively wrong. A communication theorist who was analyzing how people actually spoke, would be quite interested in this usage. He would want to know who used utterances of this type, in what context, and why. The linguist would want to explain the origins of the utterance and how it fits into current theories of grammar.

Prescriptivism is a remnant from the days when Latin was considered the perfect language. Most of the first literate people, that is, people able to read and write, were members of the church and church documents were written in Latin. An earlier popular grammar book was written by Bishop Robert Loth and he, among others, prescribed how language should be rather than how it actually was. These prescriptive grammarians tried to force fit English syntactical structure into Latin structure. So because Latin nouns had six cases, English nouns were supposed to have six cases. Rules of Latin were often indiscriminately applied to English. When students are taught not to split infinitives it is because they cannot be split in Latin. The difficulty is that the rule is logical in Latin because infinitives were one word and of course one word should not be split. But in English most functions are indicated by particles so inserting a word between two words is plausible. It is quite communicative to say that you are going "to diligently inquire . . ." rather than be constrained by a rigid rule that says you must say, "to inquire diligently . . ." It should be acceptable "to consciously split infinitives."

Syntax contributes to meaning in English in some important ways. Latin, as we have learned, is a much more synthetic language and less reliant on syntactical order for meaning. Latin syntax is called *free syntax* because it is permissible to arrange word elements in any number of ways because the inflectional endings in words communicate the subject, verb, and object of the sentence. The sentence "The dog bites the man" can be written in Latin as either *Canis mordet hominem; Canis hominem mordet*, or *Hominem mordet canis* because the subject and object are inflected into the words *canis* and *hominem*. Something (a dog) is doing something (biting) to something else (a man). In English if you said "The man bit the dog" you will have radically changed the meaning of the sentence. English syntax is called *restricted syntax* because the function of words is determined by their position in the string of words that make up the sentence.

The extent to which syntax contributes to the meaning of a sentence is called *structural meaning.* Lexical meaning is typically within the purview of semanticists and pertains to what words symbolize and their denotations and connotations. We obtain lexical meanings from dictionaries and other resources that document definitions, origins, and common usage. Structural meaning depends on a formal analysis of how words combine. In the sentence, "The friend of the mother and the father will arrive soon," it is possible to attach two different meanings to the sentence. One person, the friend of the mother and father, may be arriving; or, two people—the friend of the mother, and also the father—may be arriving soon. The ambiguity in this sentence is called structural ambiguity because it is attributable to more than one way for the word elements to combine into meaning. The sentence would be lexically ambiguous if there were a word that we did not understand.

Function words and inflections are another way that structural devices contribute to the meaning. *Function words* are lexical devices that serve grammatical purposes and do not refer to specific objects or ideas in the world. Words such as "but," "and," "the," "any" are function words. These elements of a sentence have no meaning in isolation but serve to signal the listener to combine or relate groups of words in a particular way. What if I tell a child that he or she can have "cake and ice cream" but I really mean to say "cake or ice cream." The resultant difference in meaning is considerable because "and" instructs the hearer to include both elements on either side of it (cake and ice cream), whereas "or" implies one element but not the other. English is less inflected than a language like Latin because we use more function words such as articles and prepositions to indicate the case function of the word. In Latin *homo* means "the man" as the subject of a sentence. In English we use the definite article "the" indicating a specific man and its function as the subject of a sentence is dependent on its position in the sentence: "The man (subject) hit the ball." If "the man" is in the object position the Latin term is *hominem* but the English equivalent is still "the man:" "The ball hit the man (object)." Again, Latin is inflected and builds the function of the term into the word itself, where English uses functions words such as articles and prepositions and relies on syntactical order.

Syntax, like phonology and morphology, is rule governed. Any sentence can be decomposed and altered by the application of certain rules. Consider the following sentence as an example: "The teacher yelled at the students." The hearer (or reader) of the sentence presumably understands the meaning of the lexical morphemes (teacher, yelled, student) and the way in which the functions words direct the relationships among the elements of the sentence. But it is also possible to group these words into phrases that make the structure of the sentence more apparent.

The combination of the first two words is called a noun phrase. Syntactic rules state that noun phrases can function as subjects or objects of sentences and only noun phrases can do so. "The teacher" is the subject noun phrase and "the student" is the object noun phrase. There is always an adjective slot for use at the speaker's discretion. I can modify the nouns by inserting an adjective into the position preceding the nouns. I could say, "The nasty teacher yelled at the poor students." It is permissible to insert any number of adjectives into the adjective position. It would be grammatical for me to say, "The big, ugly, weird, strong, strange, intelligent, aggressive, nasty teacher. . . ." Such a construction would be strange and perhaps in poor style, but it is perfectly grammatical. Verb

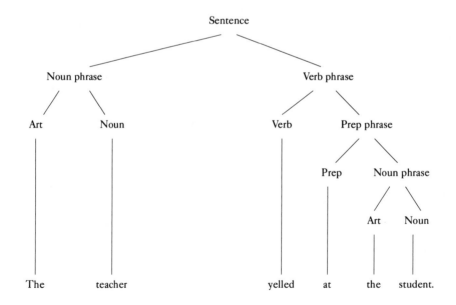

FIG. 2.1. Phrase Structure Diagram.

phrases can contain verbs, noun phrases, and prepositional phrases. Figure 2.1 indicates all the elements beneath the verb phrase.

When people are learning a language they "understand" these rules and permissible sequences at an unconscious level. Which of the following can legitimately complete the blank?

"The room————————."

a. big class

b. because the application

c. emptied quickly

d. the person

A native speaker "knows," even if only intuitively, that c is permissible because the sentence must contain a verb phrase. Knowledge of these rules is valuable because they allow you to make sense of sentences that you have never encountered before. You do not learn a language by memorizing sentences that are allowed. You learn a few rules and apply them in an infinite number of cases. Your knowledge of structural rules is central to the production and interpretation of sentences and the example below is a rather dramatic illustration of this point. What if you encounter the following sentence: "The sluddish porgath boffed opily in the gert."

If you were asked to identify the subject of the sentence you would have little trouble naming the "porgath" as the subject of the sentence. Now, what is that porgath like? It is sluddish. What is the porgath doing? Boffing. How is it doing it? Opily. Where is it doing it? In the gert. You "know" these things about the sentence because the sentence satisfies certain syntactical rules (and phonological ones). The sentence is grammatically correct, but semantic nonsense.

Most contemporary linguists are more concerned with the rules that account for the string of words in the sentence than with the semantics of the sentence. Applying meaning to the sentence, according to many linguists, is simply a matter of establishing references to the empirical world for the each word. The lexicon (vocabulary) is often considered the simplest part of a grammar. Assume we had the following dictionary definitions for the words used previously (eliminating the function words):

sluddish *adj*. Slow, not moving quickly.

porgath *n*. A bear-like animal having a long snout and shaggy hair.

boffed *v*. To swim or move through water.

opily *adv*. To be happy or do something in a happy state.

gert *n*. A shallow body of water.

The sentence would be about a slow bear-like animal that was swimming happily in some body of water. But many linguists assume a structuralist perspective where word order and formation rules for sentences are considered the basis of the grammar of a language. Words and their definitions and etiologies usually play a very small role in the world of the professional linguist. And as linguistics continues to develop, especially under the influence of Chomsky, rules that can account for the infinite variety of sentences a native speaker can utter have become the dominant direction for research. The contemporary linguist has been accused of concentrating on structure and ignoring meaning. The accusation is somewhat exaggerated but structuralism remains the prevailing power in linguistics.

Linguistics and Communication

The scholarly tradition of linguistics is only marginally concerned with communication. The term *communication* appears in much linguistic literature but usually as a way to refer to the general function of language and not as an object of study unto itself. In fact, traditional linguistic inquiry is driven by a set of assumptions that removes communication from consideration. But language is a group as well as an individual possession. Communication is its primary function even though, for all intensive purposes, the tradition of linguistics ignores communication. The major emphasis has been on assuming language to be an autonomous system and explicating its formal characteristics. But communication has been ignored for another more simple reason: Communication is complex and more difficult to study than phonology or morphology. Communication is more dependent on meaning, context, and individual cognitive and perceptual apparatus than anything else. We must certainly understand the formalities of linguists but they are less pertinent to communication than a number of other principles and theories. Consider the following sentence: "I like my apple."

We have seen all the linguistic issues one could bring to bear on this sentence. But things get a little more difficult when we enter the realm of meaning and communication. The "communicative" function of this sentence is difficult to analyze. An "apple" could refer to a fruit or a make of computer. Although any theory of semantics can account fairly easily for the two references for "apple," the semantics of the verb "to like" are more difficult. What does it mean "to like?" And how about all of the different ways that the same word can be used. In some ways these questions pertain to cognitive processing and are treated in chapter 3. But what are the other effects and consequences of this utterance? What if the person who spoke just before the utterance said, "My IBM computer is the best made" and you followed with "I like my Apple." How does the utterance *function*? What is its meaning? Would you then be having what we call a *disagreement*? What if these are the words of a salesman and a potential customer? Then they function and mean something a little different. Speakers learn sounds and grammatical forms to be sure, but they also must learn how to use language in different circumstances. Communication is essentially a matter of situated language use. Most of the remainder of this book is devoted to understanding the principles and forms of communication; or, how language is used in situations.

3

Language and Cognition: The Mental Machinery of Communication

The mind is the bridge that connects the body to the soul; it should be possible for the mind to explain the relationship between genetics, cell structures, and so forth, and the roles and problems of men and women in society. But it cannot do it very well. The realms of physiology and culture are incommensurate and rely on different vocabularies. It is as if we were trying to build an explanatory link between the sound of a drill on a construction crew and the music of Mozart; it cannot be done.

But there is one vocabulary that just might help us with this connection. It is the domain of symbols, their systems and products. Symbols like words or icons, symbol systems like language or math, and the outcomes of symbol systems like theories and explanations allow us to traffic in the realms of "noise" and "music"; symbol systems can provide at least some links between biology and culture. This is true because all knowledge must be cast in a symbol system of some sort. Biology and literature may be quite different, but both must be understood, and in some senses are constituted, in accordance with a symbol system. Our ability to symbolize is a major fact of our human nature. Other species in the animal kingdom cannot do it. Although we do not "will" things into existence, we can only know them through symbols. Inanimate objects such as rocks and trees exist separate from our knowledge of them and have functions and processes of their own, but as soon as we approach an object and label it or try to understand something about it we must rely on symbols. Even the act of labeling an object (e.g., "rock" or "tree") establishes a symbolic relationship because the label is not the thing itself, and the label influences our understanding of the object. This is especially true for objects or ideas that do not have clear referents; labels such as truth, beauty, justice, and freedom do not refer to the empirical world so their ability to define the nature of something is even more powerful.

All acts of cognition are symbolic. A child is born capable of performing certain biological functions such as sucking, crying, and so on, but the child is also biologically prepared to think and symbolize. At first a newborn will suck anything because the response is instinctual, but very soon the child "knows" what to suck and what to avoid because he or she has categorized those objects that are pleasurable and productive and those that are not. This categorization is the child's first experience with meaning and rudimentary cognition. Humans must interact—that is, communicate—with the world. We are in one instance born alone as a sophisticated problem-solving machine, and in another a product of a culture that we must "experience" and shape ourselves to conform to.

The perspective held by Noam Chomsky (1975) is the one most in accord with a view as humans as a problem-solving machine. Chomsky's Cartesian linguistics assumes that the environment plays a limited role in the development and performance of human skills. Language development in children is, according to Chomsky and his associates, a matter of triggering predetermined principles. The mind is anything but a *tabula rasa*; rather it is composed of a set of laws and rules that will lay dormant unless triggered by environmental stimuli, but such laws and rules are not created or fashioned by the environment. Chomsky's perspective has been useful in many ways because it serves as an important adjustment to empirical accounts of cognitive development. It seems unreasonable to assume that fundamental cognitive skills are *learned* in the traditional learning theory sense of the term.

Chomsky's arguments are weak, however, because they do not recognize the importance of symbolic capacities and the fact that human cognitive abilities are awash in meanings and interpretations that vary across cultures. Other theorists such as Scribner and Cole (1981), and most notably Geertz (1972), work in direct opposition to Chomsky by maintaining the primacy of culture. These scholars maintain that the forms and powers of culture are responsible for individual development. They deny the mentalism of generations ago, which assumed that individual capabilities were biologically determined, and the claims of theorists like Chomsky who assign a very minor role to culture.

These culturalists stress the extent to which cultural symbols and collective wisdom are responsible for ideas and ways of thinking. They would agree in some sense with Chomsky that there are core intelligences that are common to all people and cultures. But rather than assuming that humans are an autonomous calculating device, they propose that the systems of meaning and interpretation in cultures influence these core intellectual apparatus and are essentially responsible for their nature. Theorists such as Geertz assume that the mind is a cultural achievement. An individual's cognitive powers are absorbed from outside him or herself.

LANGUAGE AND MIND

It is possible to forge a path somewhere between a Chomskian preoccupation with innate intelligence and claims for the primacy of culture. There is a position that assumes the centrality of innate human intellectual abilities, and the extent to which these are influenced by cultural practices. Such a position is "symbolist" in nature. It relies on the writings and theories of people like Cassirer (1953–1957) and Susan Langer (1942) and distinguishes humans from other organisms by their ability to use symbolic vehicles to express and communicate meanings. Language is the fundamental symbolic vehicle of all cultures and it alone is both an integral part of our biological storehouse of intelligences, and the cultural structures that form our ideas and ways of behaving. In my view, along with David Olson (1970a), Howard Gardner (1985), and others it is the deployment of various symbol systems that accounts for our distinctive human nature. Any of us may be skilled at math, language, music, or visual arts but all of these are symbol systems that operate according to intellectual principles and are, of course, culturally specific. The more specific relationship between mind and natural language is of concern to communication. Although there are other systems of symbolization, natural language is the most fundamental. It pervades mental life but does not constitute the whole of mental life. We possess emotions, feelings, and prelinguistic cognitions that are not language-like. But here we examine models of language and cognition and take up issues in language and mind as they relate to communication. In his provocative book *Frames of Mind* (1985), Howard Gardner discussed other symbol systems or intelligences such as musical intelligence, spatial intelligence, and bodily kinesthetic intelligence and he concluded that people vary with respect to skills in these areas. But linguistic intelligence is the heart of mental life. As we proceed it becomes clear that language and thought are inseparable, although language is only one of the many factors that constitute our "humanness."

Language and Thought

In recent years there has been a continuing debate that pits "behaviorists" against "mentalists." A generation ago there was no such debate because most scholars assumed a behaviorist position that language learning was essentially a complex stimulus–response system learned like any other habit. B. F. Skinner (1957) in his book *Verbal Behavior* wrote that conclusions derived from laboratory work on rats were sufficient to describe human language behavior. John Watson, the father of American behaviorism, assumed that thought and speech were the same thing; he wrote that thought processes were directly related to motor habits in the larynx. The eminent Soviet psychologist L. S. Vygotsky took a less extreme position. Vygotsky (1965) argued that language and thought are very close, perhaps isomorphic, in a child when he or she is learning to think and speak. When a child thinks, he or she speaks. But as the human organism develops it is no longer constrained by external stimuli, and thought and speech become more separate. After about the age of 6 the inner mental life of a human being becomes more autonomous. Piaget (1950) offered related arguments—and is clearly opposed to the behaviorists—by suggesting that cognitive development precedes linguistic development. He concluded that the mind interacts with the environment and gives rise to the linguistic process. Piaget's work has been very influential in convincing a generation of thinkers to take a whole view of the child and his or her development rather than adopting a structuralist position that fragments the ingredients of language and cognitive abilities.

Up to now we have been using the terms *language* and *speech* a bit sloppily and it is important to make some distinctions. The early behaviorist position is really quite easily discarded because they failed to recognize the differences between language and speech. *Speech* is a physical process. It is concerned with the physiological production of sounds. It is quite easily measurable and observable. *Language* is an abstract system of meaning and structures. A language is composed of symbolic elements that exist on a variety of levels (e.g., phonemes, morphemes), and rules for arranging and using these elements. The behaviorists were talking about speech and thought, not language and thought. The biological processes that govern speech are perhaps related to thought in some interesting manner, but these processes are probably quite separate from the mechanisms that describe language and thought. The cognitivists such as Piaget were essentially interested in language and thought, or the structures that relate inner linguistic processes with cognitive ones. It is certainly easy to demonstrate that physiological speech is not necessary for thinking that relies on linguistic principles.

It is also true that thought is not just inner speech, where inner speech is used to mean a one-to-one mapping between an idea and spoken words. The map that guides us from a thought to a particular verbal expression is surely a complex and poorly understood one; a map with little detail. The same thought can be expressed with many words. If I wanted a friend to open a door I could say it in any number of ways using a variety of words and sentence structures. I do not "think" the request in an analytic manner where I imagine each separate word and action. Thoughts seem to be present all at once and then sent elsewhere for processing where they are packaged and made suitable for expressions in speech. Language is only one system of representation. Artists, scientists, and mathematicians, all report that their insights come in many forms and often do not even resemble language. But language is the system of representation that concerns us here, and even though there are other interesting and provocative symbol systems, we must now turn our attention to specific models of language processing and representation.

PSYCHOLINGUISTICS

The word "psycholinguistics" refers to the psychological principles involved in how language is processed and represented. Before 1957 psychologists were not very interested in language in the same way as linguists. Psychologists assumed that language was some sort of complex word association established through reinforcement, the position essentially espoused by B. F. Skinner (1957) in *Verbal Behavior*. Most psychologists were not very familiar with particular issues in linguistics and their attempts to develop suitable theories about psychology and language—psycholinguistic theory—rested on an inadequate description of language in general. But in 1957 Chomsky published *Syntactic Structures* and radically changed the direction of linguistic work: New issues came to the foreground and old ones receded into the background. You will recall from chapter 2 that until 1957 the Bloomfieldian tradition was strong in linguistics and Bloomfield was very influenced by the behaviorism of his time. He worked toward an inductive description of language that was free of assumptions about cognitions and mental states in general.

Insufficient generality and theoretical depth was one of the consequences of Bloomfield's preoccupation with the descriptive facts of language. A Bloomfieldian approach failed to account for a number of "facts" of language because it assumed that language could be modeled as a Markov process with probabilistic functions that describe the left-to-right movement of a sentence as in the following sentence: "The man who works in the building eats here often." Analysis of this sentence would assume that "man" follows "the" with some probability and according to a linguistic principle connecting definite articles to nouns. The same is assumed to be true of all other words in the sentence, but we run into difficulties when we encounter "eats" following "building." Buildings do not eat and these words are unrelated because "eats" refers to "man" in this sentence, and "man" is six words back. Because embeddings in sentences are unlimited, a left-to-right surface structure cannot fully describe sentences. Chomsky (1957), in fact, showed that it was impossible.

Another problem with Bloomfieldian linguistics was that it had trouble with ambiguous sentences such as: "The shooting of the hunters was terrible." The sentence is ambiguous because it could mean that the hunters were poor shots, or that it was too bad that hunters were shot. The words have different grammatical functions depending on how you interpret the sentence. There are other problems with Bloomfieldian linguistics (see Chomsky, 1965, 1966; Lyons, 1969), but they can be reduced for our purposes to a failure to include the role of cognition in language. Bloomfield simply could not explain many facts of language, facts such as embeddedness and ambiguity. It also seems increasingly necessary to make assumptions about innate ideas and abilities as responsible for learning language. The structures of grammar were simply too complex to be learned according to the principles of behaviorism. There had to be some form of grammar programmed into the brain.

Chomsky's Linguistics

Noam Chomsky took issue with the behaviorists and the Bloomfieldian tradition in linguistics and adopted a mentalist and rationalist approach to linguistics. The publication of *Syntactic Structures* in 1957 was a remarkable intellectual achievement and produced a revolution in the study of language comparable to Freud's influences on psychology. We cannot take up the full details of Chomsky's work here but the interested reader is referred to original sources, or accounts for newcomers that appear in Langacker (1973), Lyons (1969), and Liles (1971). Moreover, many of the technical and philosophical details of Chomsky's writings are of less concern to us than his influences on psycholinguistics and language processing. In many ways, Chomsky's work is only tangentially related to principles of communication because he stated rather emphatically that language use—the essence of communication—holds little interest for him. We see later and in other chapters that Chomsky relegated communication to linguistic performance and fails to treat it seriously. We also see, however, that Chomsky has been criticized for failing to understand language as fundamentally a communication process (Searle, 1974), and others have tried to adjust his theory to include the semantic and communicative components of language. We delve into Chomskyian principles and contributions only as far as necessary to understand current thinking about the relationships between language and mind. Communication is assumed to rely on linguistic processing because human decisions about meaning, the effects of messages, and various communicative skills are dependent on how language is processed.

Sentence Units and Grammar. Bloomfieldian linguistics was a sort of verbal botany. All the little parts and elements of language (e.g., phonemes and morphemes) were classified and organized into different levels. Meanings were assumed to be patterns of stimulus and response and within the realm of psychology. Chomsky found that the methods he had been taught as a graduate student worked well enough with phonemes and morphemes because there was a finite number of them. But the number of *sentences* in a natural human language is infinite. Humans can produce an unlimited number of sentences and any single sentence can be made even longer and modified by adding adjectives. For instance, the following sentence is grammatical: "The little boy who walks home from school every day with his friend went into the store to buy some penny candy for his sister who drives her red sports car home every day."

Such a sentence is grammatical although it is not one we would likely use because we might lose track of what we were talking about. The addition of an infinite number of adjectives or relative clauses would lengthen the sentence yet it would remain grammatical. But we do learn to produce and comprehend an infinite number of grammatical sentences. How can this be? We certainly do not learn by memorizing all of the sentences that we use. People utter and comprehend sentences all the time that they have never been exposed to before. It must be that we do not learn sentences themselves but a finite set of rules for producing sentences. Also, as we said before, the surface structure of a sentence is not sufficient for understanding a sentence. Therefore, we must know something about sentences at a deeper and more fundamental level than what we see and hear. It is the relationship between this deeper level and the surface level that concerns Chomsky. He changed the goal of linguistics away from the classification of linguistic elements toward creating a theory that accounts for all sentences. The theory would describe which strings of words would be counted as sentences and the structure of these sentences.

The theory should generate sentences such as "Willie was in love with Margaret" but not "Love in Margaret Willie with was." This is the point at which Chomsky becomes significant to psycholinguistics. Chomsky claimed that humans had a "tacit" knowledge of grammatical rules that was biologically grounded. The grammarian's ability to generate these rules was proof that they existed. Chomsky took this assumption to be a rationalist view of linguistic knowledge, and associates his work with Descartes and Kant who believed that certain parts of our cognitive machinery were innate. A child is presumed to be born with a universal grammar—a set of principles common to all languages—and this universal grammar is what allows the child to learn language so effortlessly. The child "learns," in the behaviorist sense, a particular language but he or she does this from the foundation of universal grammar. This universal grammar is part of a speaker–hearer's knowledge of language and is called *linguistic competence* by Chomsky. This places linguistics as part of cognitive psychology and in the province of the psycholinguist, whose job it is to describe the processes that access and utilize language. Competence is part of the code for all speaker–hearer's, it is part of the mental equipment of the language user. The psycholinguist is in the business of describing this mental reality that is responsible for actual language learning.

Linguistic performance, on the other hand, refers to actual language behavior in concrete situations. It is concerned with the actual languages that people speak and all of the situational and psychological influences that come to bear on members of a speech community. The actual words, sentence structures, slips of the tongue, false starts, and so on, that characterize everyday language behavior is the province of linguistic performance. Chomsky's distinction between competence and performance is important because it is a distinction between the mental knowledge necessary for language and a theory about implementing that knowledge. Overt language use (communication) reflects how language is processed and understood, and results in theories that produce idealized versions of the processes that determine language behavior. Chomsky argued that in order to understand language performance it was necessary to understand the structure that generates performance along with other necessary psychological faculties such as memory, attention, recall, and so on.

Chomsky therefore returned linguistics to the realm of psychology, something that Bloomfield worked so hard to avoid. Chomsky's work stimulated a tremendous amount of research and model building regarding the cognitive processes necessary for language processing. Much of the current work in artificial intelligence, teaching computers to think and make decisions, can be traced to Chomsky's earlier theorizing about the competence/performance distinction. The competence/performance distinction has also been roundly criticized (Kaufer, 1979; Searle, 1974; Sutherland, 1966) and we take up some of these criticisms in a later chapter. But first it is important to fill out Chomsky's theoretical position and to examine some of the models and thinking about language processing.

Linguistic Universals. Conceiving the mind as a predetermined entity that influences the structure of language is a logical consequence of Chomsky's position, especially the principle of linguistic competence. The argument is that this innate mental structure is uniquely human. It follows, therefore, that all human language should have a common form. One goal of the psycholinguist is to explain a language in such a way as to show that language is a logically produced variant of the universal structure. This allows for knowledge claims across languages rather than just within them. Some of the universals are phonological, syntactic, and semantic units. All languages, for example, have grammatical classes such as nouns and verbs, and sentence structures that can be classified as having a subject and a predicate. It is also possible to identify articulatory and acoustic properties of sounds that are universal. And the fact that children of all languages go through the same phasic development during language acquisition has been used as an example of universal structures that direct the nature of language. At best language universals are generally plausible, but they have yet to be identified and stated in a particular way.

Transformational Generative Grammar. Transformational generative grammar is a key component of the Chomskyian system and another logical consequence of Chomsky's arguments and philosophical assumptions. Transformational generative grammar is a detailed and precise theory and the reader is referred to Chomsky's original work or Searle (1974) for the most complete explanations.

If there are innate structures that direct the form of language then the goal of the linguist is to state the phonological, syntactic, and semantic rules that describe this knowledge that a person has. The grammar is *generative* because it must be capable of producing an infinite number of sentences even though only a few sentences are actualized in a particular situation. The sentence that I have just written or a particular one that I uttered in class the other day are sentences that I have never produced before, and more than likely the reader or hearers have never encountered those exact sentences, but they are still grammatical and understandable. Chomsky's grammar must be generative because the theory requires that it be possible for a few rules to "generate" an infinite variety of sentences for situations. A second use of the term *generative* by Chomsky pertains to the necessity for rules that produce sentences without conscious thought. Sentences must be produced automatically and mechanically.

It is interesting to note that Chomsky's use of the term *generative* parallels historical uses. Earlier grammarians in the rationalist tradition wrestled with the notion that the mind had an innate language capacity to create unlimited sentences. These grammarians failed to establish a workable scheme, but they recognized the issue. On the other hand, Bloomfieldian linguists had some success at mathematical precision for producing sentences but did not recognize the importance of the first use of generative. Chomsky acknowledged the importance of both uses of the term and incorporated them into his theoretical models.

The grammar is *transformational* because it includes certain types of rules that perform transformations. These rules operate with logical precision but the principle behind the rules is really quite simple and necessary for the theory. The core of the theory makes it necessary for a few rules to create an infinite number of sentences. These rules exist to perform transformations on *deep structure* and produce surface structures (actual sentences). Deep structure is part of the innate knowledge of the language user and is common across all languages. Surface structures are what differentiates individual languages. Consider the following sentence: "Karen, who is a good cook, made the pasta dinner."

The sentence is derived from a complex conceptual or deep structure. We can use our intuitions to see that the sentence can be analyzed as being composed of a matrix sentence and embedded sentences. The matrix sentence is the elemental proposition of the sentence and corresponds roughly to an affirmative declarative sentence.

Matrix sentence:	Karen made the dinner.
Embedded sentence:	Karen is a good cook.
Embedded sentence:	The dinner is pasta.

We can parse the sentence into phrase structures (see chapter 2, p. 39) and conceptualize the sentence as diagrammed in Fig. 3.1. These sentences are represented in deep structure and must be "transformed" into the surface structures that we commonly employ. The transformation rules allow us to make alterations so that we can represent deep structure in surface structure.

Notice that the embedded sentences are governed by the matrix sentence. We need the transformation rules to delete and rearrange various aspects of the embedded sentences so they will be represented in the matrix sentence according to surface structure principles of the language. An example of a transformational rule would be one in which "Karen is a good cook" becomes a relative clause, and "The dinner is pasta" gets transformed into an adjective. An adjectival insertion rule, then, states that if the noun of an embedded sentence is the same as the matrix sentence it is permissible to delete the noun and move the adjective to the front of the same noun in the matrix sentence. The same basic rule applies to the subject Karen and the fact that she is a good cook. Karen can be deleted in the embedded sentence and replaced with the relative pronoun "who." The argument is that these two transformation rules operate on the deep structure to produce the surface structure sentence "Karen, who is a good cook, made the pasta dinner."

It is important to note that this is a theoretical representation of the knowledge that a speaker should have to produce language in the way that we do. It certainly is not the case that the mind actually goes through this process. The goal of the theorist is to construct a formalism that represents "tacit" knowledge, not consciousness. Chomsky did argue that grammars should reflect what is stored in the mind, but it is unlikely that there are parallels between the constraints of formalism and the way the mind works.

Grammar and Psychological Reality. The 1957 version of *Syntactic Structures* focused on syntax more than meaning or sounds. The result was a shift away from meaning and a move toward studying types of transformations. In *Aspects of a Theory of Syntax* (1965) Chomsky specified the deep structure–surface structure distinction and at least addressed the issue of semantics. But his critics suggested that meaning was more central to demonstrating how sentences work than perhaps syntax, or at least more important than previously assumed. One line of work began to examine how "real" grammars are, that is, whether or not it was possible to find empirical illustrations of these abstract cognitive models. A number of investigations tried to assess the reality of transformations.

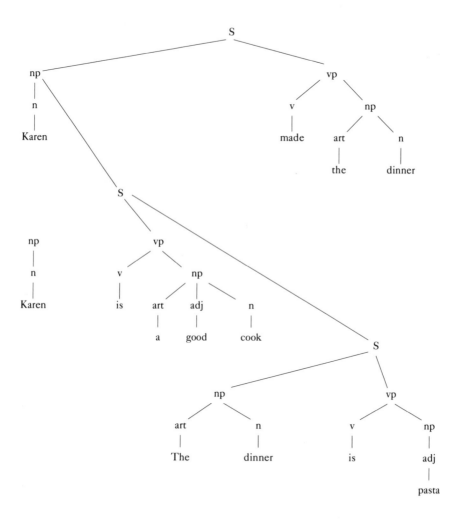

FIG. 3.1. Diagram of sentence relationships.

The assumption was that sentences that required few transformations would be easier to recognize or manipulate in some way than sentences that required more transformations. One investigation (Miller & McKean, 1964) measured how long it took subjects to match active sentences with passive ones and found that it took longer than to match affirmative sentences to negative ones. So matching "Bill liked the dog" to "The dog was liked by Bill" was slower than to a corresponding negative sentence such as "Bill didn't like the dog." These results were assumed to be supportive of the psychological reality of transformations because passives are regarded as linguistically more complex than negatives. Other studies (Gough, 1965; Slobin, 1966) asked subjects to determine the truth value of different sentence types (e.g., passive–negative, active–affirmative, passive, negative) in relation to pictures and various situations. These studies used response time as a measure and found that passives required more time to evaluate than active sentences. Further investigations (Johnson-Laird, 1969) used quantifiers in sentences such as "All philosophers have read some books" and "Some books have been read by all philosophers" and found that subjects confused the explanation of the sentences. Even though each sentence is ambiguous in the same way, the first sentence is typically interpreted as "some book or other" and the second sentence as "some books in particular." Findings in experiments such as these caused researchers to alter their grammars because underlying meaning relationships were perhaps accounting for results as much as the proposed theoretical assumptions.

Current work takes a much more skeptical approach to relating grammatical descriptions to mental operations. Few theorists believe that such mental operations will be revealed in a response-oriented task. And psycholinguists are hesitant to directly equate linguistic complexity to mental operations. There are any number of immediate difficulties with this research. One is with the relationship between "generation" and "production." It is assumed that grammars generate sentences and speakers produce them, but are these processes the same or are they different in some fundamental ways? The term *complexity* is also full of problems. Should complexity be measured by the number of transformations, type of transformation, sentence structures, or semantic relationships? Other questions persist such as the relationship between sentence structure and memory. And it is debatable whether syntactic and semantic information are treated alike in memory or by the generative grammar. There are many ambiguous and contradictory results. The mind is the blackest of all black boxes and its inner workings are not very accessible.

But these problems suggest an alternative approach that is more characteristic of current work in psycholinguistics. Such an approach makes inferences regarding the human mind on the basis of knowledge about language. It continues the direction in science of creating abstract models or "useful fictions" that are logical characterizations of the phenomenon of interest, namely, the human mind. If language is a complex rule-governed system, then the mind must be built to handle the system. There must be a theory of language in order to have a theory of mind and both must be defensible on logical and empirical grounds. Investigators today are interested in developing models of how language is processed. They approach the problem bit-by-bit rather than searching for an all-encompassing principle or generative mechanism that presumably explains things in a simple way. The next section continues much of what Chomsky started by examining issues in word recognition, syntax, and related problems. The notion of meaning and attendant cognitive implications as they relate to semantics, discourse, and text are so central to communication that they will be taken up in separate chapters. We can divide language-processing issues into three general areas: word recognition, structural relations (syntax), and message-level processing. The remainder of this chapter is devoted to word recognition and structural relations.

WORD RECOGNITION

One of the first language-processing problems to be solved is how individuals recognize and process words. It is possible to divide this process into two general areas where the first is related to language comprehension, or how we perceive and establish the meaning of a word, and the second to language production, or how we select a lexical item for expression. Most of the discussion in this section deals with word recognition and comprehension. The question here is: How do we identify words in spoken and written communication? There are differences in processing between spoken and written words and we attempt to deal with those differences. Most of the research uses printed words rather than spoken or cursive script because of the ease in producing and interpreting research material. An important exception is Marslen-Wilson and Tyler (1980).

The Lexicon

Establishing meaning is the purpose of listening or reading. This is accomplished by taking incoming stimuli from visual or auditory cues and activating a sort of warehouse of knowledge about words. An individual's knowledge of words is called *mental lexicon*. It is a "mental" lexicon because even though it has dictionary-like entries, it is quite different from a standard dictionary. The mental lexicon contains word meanings and information about pronunciation and usage but the mental lexicon is organized differently than a dictionary. The mental lexicon has rules for making "decisions" about meaning because humans, unlike dictionaries, must make choices about how a word is being used at a particular time. The first thing a listener or reader must do is utilize information that aids the word recognition process. There are two types of information available for use: perceptual and contextual.

Perceptual Information. Perceptual information comes from detecting visual cues that signal recognizable patterns and shapes. In the case of the reader this is lines and shapes that allow for the identification of letters and words. As the reader of this book, you can recognize the following letter strings because you have a set of recognition units that allow you to process the sequence as meaningful (BOOK, COMPUTER). We learn visual recognition cues for writing when we are very young because writing is important in our culture. There are other forms of visual symbols that are increasingly important in contemporary culture, although they are more ambiguous and therefore more difficult to understand. After identifying individual letters of a written word you must then recognize familiar letter strings that constitute words. Again, words such as BOOK and COMPUTER will be simple enough because they are consistent with rules of visual signals and phonetics. But what about a letter string such as PORGATH or QZRTGPMGV. These words are unfamiliar so you have no way to use them as indicators of meaning. But PORGATH is pronounceable because it adheres to phonetic rules. An adequate theory of visual word recognition must include rules for converting letters to sounds before searching for meaning. PORGATH "sounds" like it should be meaningful or might be an actual English word; but with QZRTGPMGV we do little more than identify individual letters. In fact there is evidence to indicate that we do not even attempt to find meaning for nonsense letter strings (Stanners & Forbach, 1973).

This requirement for converting letters to sounds has been called *phonological recoding.* The argument is that spoken language is cognitively prior to written language and that visual patterns must be converted to phonological ones that are consistent with spoken language. It has been suggested that we learn a set of rules called *grapheme–phoneme correspondence rules* that translate visual letter patterns into the sound patterns of the language. The evidence for the phonological recoding hypothesis is indefinite. Some earlier work by Rubenstein, Lewis, and Rubenstein (1971) compared pronounceable nonwords (e.g., porgath) to pseudo-homophones (e.g., brane), which are words that sound like real words. They found that pseudohomophones took longer to reject and suggested that this was because the sounds activated a lexical search that took some time before the search could be rejected. There is other supportive data in Meyer, Schvaneveldt, and Ruddy (1974).

But Kleiman (1975) produced the most compelling evidence against the hypothesis. He argued that if we recoded a visual stimulus into a phonological one there should be a problem if people had to speak while making the recoding because both tasks require phonological processing. His research was supportive of his assumption and resulted in what he called the *dual access hypothesis*. This hypothesis suggested that words can access the mental lexicon by either direct visual access or phonological recoding. Although the dual access hypothesis is popular, there are continued efforts to explain results by positing new theories.

Analogy theory is one such effort. This work (McClelland & Rumelhart, 1981; Rumelhart & McClelland, 1982) maintains that visually presented words have only one path to the lexicon rather than two, and the path is through the activation of entries in the lexicon by visual stimuli with similar spellings. Moreover, the Rumelhart and McClelland models uses some *top–down* processing and also does not require one type of processing to be complete before beginning another. We have mostly been talking about word recognition as a bottom–up process—that is, recognition and access to the lexicon is controlled by incoming visual stimuli. Top–down processing uses stored knowledge and experience to interact with the external signal stimuli information to influence what is perceived. Rumelhart and McClelland claimed, and supported through their computer program, that strings of letters begin stimulating recognition and this in turn activates possible words. These word activations in the lexicon then feed back down to the letter recognizers and "help" with that process. So, if I am trying to read the word BOOK I begin by identifying the letters B,O,O, and K but before even finishing the letter recognition the initial letters begin activating related BOO words. This feeds "down" to the letter detectors so the final recognition is a combination of information from below (printed word) and above (stored knowledge about words with similar visual input). Information can, as Rumelhart and McClelland put it, "cascade" from higher to lower levels. The model has a number of strengths, not the least of which is that it shows how higher levels of processing and general knowledge interact with moment-to-moment stimuli to affect consciousness and experience.

Clearly, most research on visual processing uses printed letters and words. But it has been known for some time that there is also a visual aspect to listening and processing speech. Research on processing speech during face-to-face encounters indicates that listening has a visual component to it that is responsible for some perceptual information. Some early work found that having an opportunity to view a speaker's face improved recognition of sounds and words. But later investigations (McGurk & MacDonald, 1976) suggested that visual information interacts with sounds in some complex ways. In one study, subjects viewed a videotape of a speaker saying one thing but with the words replaced by a different soundtrack. They found that watching lip movements for one sound while listening to another sound resulted in an altered perception of what the speaker was saying. The researchers concluded that the visual and auditory signals must be consistent before processing and recognition, because the visual and auditory combine to form a single perception.

Contextual Information. Contextual information comes from the meaning environment of a word. More specifically, it is the influence of the preceding text, accompanying pictures or illustrations, and shared knowledge on the probability that a word will access the lexicon at a particular speed. Word context is an important source of information and there is little doubt that word associations improve recognition. If someone sees the words *wheels car* presented either together or one after the other, a decision about their meaning will be faster than if the person had the words *wheels sugar* presented (Meyer & Schvaneveldt, 1971). It is also easier to recognize a single letter in a familiar context than in an unfamiliar or uncommon one. It is easier to identify the letter *a* in the word *band* than it is to pick it out amid a string of Xs. The McClelland and Rumelhart (1981) work discussed earlier also utilizes context effects during word recognition because it uses stored knowledge to make a decision about a word. As the beginning letters in a string unfold they provide a context for recognizing the word.

A final decision about word recognition must include a mechanism for checking context. Norris (1982) offered a *checking model* by arguing that during word recognition the lexicon is continuously outputting words that are consistent with the perceptual analysis. These words are compared to the context to see how well they fit. Context in this case works with the perceptual system by contributing to the probability that a word will be recognized. Contextual information is not separate from perceptual information. Both interact with each other to increase or decrease the evidence required to recognize a word.

Marslen-Wilson and Tyler's (1980) model uses left-to-right processing assumptions. They claimed that letters are processed from beginning to end and early perceptual data calls forth a set of words that are candidates for recognition. One problem with any model based on a left-to-right processing assumption is that it cannot explain words that are mispronounced at the beginning. There is no component of the model that explains why you understand when a drunk says "dink" for "drink." Processing auditory input is probably not a matter of extracting phonemes in sequence the way written alphabetic letters are processed.

Context in language processing is more than the sounds or letters that precede or follow something, it includes word and sentence contexts. Some early studies showed that if a context were established for a series of words to follow then subjects could recognize them easier. If, for example, you were "primed" and told that all the words on a list to follow referred to "automobile" then you would be likely to understand "brive" as "drive" or "bunk" as "trunk." This is a very consistent research finding throughout the language reception literature. The recent theoretical principle that has been invoked to explain this phenomenon is *spreading activation*. This principle holds that the lexical entries that are activated by automobile "spread" to related concepts such as "trunk" and "drive" (Collins & Loftus, 1975).

There is a final issue of interest with regard to the roll of context on language reception. There are data to indicate that the importance of context differs dramatically with respect to its significance in processing print versus speech. Henderson (1982) and Stanovich and West (1983) suggested that the nature of the communicative signal—whether print or speech—determines the role of context in processing. Context seems to play a very important role in speech processing and a less important one when processing printed matter. Normal speech is not a very high quality carrier of information. The printed word is highly coded in that there is one or relatively few ways a printed word can be informative. The printed word has its own context and it is not bound in time. You can read the same book any day of the week and the signal will be the same. But natural language is full of imprecisions, flawed articulation, background noises, and more importantly, it is most meaningful within an immediate temporal context. Words removed from the context of a conversation become much less intelligible. The difference is one of "bottom-up" versus "top-down" processing. Reading the printed word relies on extracting information from the printed signal, whereas listening to a speaker involves applying generalized cognitive structures to the information contained in the speech. There is evidence (Stanovich & West, 1983) that this is attributable to the quality of the signal because there is increased use of context and "top-down" processing in studies where the written signal has been degraded. We see later that processing spoken communication (discourse) involves some unique psychological processes.

Accessing the Lexicon

Words are recognized using perceptual and contextual information that is either part of a stimulus (spoken or written language) or a context. We have been examining theories of recognition and how the lexicon is accessed is part of those theories. There are two general models that depict how the lexicon is accessed, namely, direct access models and search models.

Direct access models assume that the perceptual information from a written or spoken word directly accesses a set of features. Morton (1970) called these features *logogens* and there is a logogen for every word. Simply, if the input from perception contains a quality of a particular logogen then that logogen is activated. At the beginning of perception all logogen candidates are aroused but at one point a decision is made and one logogen is available for response, whereas the others are deactivated. If, for example, I encounter the word COMPUTER I begin activating related logogens at the moment that I recognize the shape of the first letter. After I decide that the word is COMPUTER the system prepares for the next input.

The logogen model has met with considerable success. It can account for a variety of known effects in language processing. We know, for example, that words that are encountered frequently are recognized and processed more quickly. The logogen model has a component that explains how this is accomplished while language is being learned. A logogen that fires more often will fire more quickly. The converse is also true. Nonwords are rejected by the logogen model because they contain no recognizable features. And the importance of contextual information is taken into account by the models use of a priming technique where information from a cognitive system is primed by the perceptual data and then used for interpretation and stored for future information.

The second approach to accessing the lexicon makes use of a search through the lexicon. This approach denies that there is direct access. At the extreme is the complete search approach where the entire lexicon is searched whenever a word is encountered, but no one has ever seriously proposed that we search every entry in the lexicon before recognition. It is more sensible to assume that the cognitive system is ordered in some way to ensure more efficiency and economy. Most search models are mixed models where some part of the lexicon is selected for search and then reduced to manageable size.

One theorist (Forster 1976, 1979) posited an important version of a mixed model by claiming that access files are used before the lexicon is searched. The access files are separate from the mental lexicon and allow for a search of its entries before moving to the lexicon. The argument is that you have one access file for printed words, a phonological file for recognizing spoken words, and a syntactic and semantic file that allows words to be inserted in sentences. After extracting data from all access files it searches for a corresponding entry in the mental lexicon. Forster's model accounts for known findings fairly well. Rapid recognition of common words occurs because entries in the files are assumed to be in order of frequency and input is compared with high frequency words first. Low frequency words, on the other hand, require many comparisons and take longer to process. Nonwords that might be close to real words are even more time consuming because similarities are processed but need to be rejected. If you encounter input such as COPMUTER it activates COMPUTER and related entries but must ultimately reject each. Finally, the importance of context in word processing is explained by configuring the lexicon in such a way that related words are organized closely in cognitive space. Activating one word then makes it easier to activate a related one.

Recognizing words and making them available for processing is perhaps an important early cognitive function in language processing. Perceptions of written and spoken language, along with contexts, are the primary sources of information about words. Earlier in this chapter we credited Chomsky with making significant contributions to psycholinguistics. But although Chomsky had very little to say about perceptual processes involved in word recognition, he was very interested in the structural relations between words. Now that the words in a sentence have been recognized and described syntactically, the language-processing system must establish the structural relationships between those words so that it can establish the message of a sentence.

STRUCTURAL RELATIONS

Structural relations, for the linguist and psycholinguist, is the problem of serial ordering of words within a sentence. *Syntax* is the term most commonly used to describe this characteristic of language. In the early days of behaviorism in psychology, syntax was assumed to be a string of stimuli and responses, although psychologists devoted very little time to syntax or grammar. Before Chomsky and contemporary work in psycholinguistics there was an emerging research tradition in information processing. Miller (1953) was conducting studies of sequential dependence to test how well subjects could recall a string of words that differed in their approximation to normal English. The results led Miller to conclude that people could learn material, not from meaning, but from short-term associations. This preserved the tradition of stimulus response explanations in psychology, and made it possible to continue to ignore the problem of meaning.

In *Syntactic Structures* (1957) Chomsky, of course, showed that the stimulus–response behavioristic paradigm was unsuitable to explain language processing and syntax. As we saw earlier, he required considering underlying structure as well as surface structure, and showed how these two might be related by transformation rules. Chomsky suggested that the number of transformation rules might vary according to the type of sentence being processed.

The psychological implications of the relationship between transformation rules and syntax became very exciting for some psychologists. It inspired many to reason that the more transformations required to process a sentence the more effort and perhaps time would be required of subjects. This line of thinking became known as the *derivational theory of complexity* and it stimulated considerable research. Psychologists assumed that the more transformational operations required to recover deep structure, the longer it would take to comprehend a sentence and the more difficult to memorize. Thus began psycholinguistic research. Some of this work is discussed in this chapter (pp. 51–55) and more particularly in Slobin (1971) and Fodor, Bever, and Garrett (1974). The derivational theory of complexity is of historical interest but has been abandoned because of alternative explanations of results and the fact that the theory was essentially untestable (Garnham, 1983). More recent theories do not depend on the assumptions about the effects of transformations, and rely on a more important role for semantics and the lexicon.

Models of Computing Syntactic Structure

The difference between the linguist and the psychologist led to revisions of the derivational theory of complexity. One problem was that psychologists conducted experiments assuming direct link between linguistic models of grammar and transformations, and psychological issues in perception and memory. Fodor and Garrett (1966) argued that a linguist's grammar may not be related to psychological mechanisms of production and comprehension. They cited numerous problems with experimental procedures such as the length of sentences, where they found that subjects recalled shorter sentences faster even when those sentences involved more complex transformations. Psycholinguists were now in difficulty because they had accepted the competence–performance distinction, and a linguistic theory as a psychological one. They realized that they had to construct their own abstract theory.

Fodor and Garrett (1967) began this work by arguing that the complexity of a sentence, with respect to producing surface structure from deep structure, did not necessarily correspond to the complexity of the perceptual process necessary to establish base structure from surface form. Another way of saying this is that grammar influences output but not input. They would accept that deep structure generated surface structure but suggested that the process of comprehension (converting surface form to base form) was achieved by computing deep structure relations from cues in surface form along with information in the lexicon.

The verb *complexity hypothesis* was one test of the problem and Fodor, Garrett, and Bever (1968) designed an experiment to see if perceptual processing of sentences varied as a function of verb structure. They reasoned that the more verb associations in a lexicon, that is, the greater the structural ambiguity of a verb, the longer it would take to process. The verb *discuss* is a simple transitive verb with a simple structure. But the verb *believe* can take several structures such as:

I believe John.
I believe that John . . .
I believe John to be . . .

Research results support the conclusions that verbs with more complex lexical structures take longer to process and that a person applies this information when working to comprehend a sentence.

This work is significant because it does not rely on assumptions about transformations; rather, attention is turned to the lexicon and more general issues in meaning. Other research (e.g., Hakes, 1971; Holmes & Forster, 1972) supports and modifies the work begun by Fodor and Garrett, but their work is seminal because they established research on syntax as an important aspect of psycholinguistics. There are many questions to be answered and problems to be solved but psycholinguists were now free to pursue their craft from a psychological perspective. They were no longer dependent on linguistic theory. There continues to be models of parsing in psychology and other disciplines—Kimball (1973) and Frazier and Fodor (1978) are excellent examples of complete theories—but some of the most powerful parsing devices and theories of parsing have emerged from the artificial intelligence literature. These are the parsers used by computers designed to model human intelligence.

Augmented Transition Networks

One of the goals of artificial intelligence work is to teach a computer how to process natural language. To do that the computer must model human language processing, which means that the computer must have a technique for assigning structural relations to strings of words. The most successful systems for solving this problem are called *augmented transition networks* (ATN). The work in computer science has prompted some psycholinguists to try to assess the "psychological reality" of these parsing systems (Johnson-Laird, 1983). An ATN is composed of a set of transition networks that looks for various components of a possible sentence. Figure 3.2 is the simplest version of an ATN because it begins at the sentence level and requires the computer to find a noun phrase and then a verb phrase. It also must assign a subject to the sentence.

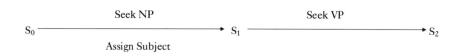

FIG. 3.2. Simple ATN.

When a noun is found it can make the transition to a verb phrase. A real ATN must be capable of identifying complex sentences, with embeddings of all sorts and a variety of sentence structures. The network is trying to traverse arcs so it can move from one area of the sentence to another assigning structural descriptions.

An ATN is a syntactic analyzer that uses a processor and a transition network. It identifies any linguistic input as a segmented string of words. The analyzer works its way through word by word, formulating testing, and modifying hypotheses about syntactic structure. Because a sentence is a complex pattern of words, the main problem for the ATN is recognizing patterns in the form of clauses and phrases. The process works something like this: In the sentence "The boy hit the ball" the processor begins with the first word. The only arc leaving S_0 is SEEK NP or an indication that the system will make a transition if the current input is part of a noun phrase. The processor executes SEEK A NOUN PHRASE. It searches the noun-phrase patterns in the processor and compares patterns against the input. The noun-phrase network in the processor has a component that says CAT ART or that processing can continue if the current input can be CATegorized as an ARTicle. The processor looks up *the* in the lexicon and because the condition is satisfied it moves to the next function, which is to identify *the* as the determiner in the noun phrase. The processor then moves to the second word in the sentence.

Eric Wanner introduced ATNs to psycholinguistic research and the work of Wanner and his associates (Wanner & Maratsos, 1978) is the most complete and powerful. ATNs have been used successfully to analyze information about lunar rocks, and they can model human sentence parsing quite well. Wanner and Maratsos (1978) gave three reasons why they believed that ATNs correspond well to the operations of human comprehension. First, data indicate that humans process sentences sequentially and ATNs are designed to do the same thing. Humans may not process exactly left to right and word by word, but evidence is clear that what comes first in a sentence is processed first. Second, a human listener has knowledge of linguistic structure and actively applies that knowledge. Physical cues such as tone and punctuation facilitate understanding but they are not necessary for establishing the component structure of a sentence. And finally the ATN, like its human counterpart, is organized into tasks. One part of the network is assigned to work on phrases, another clauses, and so on.

Psycholinguistics is important to communication because it attempts to describe how language works and the role of cognition in that explanation. Whether linguistic knowledge stored in the mind corresponds to grammar or any known process is a matter of further question. Chomsky believed that it does and he, from a psycholinguistic point of view, is a most important figure in linguistics. Chomsky introduced precision and theoretical analysis of such elegance and penetration that he was able to show the inadequacy of behaviorist accounts of linguistic behavior. The goal of psycholinguistics has been to build models of the mind and its role in language processing. Recognizing words and establishing structural relations are processes that must be part of any such model. But since about the end of the 1960s, with a few exceptions, there has been a leveling of interest in theories of word recognition and syntax. Nevertheless, this leveling was short lived because the surge of interest in artificial intelligence has stimulated new work in parsing—notably augmented transition networks. But *meaning* is the final goal of language and communication and the remainder of this text is devoted to issues in meaning. After considering some technical issues in the concept of meaning, we turn our attention to discourse and message levels of significance.

4

Meaning

The "meaning of meaning" is probably the single most controversial issue common to linguists, communication theorists, logicians, and psychologists alike. In the previous chapters we have examined formal issues in language and communication with an emphasis on the linguistic system; and syntax, structure, and cognitive processing in particular. We come now to the essence of language and communication—the meaning system. Assuming one accepts the obvious fact that the entire nature, structure, and development of language is as a vehicle for communication or meaning transmission, then it is certainly odd that linguists, psychologists, and communication theorists have spent little time studying meaning or they avoid it altogether. The Bloomfieldians, who were behavioristic, avoided the problem of meaning by relegating it to psychology. Bloomfield (1933) knew that meaning was the weak point in linguistics and his successes would have been limited had he concentrated on this problem. Chomsky escaped the problem by assigning syntax to the central role in grammar. This does not detract from his contributions to linguistics and psycholinguistics, but syntax is not meaning and, as Chomsky freely admitted, the "understanding" sense of meaning is far removed from computing syntactic structure.

The Problem of Meaning

People have little or no difficulty working out the meaning of most of what they hear or read, yet the concept of meaning is complex and difficult to explicate. The syntactician has worked out models that describe what the human language processor must do in order to comprehend and produce sentences. He or she has established some plausible explanations of how it is possible for people to organize morphological units into logical sequences. The semanticist or meaning theorist must do the same; however, the domain of meaning is more stubborn and intractable than syntax. It does not lend itself to neat logical analyses. Nevertheless, a complete explication of meaning must account for certain qualities of language. Some of these qualities, as they pertain to words, are listed below. We comment on difficulties when processing sentences later.

   1. Many words are *associated* with one another. Things would be simple if the world were divided into neat units and there was one word corresponding to one idea or thing. But there are many shades of meaning that are communicated by a set of related words.

- ghost, spirit, apparition, spook, poltergeist
- cheat, swindle, fleece, rip off, defraud

   2. Words are *ambiguous*. They can take more than one meaning in a sentence.

- This plant is tough. ("skin is thick" or "healthy")
- Don't dribble. ("bounce the ball" or "drop food")

   3. Words can be *redundant*. The meaning of one word can be contained in the meaning of another.

- He killed him dead
- We paired them in twos.

   4. Poetic uses of language result from the possibility of combining words in some strange ways. One can place *contradictory* and *anomalous* words together to create interesting and new meanings.

- The sun kissed the forsythia bush (anomaly)
- When he stood there was a thunderous silence (contradictory)

Some semblance of communication occurs because we assume that we have knowledge of the meanings of these words—and how they are formed into sentences—and this knowledge is shared among language users. But knowledge of words and their meaning is not equally distributed in the population and many confusions, distortions, and general breakdowns in communication are attributable to uncoordinated knowledge of word meanings. The ability to understand someone is not the same as the ability to understand the concept and nature of meaning. Although there are a variety of issues involved in understanding "meaning" one distinction is of particular importance. It is the difference between *reference* and *sense*. A word has a referential quality in that it refers to or stands for something in particular. The referent for a word is typically one thing or idea and represents its core meaning or what the word denotes. The word "Karen" as in "My wife Karen" denotes a specific person. The word "chair" in the phrase "My chair is comfortable" refers to a single empirical object. Any word such as "run," "hit," or "blue" has a set of objects or qualities that it denotes. The *sense* of a word, on the other hand, is related to the practical and common uses of a term. All the possible dictionary entries for a word roughly correspond to all the possible senses of a word. The word "chair" can refer to the object I am sitting on, but I can also say "I am going to chair the meeting." This is a different sense of the word. In the sentence "My son swung at the ball, and his mother, at me," the word "swung" is used in different senses. Both refer to the same essential physical activity, but they have different purposes, motivations, and goals.

There are other "senses" of the word *meaning* that are more applicable to communication issues. When you ask the meaning of a word such as the word *computer* in the sentence "What does the word computer mean?" you are asking about a class of objects and qualities. You would be correct if you said that a computer was a machine that performs calculations of various types. The meaning refers to abstract qualities. But in actual utterances, phrases, or written sentences words typically refer to specific things. If you asked "Where is my computer?" you would be asking about a specific computer and the answer would require knowledge of the world, or reference to facts that you understand. The interesting distinction is that human communicators are rarely in doubt about the meaning of individual words uttered during actual communication. If I asked someone about the location of my computer they would know what I meant and would answer in accordance with their knowledge of its whereabouts. But, curiously, if I asked someone for a complete and exhaustive definition of a computer they would have trouble satisfying my request.

The point here is that words and sentences denote specific things and have a variety of senses about them. A complete theory of meaning must account for both types of meaning. A native speaker computes both types of meaning for a word and, more importantly for communication, a speaker can make educated decisions about the variety of possible senses of a word or phrase. This is called *comprehension*. It is also true that if I ask you about the location of my computer you might understand my question as an "accusation." There might be a subtle implication that you acquired my computer unlawfully; only our relationship and general knowledge about things would decide whether or not this implication was warranted. A native communicator listening to the example sentence would be looking for various sorts of significance. A complete theory of semantics should be capable of accounting for the many senses of words and utterances.

SEMANTICS

A theory of semantics is a theory of meaning and probably the most difficult and troublesome aspect of a general theory of language. It was no accident that Bloomfield and Chomsky chose to relegate semantic issues to other disciplines because it poses some of the thorniest problems. In 1938 Morris established a division of semiotics into syntactics, semantics, and pragmatics. The distinction between semantics and pragmatics was that semantics was the study of the relationship between signs and objects, and pragmatics was the study of signs and their users. Pragmatics is concerned with all of the various and unique uses that language users (communicators) have for words and phrases. It is how words actually function in communication. In the sentence "I like your new hair," the words "new hair" do not literally refer to new hair but to a cut or style of hair. It is a meaning that expresses the relationship between language users and words. For Morris, semantics was the study of a word and what it referred to, but it is quite difficult to make a clear distinction between semantics and pragmatics using Morris' distinctions.

We use Gazdar's (1979) distinction between semantics and pragmatics by assuming semantics to be truth conditional and pragmatics to be nontruth conditional. The circumstances in which a sentence would be true are the truth conditions of a sentence. If we can understand how a sentence is a correct description of a situation then we have established the truth conditions of the sentence. Pragmatics, on the other hand, has become increasingly important in the last couple of decades because it is concerned with the practical conditions of an utterance. Pragmatics and related topics such as implicature, presupposition, and conversational mechanisms are more central to communication and are discussed in more detail in subsequent chapters. There is a tendency in linguistics and in communication in particular to concentrate in the future on larger units of meaning that do not lend themselves too easily to strict logical analysis. Stories, narratives, and larger textual units have an order and structure beyond isolated sentences. We consider some of these issues later.

Structural Semantics

The branch of semantics that is the most formal and logical is called *structural semantics*. Structural semantics is a formal logic that many people have difficulty understanding because so little of our everyday use of language is comparable to formal logic. The purpose of structural semantics is to specify how sentences come to be true given the words in the language, and the way in which the syntax organizes the words. Logicians such as Frege (1879/1972) claim that natural language can be expressed in a form of predicate calculus. The goal is to take the components of a sentence and provide a precise translation into the calculus.

Structural semantics does not produce meaning for words, rather it produces a complex expression of objects. The theory begins with a model that includes an *object language*. The object language pertains to the specific objects that parts of the natural language refers to. Thus, the name for something, such as *house*, will refer to a set of objects (the class of houses) that it denotes. Structural semantics assumes that meanings have already been assigned to words. The theory is not concerned with the actual determination of meaning or providing clues to common usage. The particular objects of a sentence must then be organized according to a syntax. The component parts and the way in which they are organized determine the meaning of a sentence. There is a corresponding semantic rule for each syntactic rule. These rules are a metalanguage that allow for statements regarding the object language. They are comparable to syntactic rules that we encountered earlier such as S $\rightarrow$ NP + VP, which means that a sentence (on the left side of the equation) can be rewritten as a rule on the right side of the equation, or as being composed of a noun phrase and a verb phrase. The semantic rule would be as follows: The sentence is true if the object(s) expressed by the noun phrase is in particular relation to the object(s) denoted by the verb phrase. So the sentence "Steve hits" is true if there is someone called Steve and he hits.

Semantics and Truth. In structural semantics a semantic theory is a theory of truth. A goal of semantic theory is to state that something is true of false, and to do that we must distinguish between sentences in a language that are *linguistically true* and those that are *empirically true*. A sentence is determined to be linguistically true if its truth is established by its structure and semantics of the language and not by checking facts in the nonlinguistic empirical world. A sentence is empirically true if we must confirm it by checking the empirical world as to its correctness. Most communication is of this latter type. If I say "My briefcase is on the desk," then the sentence is empirically true if the briefcase is actually on the desk. But consider the following sentences and note how it is possible to establish their truth value without reference to the empirical world.

1. The window is either open or it is not open.
2. If Don and Bob like baseball, then Don likes baseball.
3. The window is open and it is closed. (False)

These sentences are called *analytical sentences* because their truth value is determined by logical connectives such as "either," "if," and "then." Sentences 1 and 2 are true and Sentence 3 is false. We can see that the form of these sentences makes them true and not their empirical content. They can be cast as logical equations because Sentences 1 and 2 can take the forms:

4. Either S or not-S.
5. If S and S', then S.

but Sentence 3 is false because the following equation cannot be true:

6. S and not-S.

The sentences in Examples 1–3 are true because the words "either," "and," and "if" are logical terms that dictate how one part of a sentence should relate to another. But in the following sentences terms are descriptive of certain subject matter and while it is possible to generate their logical forms, it is also possible to produce false sentences:

7. If Bill is a genius, then he is intelligent.
8. If the perfume was fragrant, then it was scented.
9. If Bill is a genius, then he is dumb.

Sentences 7 and 8 are true and Sentence 9 is false. The first two sentences are true because the key terms each imply one another. To be a genius is by definition to be intelligent, and anything that has a fragrance has a scent. In Sentence 9 we have related two terms that cannot be true so the sentence is false. These three sentences can be cast into logical forms quite easily.

10. If Bill is G, then Bill is I.
11. If perfume was F, then it was S.
12. If Bill is G, then Bill is not D.

The types of sentences in Examples 7–9, and their logical forms in 10–12, are called analytic sentences because they are true by virtue of their semantic nature.

Entailment. One other function of a theory of truth and semantics is *entailment*. Simply, entailment means "follow from" or that the truth of one sentence guarantees the truth of a second as in Examples 13 and 14.

13. Bill is a man *entails* Bill is a mammal.

14. Karen awoke at 5:30 *entails* Karen was asleep immediately prior to 5:30.

Logical entailment is a goal of a formal theory of semantics, but it is often difficult to achieve because the logic of semantic structure is not always clear. Words such as "man" and "mammal" or "color" and "blue" imply one another and can be written as analytical sentences. The language of some natural sciences (e.g., chemistry, physics) begins to approximate the type of semantic precision necessary for exact description and analysis. The specificity of the language used to describe a chemical process, for example, and the close relationship between a term and its referent, makes it possible for these sciences to be more exact. Some sentences do not easily entail others, such as Example 15 does not necessarily entail Example 16.

15. Don cleaned the house.

16. The house was clean.

There are situations in which Example 15 would be true but 16 would not be because it is possible for Don to engage in house-cleaning activities, but have the house still not be what we would call clean.

The types of sentences in Examples 15 and 16 are more like the sentences in natural language during communication because the meaning of words change according to usage patterns and individuals. Because it is not possible to have an objective measure of a clean house, or a definition that would represent complete consensus, Sentence 16 cannot be an entailment of 15. In short, very little of our everyday language takes the form of logic that can be expressed in a formula. Formal logic and theories of truth have really very little relevance to natural languages—that is, little relevance to the way people actually use language. This is because sentence comprehension also requires general knowledge about the world, it requires individual language users to bring background information and presuppositions that are necessary for comprehension. It is important to underscore that truth conditional semantics has solved certain problems in linguistics and is quite useful for recognizing where literal meaning ends and inferences using background information begins. Literal and propositional meaning has been the province of traditional linguistics, and context sensitive meaning is in the realm of pragmatics and communication.

The gap between formal logic and natural language has been bridged by developments in two areas. The first is contextual semantics, which is so central to communication that we take it up in chapter 5 and various remaining chapters. Contextual semantics is about how people actually use language (communicate) and assign meaning to utterances that are not truth conditional. But within the realm of logic perhaps the most important concept for semantics was that of possible worlds (Kripke, 1963). This work emerges from *modal logics* that are used for analyzing possibilities, probabilities, beliefs, and so on. The concept of possible worlds makes it possible for a statement not to be true or false, but true or false within a possible world. The sentence

   17. It is possible that David is friendly.

is true if there is at least one possibility that the sentence

   18. David is friendly.

is true. Modal logics allow for the application of semantic theories to natural language. They help semantic theories predict semantic entailments that any correct theory of semantics must produce.

Structural semantics has little bearing on actual language use and communication. And the reason for this, as we have seen, is that the logical calculi of formulae do not correspond well to natural language, and that the proper unit of analysis might not be the sentence. In later chapters we see how examining every sentence of a text, regardless of context, can be misleading. When considering entire texts and sequences of interaction, according to standard structural semantics, it is necessary for every sentence in a text to be true if the entire text is going to be true. Such a requirement leads to some logical inconsistencies that cannot be resolved because the structure of a text, and not only truth values, can determine whether or not a sentence is true.

Lexical Semantics

Lexical semantics is the study of word meanings. In chapter 3 we described the mental lexicon and processes responsible for word recognition, storage, and access. The question here is how communicators decide on a meaning for use in understanding discourse. In the formal theories of structural semantics the meaning of a word is assigned (e.g., *book* denotes a set of books), and truth conditions result from logical formulae or the structural relations between words. But lexical semantics must explain how people understand words and what cognitive processes interact with this understanding to produce meaningful communication.

We noted earlier that the behaviorist Bloomfield assigned the study of meaning to other disciplines, namely, psychology. Phycholinguists have undertaken this assignment by concentrating on the mental activity that language reflects. A few early behavioristically oriented psychologists (e.g., Mowrer, 1954) began to argue that traditional principles of conditioning could account for meaning, but it was Osgood, Suci, and Tannenbaum (1957) who presented the first important conception of the nature of meaning. Their theory was based on principles of learning and mediation, which argues that people learn meaning by learning to make internal representational responses to words. These internal responses are an image of actual things represented by words. Words are signs for particular things and these internal mediating responses to words are the meaning of the word. Osgood suggested that an individual's response to some object or idea becomes part of the sign or word representing the object or idea. In this way, meanings vary from one person to another depending on the person's behavior toward an object. Osgood and his associates created the semantic differential scale that was a measuring instrument designed to measure meaning by locating a word in what was called *semantic space*. The semantic differential was a theoretically sound measuring device that generated large amounts of research (Snider & Osgood, 1969).

Linguists such as Fodor (1965) pointed out that Osgood's theory was little more than a direct conditioning model that Osgood was supposed to have rejected. The mediation model still holds that there is a direct relationship between the meaning of a word and the object that it represents. And a most difficult problem for mediation theories such as Osgood's is that language is not dependent on external stimuli, either for its acquisition, production, or comprehension. In many important respects Osgood had done little more than cast the simple theory of meaning, which is that words got their meaning from ideas in the mind, into some formal psychological theorizing.

The earliest work in lexical semantics was inspired by transformational grammar. In Chomsky's first book (Chomsky, 1957) he did not even mention issues in semantics. But in his second book (Chomsky 1965), he proposed what is known as *standard theory*. Standard theory builds on ideas proposed by Katz and Fodor (1963), in which they stipulate that meaning can be described as a set of features that define a word. The communication theorist and linguist are concerned with the concept of a word. There is no single thing, for example, that is a *dog*. The word *dog* refers to a concept or a sense in which things belong to a conceptual class called *dog*. A word spoken in an actual communication situation is only a single instance of a meaning, but it is the underlying sense of the word that defines the instance as correct or appropriate. We need to have a lexicon (dictionary) and rules for combining words.

Katz and Fodor suggested that each entry in our cognitive lexicon was defined according to features (markers) of the entry compared to all other entries. There would be a marker for every meaning associated with a word. The word "drill," for example, would have one semantic marker for the concept of "machine that makes a hole," and another marker for "routine practice." A further example might help by explaining the way in which the words "women" and "man" would be defined and distinguished by the semantic system. We would say that a women was "human" (expressed as +HUMAN) and +ADULT, +ANIMATE, +FE-MALE. A man would be +HUMAN, +ADULT, +ANIMATE, +MALE. All semantic markers apply to both except the +MALE and +FEMALE distinction. The markers specify both their similarity and differences. The markers also state how "man" and "women" are more similar to each other than they are to "drill," for example.

After enumerating all semantic markers for the lexical items in the language, the theory still needs rules to state what syntactical combinations are permissible. The rules must lead to acceptable grammatical sentences and be specific enough not to produce sentences such as "The drill is thinking about dinner" because inanimate objects do not have cognitive capabilities. A sentence such as "The man is thinking about dinner" would be acceptable.

Chomsky (1965) introduced semantics into his generative grammar by positing a semantic component that interpreted the meaning of a sentence by a set of rules. Word meanings were conceived to be composed of bundles of features that were interpreted in deep structure and transformed into surface structure. Grammatical elements and their arrangement in deep structure are the input into the semantic component. The semantic component interprets the input and provides "readings" of the sentence. If the sentence can have four meanings the semantic component should duplicate the four meanings. If the sentence is nonsense then there should be no readings. If two sentences mean the same thing then the semantic component should produce the same reading for both sentences. The semantic component of Chomsky's model should be able to represent a native speaker's understanding of nonsense, synonymy, contradictions, and ambiguity.

Since Chomsky introduced semantics into his generative syntax there have been a number of variations posed. The position known as generative semantics (see Lakoff, 1968; McCawley, 1968) was a response centered around the idea that syntax and semantics could not be separated. They argued that the semantic component did not merely interpret the syntactic component; rather, sentence generation began with semantics. Fillmore's (1968) case grammar is another approach to semantics. He introduced "cases" that were syntactic–semantic relations in deep structure. This allowed for the introduction of semantics into deep structure. In 1971 Chomsky modified his position and moved closer to the generative semanticists. He still maintained the separation of syntax and semantics but now has an interpretive component that applies to both deep structure and surface structure.

Research and Lexical Semantics

There is still no accepted theory of semantics. But linguists and psycholinguists continue to grapple with the problems. It is currently a time of very active research in the area because of an increase in interest in cognitive processes and artificial intelligence. In the 1970s there was even more theorizing about semantics and cognitive processing, for example, Bresnan's (1978) lexical interpretive model, and changes in Fodor's position (Fodor, Fodor, & Garret, 1975), and a dramatic increase in research and empirical demonstrations. Katz and Fodor's feature theory, along with other models of meaning and cognitive processing, were the subject of experimentation.

There is an important distinction between semantic representation and semantic processing. The mental lexicon is a storehouse of knowledge about words but it does not contain practical information about words. It has instructions about where to go for information. Information about the actual meaning of a word is stored in a second semantic location called *semantic memory*. This memory contains actual word meanings that correspond to meanings in ordinary communication. Where Chomsky and others worked to identify the theoretical aspects of semantics that must be understood in order to use language, psycholinguists must explain and empirically demonstrate how words relate to the world and what processes the human communicator uses to access these words.

Feature Theories. Semantic feature theories were used to account for word association tests. McNeill and McNeill (1968) argued that if word meanings were made up of sets of features, then people were most likely to respond to a stimulus word with one that had many features in common. Moreover, their arguments were bolstered by findings that children associated words that were more logically related than semantically because children would have fewer features to associate with a word. So a child would see "deep" and "hole" as more related than "deep" and "shallow" because deep–hole is syntactically related.

Feature theories were also influenced by the research on memory for sentences. A number of researchers (e.g., Sachs, 1967) found that the semantic message of a sentence is what people remember about sentences, and the syntactic structure fades quickly. If subjects were exposed to a sentence such as, "The rock was small" they were likely to recognize the sentence "The rock was not big" as one they had seen before. Clark and Clark (1968) thought that markedness could explain sentence memory experiments. They argued that when people heard words and sentences they extracted semantic distinctions in the form of features. Recall of sentences was assumed to be a reconstruction of semantic features.

They reasoned that simpler terms (terms that are unmarked or have single features) would be easier to recall than more complex terms. Data from experiments conducted by Clark and his associates support the assumption that unmarked terms were better recalled than marked forms.

This general theoretical work was extended to the reasoning process by Clark (1969). He wrote that reasoning was essentially a linguistic process where in processing a sentence a person first drew on primitive functional relations to construct the sentence. A person first worked out the functional relations in a sentence such as the subject-of, predicate-of, verb-of, and so on. After these functional relations were established language users would disambiguate words on the basis of feature complexity. In some experiments Clark asked subjects to respond to reasoning problems such as *If John is better than Pete, and Pete is better than Dick, then who is the best?* and predicted that answers would be more accurate and rapid than with problems such as *If John is not as good as Pete, and John is not as bad as Dick, then who is worst?* This prediction was based on the primacy of functional relations and lexical markings in the first problem. Although there are other accounts of these data, Clark's work was very influential and remains as a significant example of the relationship between linguistic and higher order cognitive processes such as reasoning.

The assumption of decomposition is one problem with feature theory and the research it spawned. It is counterintuitive and unlikely that comprehension is dependent on semantic decomposition. In a question such as "Where is the paper?" it is probably not necessary to decompose the term *paper* in order to answer the question. In one experiment Tabossi and Johnson-Laird (1980) demonstrated that decomposition is context sensitive, and that some aspects of meaning may be processed separately. Subjects read a sentence such as

19. The goldsmith cut the glass with the diamond.

and were then asked one of two questions either

20. Are the diamonds hard? OR
21. Are the diamonds valuable?

Their theorizing predicted that the introductory sentence would prime the first question but not the second and subjects would answer the first question more quickly. Their data show that some aspects of meaning may be processed differently than others, and that this may have less to do with semantic features than with language contexts.

Network Theories. Another metaphor for explaining the meaning process is based on assumptions advanced by Quillian (1968) and Collins and Quillian

(1969). Quillian used a computer memory model to argue that the meaning of a word is determined by its location in a semantic network. Words exist in a super-set of other words and have what are called *pointer properties*. That is, each term relates to a category name, which in turn is a member of another category. A spaniel is a dog, a dog is an animal, and so on. Concepts in the network are represented by nodes and these nodes are linked according to specific types of relationships. One relationship is set membership (Spot is a dog), a second is set inclusion (dogs are animals), a third is part–whole relations (a paw is part of a dog), and finally property attributes (dogs bark). So a dog is an animal with a paw and barks, but there would be no pointers to "wings" because this is not a property of dogs.

It follows from Quillian's work that a word located close to related words in semantic space should be easier and quicker to identify. It should be easier to associate the word "bark" with "animal" or "dog" than with "fish" or "bird." Collins and Quillian (1969) tested this assumption and found that reaction time was quicker for related categories. Semantic network theory is somewhat more useful for communication theories because the theory approximates how language is actually used rather than the formal properties of feature theories. Meaning in natural conversation is often concerned with implications and unspoken assumptions that depend on networks of relationships among words. Network theory is a better psychological theory of language processing and performance because it represents the knowledge necessary to use language.

Network theories of lexical processing have moved more toward representing actual language use in its models. One early problem with semantic network theories was that it was easier to verify words that were used more often than less typical relations, even though they were at the same level in the network. For example, it is easier to verify that a robin is a bird than it is to verify that an ostrich is a bird even though they are at the same level of the network and should take the same amount of time. Rips, Shoben, and Smith (1973) found that it was quicker to verify that a dog was an animal than a mammal, even though the hierarchy is dog–mammal–animal. These findings clearly indicate that common usage and communication patterns influence processing. Rosch, Mervis, Gray, Johnson, and Boyes-Braem (1976) showed that some semantic categories are basic and develop early. Collins and Loftus (1975) helped clarify these earlier theoretical anomalies by establishing the principle of *spreading activation*. Spreading activation argued that nodes were accessed according to contextual cues and that links between terms varied in strength. It is more difficult for activation to spread along weaker network links (e.g., links such as ostrich–bird versus canary–bird).

Work with computers and artificial intelligence continues to advance theories of semantic networks. Computer modeling requires researchers to state precisely categories and relations among them. Winograd (1972) has been influential in convincing others to appreciate the extent to which knowledge of the world is necessary to understand language. The following two sentences illustrate the sort of problems that must be solved:

22. The council banned the protestors because they feared violence.
23. The council banned the protestors because they advocated violence.

In the first sentence the pronoun *they* refers to the council and in the second it refers to the protesters. The two sentences are structurally equivalent. A reader or hearer would assign *they* to the correct referent and comprehend each sentence only if he had general knowledge about meetings and protesters. A computer would require an enormous amount of programming to equip it with such knowledge.

Meaning, Knowledge, and Communication

More recent research takes a somewhat different approach to the problem of meaning. Many contemporary psycholinguists and communication scholars assume that language is essentially a tool for communication and the exchange of knowledge between speakers. The meanings of words, therefore, are dependent on the cognitive and conceptual systems of the speakers and listeners and the context in which they are communicating. A specific message is determined by the situation in which an utterance is made. This work is central to communication theory and rests on the assumption that meaning is *constructed* by a speaker–listener relationship in a context, and is somewhat less precise than implied by feature theory. When one considers the broader extralinguistic context of meaning, analyses based on bundles of features of lexical items lose their impact.

A well-grounded and practical theory of meaning must depend on two things: the knowledge systems of the individuals involved, and the communication between people. During the process of communication decisions about what utterances "mean" are not based on features, but on the communicator's knowledge of intentions and what he believes to be the referents for the lexical items. Confusion and ambiguities in communication do not result from different feature of dictionary definitions of a word, but from failure to coordinate the intended meaning of an utterance from a set of alternative meanings available from the context. Olson (1970b) showed that words do not name things but they designate a referent relative to alternative referents that must be differentiated. Rather than exhausting all possible meanings a message assists a listener (or reader) in making decisions about plausible intended meaning. Communicator and listener skill depends on linguistic and cognitive resources: A person in the role of speaker must make lexical and syntactic choices that assist with differentiation among possible meanings, and a listener must incorporate the language of the speaker into his or her knowledge and cognitive resources to make decisions about meaning. Meaning is the fit between the immediate context and the knowledge system of the individual. This notion of an active cognitive individual operating within a context is central to current communication theory and psycholinguistics.

Once we establish that knowledge of the world is an important aspect of meaning, the scope of the problem broadens. People go beyond the information communicated in a single word by applying their own memory, recall, and comprehension abilities. This means that there are many more factors that influence the creation of meaning. By "knowledge of the world" we mean knowledge of general facts, probabilities, and empirical occurrences. If you know that your sister has red hair then this is a piece of specific knowledge particular to a person and may be important in some future communication; however, it is not general knowledge of the world. But you also know that all people have hair, so any randomly chosen person, whom you may have never met, is still likely to have hair. And it is also possible for someone not to have hair and they are still a human organism. This is the realm of empirical regularities that semantics and world knowledge must accommodate. In the sentence "The woman went to see the divorce lawyer," there is no entailment between the woman's own marital situation and her visiting a divorce lawyer. Although one would typically assume this relationship, there are contexts that the woman might be visiting a friend, or doing an interview for a magazine. Theories of semantics that are concerned with probabilities of events have little in common with those discussed in the beginning of this chapter that explain truth conditions. Structurally based theories of semantics determine events a sentence can describe, regardless of events and relationships that are likely to occur.

Most of the interesting questions about meaning are not truth-conditional. And the use of knowledge of the world and individual constructive processes have become central to semantic and communication theory. Communication theorists and linguists must explain how our knowledge of the world is organized and accessed by linguistic and textual cues. The next two chapters are devoted to discussing contemporary theories and ideas of semantics, and how these theories relate to the process of communication.

5

The Semantics of Communication and Discourse

We ended the previous chapter by suggesting that the concept of meaning was reliant on generalized knowledge and communicative use. People speak to individuals or groups for different reasons and the language fulfills different functions. A speaker may say, "Hey, what's happenin' " to a friend just to make contact, or pronounce you "man and wife" in a formal and legal ceremony. All of these uses of language are instrumental for human communication and part of the general theory of pragmatics. The use of knowledge about the world and how your language works to understand texts, either oral or written, is the study of language practices, or *pragmatics*. If language use (actual communication) determines meaning, then a formal theory of semantics must incorporate these principles. Chomsky showed how a speaker was required to be linguistically competent; that is, have innate knowledge about the structure of language. But we would surely want to consider any of the following as part of a speaker's linguistic and communicative competence:

1. *What's happenin'* can be a greeting.
2. *Where's my computer* is a question.

3. *Where's my computer* is an accusation.
4. *I promise to mow your lawn* is a genuine commitment to mow my lawn.
5. *Is that your coat on the floor?* is not a question but an order to pick it up.
6. *It's hot today* is a statement that it's hot.
7. *This sandwich is mine* correctly refers to a particular object that I possess.

Pragmatics is the theory of semantics that extends semantics to the realm of discourse. Semantics as a theory of truth has limited application in formal linguistics and must be broadened to apply to communicative uses of language. The issues discussed here are all concerned with discovering and applying theoretical principles of semantics to larger units of language, or to texts. The list just given provides an idea of the many uses of language. A pragmatic approach to language is concerned with how people use language to *do* things. It is an account of how intended meaning is derived from what is said (text), and information about the context.

DISCOURSE

Traditional linguistics, and Chomskyian perspectives in particular, attempts to account for an isolated sentence or piece of language that is unconnected to behavior. The data consist of "well-formed sentences" that are independent of an individual speaker or his or her purposes. It is Chomsky's expressed desire to avoid how language is used. The same is true for traditional linguistic semantics. The object of interest is a logical truth relationship and not individual or social meaning. But when the unit of interest is a functional piece of language, then we are concerned with a discourse. *Discourse* is a general term that applies to either written or spoken language that is used for some communicative purpose. A discourse is a semantic concept. It is composed of text that is orderly according to interactional, cognitive, and linguistic principles. Within the tradition of linguistics, discourse is a concern for order in language beyond the sentence level. The discourse analyst is less concerned with formal properties of an abstract and isolated language, and more interested in the communicative uses of language. Discourse is the intersection of language and communication. It is the point where the two disciplines meet.

Discourse is realized in text. *Text* is a string of language that embodies the purposes of the discourse; it is, to be more precise, the lexico-grammatical expression of a speaker's or writer's functional goals. A communicator has options in meanings and makes choices about how to use and organize language to best serve his purposes. Halliday (1978) conceptualized "text" as functionally related to the environment because a speaker or writer's semantic system is activated by the environment, and the language and discourse is shaped by the environment. The relationship between discourse and text is hierarchic because discourse is expressed in text. A discourse is a semantic system and a text is part of that system; the text is to the semantic system what a syllable is to the phonological system. But this hierarchical relationship notwithstanding, the distinguishing feature of a semantic system is its organization into functional components, not units of different sizes. There are many structure-carrying units in discourse as well as grammar and size is less important than purpose. A discourse can be a single utterance—even a single word—or a verbal exchange, a paragraph, a letter, a poster, a speech, an advertisement, a newspaper article, or any communicative use of language that serves some purpose.

Semantics, in the most general sense, is a part of semiotic theory that is primarily concerned with the creation of meaning from symbols. It is possible, although beyond the scope of this chapter (see chapter 8), to consider the semantics of paraverbal symbol systems such as body movements, sign language, visual images, films, architecture, and so on. Here we concentrate only on natural language and the various aspects of discourse. If semantics is generally concerned with meaning then the most essential operating principle of semantics is interpretation. When I speak, a hearer begins the process of creating meaning by "interpreting" what I say. He or she does something like "assign meaning X to word Y," or "utterance U counts as expression Z." So words, clauses, sentences, and sound groups of various types are the subject of interpretations. Interpretation of discourse is a matter of assigning meaning to the various textual expressions in a discourse. Some linguists (e.g., van Dijk, 1985) divide interpretation into extensional and intensional interpretation; the latter being cognitive representations and the former being referential. Hence, an extensional interpretation of a discourse specifies the properties of the discourse, and an intensional interpretation describes how meanings are assigned to an expression. But real everyday interpretations are cognitive processes employed by language users that represent discourse in their memory. People represent conventional meanings specified in their lexicon that have become part of the development of pragmatic competence in the same way that natural language develops in a conventionalized manner. But similarly, language users develop subject representations of discourse. The interpretations depend almost entirely on contexts, motivations, goals, desires, obligations, abilities, and social relationships.

Sanders (1987) argued convincingly that the most basic problem to be solved in communication is to control how one is understood. Typically, communicators want to minimize unintended responses and to maximize the possibilities of achieving their strategic purposes. To do this they must formulate messages according to the principles and conventions of social behavior, and to the requirements of the individual relationship. Interpretation is an unavoidable and inescapable cognitive response to a message. Strategic communication requires a speaker or writer to project interpretive consequences, and as one increases his or her skill at such interpretive projections he or she becomes more communicatively competent. But even the most unplanned and spontaneous communication is dependent on interpretations of linguistic and social conventions that allow for inferences beyond given information.

A second fundamental principle of discourse, and one closely related to interpretation, is "functionality." Discourse is motivated by the relationship of language to the environment and is, therefore, functional by definition. Emphasizing the functional nature of language is important because so much of the history of scholarship in language (see chapters 1 and 2) is tied up in a structural perspective. Functional linguistics is a question of language use and draws on a long tradition in sociology and anthropology (Hymes, 1974). That discourse is functional means that it is less concerned with invariant structures of language, and more concerned with the specification of speech acts or ways of speaking, the gamut of stylistic devices, variations in language use, cognitive processes involved in interpretation, strategic communication, and the matrix of social relationships that provide the contexts for communication.

INTERPRETATION AND DISCOURSE

What types of interpretation are involved in typical discourse processing? A communicator provides a respondent with input data in the form of text, which is composed of surface features (e.g., lexical choices, syntactic structures), paraverbal cues (gestural and visual signals), and contextual information. There are a number of particular textual and contextual mechanisms that contribute to interpretation and we will consider these specific mechanisms in the next chapter. Our concern here is with the general problems that a respondent must solve to interpret any communication. Sanders (1981, 1987) has been working on these problems for some time and has concluded that three types of meaning must be established in most instances. This meaning is the result of interpretations regarding (a) propositional content of utterances, (b) illocutionary force, and (c) implicatures. These meaning types, especially illocutionary force and implicatures, are sensitive to problems in meaning that cannot be solved by truth-conditional semantics. They represent attempts to incorporate background knowledge into semantic theories. It is clear that truth-conditional semantics is defective because it conceives of propositional content so narrowly and does not account for the richer and more elaborated understandings that communicators routinely have.

Language users make interpretations on the basis of any combination of three principles:

1. *Routine and conventional modes of interpretation that are presupposed.* These are linguistically determined methods of deciding how to draw inferences, most notably implicatures that are not logically entailed. These modes of interpretation also describe how we assign constitutive rules to speech acts to express a communicative function.

2. *Mechanisms in the language and culture that cause interpretants to focus on the structures of a discourse necessary to ensure that the discourse is coherent;* that is, that antecedent and subsequent components of the discourse can be related.

3. *Individual and idiosyncratic understanding of the people involved in the communication.* People form relationships with private codes and modes of understanding that can be used to establish understanding. These are based on an individual's habits and dispositions.

These types of interpretations cannot be completely separated from one another. They are normally complementary but may be treated individually for the sake of clarity and theoretical exposition. In the following we focus on the issues inherent in Principle 1. We explore the issues related to Principle 2 in the next chapter. These are the principles that extend theories of semantics to pragmatic communication and are the most important theoretically. The judgments individuals make on the basis of their own interpretive schemes are usually highly variable, difficult to ascertain, and of limited applicability. Moreover, idiosyncratic interpretations can often be subsumed by Principles 1 and 2.

When faced with a piece of spoken or written communication a listener or reader must interpret the communication in order to establish three types of meaning: propositional meaning, illocutionary force, conventional implicatures. These types of meanings must be worked out of any and every communication. They are sometimes difficult, sometimes easy, sometimes ambiguous, sometimes dependent on one another, but always a part of the semantic problems to be solved when trying to create understanding. We approach the problem of interpretation by surveying each of the types of meaning that must be satisfied.

Propositional Meaning

The propositional content of a communication is its meaning derived solely on the basis of lexical content and syntactic structure arranged and used to express the content and relations implied by the language and how it is ordered. In the sentence

1. Becker beat MacEnroe in Davis Cup competition.

the propositional content refers to two entities (Becker and MacEnroe), a relationship between them (one beat the other), and a situation in which that
relationship took place. The propositional content is derived from the vocabulary and the syntactic relationships that instruct the hearer or reader as to the
relationships among vocabulary terms. The theoretical status of propositional
meaning is debatable because some theorists maintain that it is a part of truth-
conditional semantics and can be incorporated into semantic theory (e.g., Katz,
1977; Sadock, 1974). However, others argue that truth conditions cannot account
for all of the information that is implied in an utterance.

Processing the propositional content is a necessary first step in establishing the
final meaning of an utterance. One cannot begin to understand Sentence 1 if he
or she does not understand the terminology and the relationship among ter-
minological items. The theoretical problem alluded to is whether or not this
understanding requires background knowledge or simply truth conditions. As we
develop our ideas in this chapter we see that a complete and accurate understanding of a discourse requires the listener or reader to apply world knowledge
and cognitive schema to the language in question. However, this does not negate
the fact that aspects of truth-conditional semantics influence interpretations. In
Sentences 2–5 the verb "hit" refers to substantially different things but the
different uses of the term are not coded into the nature of the verb. One is
required to have general knowledge about the world to understand the different
uses for "hit."

2. John hit the ball.
3. John hit Bill.
4. John hit a jackpot.
5. John hit the rack. (went to bed)

But it is also the case that both the literal and more metaphoric meanings of "hit"
each imply some "striking action" whether it be a bed, a jackpot, or another
person. So truth-conditional principles of semantics can account for some essential components of meaning, but they are insensitive to the future meanings that
interpreters routinely apply.

There is still debate as to whether or not pragmatic meanings are required for
a full semantic interpretation of an utterance (see, e.g., Gazdar, 1979; Posner,
1980; Sanders, 1987). But we take the position here that pragmatically informed
content is an inherent part of any communicative use of language. Sanders
claimed that only semantic oddities require pragmatic grounds to fully interpret
a sentence. In Sentence 6 Sanders (1987, p. 56) suggests that a full understanding
is metaphoric.

6. Getting pregnant and getting married is worse than getting married and getting pregnant.

The truth conditions of the sentence are such that there is no difference between "getting pregnant and getting married" and "getting married and getting pregnant" regardless of the order, but the comparative "worse than" presupposes that the two are not identical. Moreover, the communicative purpose of the utterance is to indicate that the order in which one gets pregnant and married certainly has consequences. The connective *and* is a linguistic indication that the order is important. Gazdar (1979) and Sanders (1987) suggested that the comparative—which comes first, pregnancy or marriage—can be verified or falsified and therefore is part of propositional content. The dilemma here is that Gazdar worked too hard to include pragmatic meaning into propositional content. He stated that once a sentence acquires pragmatic content its truth values can be acquired. But it remains that pragmatic meaning, or assumed relationships among things in the world, is accounting for a full interpretation of the sentence. It is necessary to attach pragmatic content to propositional content. As I stated earlier, propositional content is still basic to understanding the sentences because the vocabulary and syntax carry necessary meaning and information about the essential content of the communication.

It is possible, however, to view propositional content as dependent on background knowledge that people have about the world. Searle (1969, 1974) demonstrated that a sentence cannot be specified (truth-conditionally) without reference to pragmatic knowledge. Searle would argue that Sentences 2–5 are substantially different and cannot be compared even with a generalized semantic specification of "hit." His essential argument is that a person's knowledge of meaning is made up of a person's knowledge about how to *use* language and make sentences, clauses, questions, promises, demands, and so forth, and that people use sentences and utterances for a particular purpose. In other words, the key mistake made by Chomsky, feature theorists, and structural semanticists is that they fail to see the essential connection between language and communication. Although it seems reasonably useful to talk about the propositional content of a discourse such content is typically part of the illocutionary acts of speaking.

Illocutionary Force

The propositional content of utterances is used by speakers to signal *illocutionary acts*. This is a second type of meaning in communication. A listener must not only understand the basic references for words and syntactical relationships, but he or she must understand how an utterance is functioning. If a sign says *Attack Dog on*

Premises this is a warning about how you should behave, not a simple statement describing the nature of the animal nearby. Illocutionary acts are utterances that have social and communicative purposes. Austin (1962) and Searle (1969) described *locutionary* acts as utterances with sense and reference, they are akin to propositional content. But an illocutionary act describes the function of the locution. A speech act has illocutionary force when it does something: announce, promise, state, assert, command, request, propose, suggest, order, and so on. Austin pointed out that utterances also have *perlocutionary* effects; that is, effects on a hearer that are not part of the meaning of an utterance. The utterance "Go home!" is a locutionary act because it is well formed and makes a sensible reference to something. But it is also an illocutionary act that if said by the right person in the right context functions as an *order*. If the illocutionary act is successful and someone is sent to their place of residence, then the illocutionary act plus the consequences constitute perlocutionary effects. There can be perlocutionary effects without natural language. Nonlinguistic acts can, of course, have effects on people and cause them to behave in certain ways.

Speech act theory, and Gricean (1975, 1978) pragmatics, are the major strands of linguistic work that successfully incorporate generalized knowledge about the communication system and its functions into semantics. Searle's primary objective has been to show that propositional content is not very important and that illocutionary acts instruct an interpreter about how to use the content of an expression. This is significant because it amounts to a rejection of the notion that there are context-free meanings—meanings that can be separated from speaker goals and intentions and the generalized knowledge of an interpreter. Searle realized that important elements of meaning went considerably beyond literal meaning. It also means that communication is the fundamental unit of semantic analysis, not an abstract and rarefied system of features and markers. Semantic competence is a matter of knowing relationships between semantic intentions, rules, and situations. If a speaker says "This book is big" a hearer knows that it was said with the intention of making a statement and having a certain impact on the hearer. Searle's principle objection to Chomskyian semantics is that Chomsky treats language as an autonomous system only incidentally used for communication. Searle (1969, 1974) showed how these assumptions lead to either a circular theory of semantics or an inadequate one. Language is essentially a system of communication and it is therefore impossible to separate the communicative functions of language from accounts of the meaning of a sentence or utterance.

This weds discourse and semantics and blurs the often used distinction between competence and performance. A theory of meaning is a theory of communication and social action. Competence with the language implies a competence to perform. A language user must know more than grammatical rules and word meanings to use and understand a language competently. He or she must also know when and how to speak, to whom, in what situations, and for what desired effect. There is now a pragmatic orientation to the previously theoretical components of language.

Speech Act Semantics. Detailed examples of Searlean analyses of speech acts are readily available (see Searle, 1969, 1975) and we are brief here; nevertheless, it is important to demonstrate speech act analysis in order to show how principles of pragmatics and communication are necessary aspects of meaning. A set of rules that constitute a speech act and provide an account of how one type of meaning is produced is given here. The theoretical concern is how one discovers a set of rules that govern the use of language. Searle (1969) produced a strategy whereby we set down conditions on an illocutionary act such that if the conditions are met the act is performed. These conditions must be recognized by both the speaker and hearer, which means that the purpose of the communicative exchange is fundamental to a complete semantic account. Searle used the performative verb "to promise" as an example.

Assume that someone utters the following:

7. I promise to mow your lawn.

What we have here is that Speaker S promised that he would do Act A for Hearer H. For our analysis to be successful we need to explicate the rules and conditions that make it possible for competent language users to understand the utterance as a literal and sincere promise. We assume that both S and H (speaker and hearer) are engaged in normal communication such that there are no impediments: that both are conscious, capable of speaking and hearing the language, and so on. Searle (1969) identified four conditions necessary to perform promising.

The most basic ingredient of a promise—what separates it from other speech act functions—is that the speaker assumes an obligation to do something. The fact that a speaker does not fulfill his or her promise does not jeopardize the performance of a sincere promise. If I promise to mow your lawn but my lawn mower breaks down, I have not failed to perform or communicate a promise, I have failed to keep it. This is called the *essential condition: Speaker S is obligated to do Act A.*

A second ingredient of a genuine promise is that the speaker plans to honor the promise. Again, a speaker's failure to honor a promise does not change the nature of the act. If, however, a speaker never intended to keep his or her promise he or she is not promising genuinely or sincerely. This then is another act called "lying." This second fact is called the *sincerity condition: Speaker S has every intention of doing Act A.*

A third necessary rule for promising is the belief by the speaker that the hearer wants the promised act performed. The speaker must believe that it is in the hearer's interest to do Act A. A violation of this rule is one way to distinguish between a promise and a threat. If I say to a friend, "Pay me the money you owe me or I promise legal action" then I am not actually "promising" I am "threatening." This is called the *preparatory condition: Speaker S believes doing Act A is in Hearer H's best interest.*

Finally, there is the *propositional content condition: Speaker S predicates a future Act A.* This means that the speaker will do something him- or herself, something in particular such as mow the lawn, pay the money he or she owes, or whatever. A speaker cannot just promise anything; rather, it must be something he or she can perform and meets the conditions of promising.

The example we have just enumerated illustrates the extent to which semantics is dependent on the role of communicators and their assumptions about the world. If all the conditions are met then a promise has been made, but we can see how violating certain conditions accounts for different meanings of the same words, an issue that semanticists have grappled with for a long time. Violating the preparatory condition turns a promise into a threat. Violating the sincerity condition makes for a lie. And I can capitalize on the essential condition of promising in statements such as "I promise I didn't take your money," which is not a genuine promise but an indication that I am very committed to my statement.

The rules taken together *constitute* promising in the same way that the rules of basketball or chess constitute these games. Basketball and chess do not have an existence separate from their rules. Their rules bring them into existence. The rules of basketball and chess, just to use these examples, stipulate all of the legitimate moves and possibilities. The rules of promising or any other performative verb constitute how to perform these communicative acts. And people learn these rules while they are learning language. One part of learning a language is learning pragmatic rules, such as the ones for promising. It is easy to see how a speaker's intention to promise can be recognized by a hearer. The word "recognize" means to "re-cognize" or to invoke the perceptual and intellectual apparatus necessary for understanding. This is precisely what an individual does during communication: He or she uses the rules and conditions that he or she has acquired to disambiguate or make sense of the sounds of the other individual in the communication. So meaning in discourse or communication involves intentional language use formulated according to rules and principles acquired and understood by both a speaker and a hearer.

Speech Acts and Action. The theory of speech acts and the kind of meaning that interpretants extract from utterances that have illocutionary force are based on theories of action. Action theory is another way to describe how principles of natural language and discourse are dependent on assumptions other than truth conditional semantics. Sentences such as "There are blue birds" or "There are no blue birds" have rules for representing how the information is conveyed in such sentences. But when we do something other than assert sentences that can be verified, when we say things that function as requests, commands, promises, and so forth, proposals for truth conditions are bound to fail because they do not adequately account for all that is involved in the utterance. There are two reasons why this is true.

First, any unit of natural language functions as a speech act in the broad sense of the term. Any single word, sentence fragment, or string of words functions first and foremost as purposeful human action. Natural language carries with it information about the context and thoughts of the speaker and hearer. There is no such thing as language that is "simply words"; rather a sentence of any type is performed intentionally for a reason, on the basis of the speaker's goals and his or her beliefs about the available means of attaining goals. When I speak to someone I have reliable beliefs and assumptions about how to use language under these circumstances. Dummett (1976) has shown that understanding requires one to take into account assumptions about a speaker but also assumptions pertaining to the relationship between language and the addressee.

We can take it as a given that an explication of a speech act will not benefit by probing the physical qualities of an utterance. But all speech acts are characterized by goals, means to achieving goals, effects, and relationships. It would be possible to take any particular speech act and establish the connections between the text of the act and the goals of the utterance, strategic means for achieving the goal, relationships, or the effect. Kasher (1985) has shown how this essentially makes any piece of natural language a type of discourse with communicative value. If I say to you "What is your name?" the goal of the utterance is simply to elicit your name from you. I have used standard question formation principles in the English language. I could also, however, have said any of the following: "By what name do you go by?" "How are you called?" "Your appellation please?" "What's yer name buddy?" "How shall I address you sir?" These would all be different means to the same end and of course signal different attitudes and relationships. The individuals in a communication must also be knowledgeable about one another. If I say "I order you to leave the premises," I must be in the appropriate relational position to make such a statement. Outcomes of speech acts are more general results and consequences. The outcome of asking someone their name might be a developing friendship, an insult, or a suspicious glance. In short, language users internalize the issues and rules that preside over speech acts.

A second ingredient of the action perspective concerns the constitutive rules discussed earlier. Constitutive rules are vehicles for definitional justification. They are particularly important for semantic analyses of discourse because of the functional nature of discourse. Theorists often find the analogy between natural language and formal activity such as games a useful one. Rules belong to a family of rules and a particular rule acquires its meaning by being a member of the family of rules. So the rule that specifies how to make a touchdown in football does so because it is part of the definition of the game. One cannot independently evaluate or explain the rule for making a touchdown; it makes sense only as part of the definition of football. The same is true for natural language. An explication and evaluation of an act of natural language can only take place within the family of rules and assumptions that govern the act. These types of rules are central to the semantics of discourse because they are derived from the meanings designated by language users. Discourses do not "have" meanings, but meanings are assigned by language users in some concrete interaction. Interpretation is something that people "do." The ability to perform speech acts results from learning how to make the correct interpretations. Because language use is not random or highly idiosyncratic, and knowing a language implies knowing how to use a language, the constitutive rules for a given act should be sufficiently clear enough for interpreters to identify the act.

Implicature

Implicature is a third pragmatic problem in meaning that must be solved by interpretants. Implicatures (Grice, 1975) are part of the problems that communicator's must solve in order to accomplish understanding. They are part of inferencing in general. They are, as with interpreting propositional content and speech acts, guided by rules about what people need to know and must assume in order to make sense of or interpret messages.

Grice (1975) began with the assumption that conversation is a cooperative activity. He took it as a given that interaction is to a large degree concerted and orderly. He proposed that his cooperative principle is operative and that any deviation from the principle prompts inferences (1975, p. 49). The cooperative principle is a general assumption held by all interactants that says that when formulating what to say "make your conversational contribution such as is required, at the stage at which it occurs, by the accepted purpose or direction of the talk exchange in which you are engaged" (p. 45). This general maxim is supplemented by four submaxims that logically follow from it and if adopted will contribute to a cooperative exchange. The four submaxims are as follows:

- *Quantity*: Make your contribution to a communication neither more nor less than is required.
- *Quality*: Be no more informative than is required. Say what you know to be true.
- *Relevancy*: Be relevant. Make your contribution in accordance with the context.

- *Manner*: Be brief, orderly, and avoid ambiguity. Avoid disorganization, verbosity, and obscurity.

When a communicator violates one of the maxims and is not cooperative he or she invites *conversational implicature*. Generally speaking a conversational implicature is an interpretive procedure that operates to figure out what is going on. For example, the following conversation violates the relevancy submaxim. Assume a husband and wife are getting ready to go out for the evening:

8. Husband: How much longer will you be?
9. Wife: Mix yourself a drink.

In order to interpret the utterance in Sentence 9 the husband must go through a series of inferences based on principles that he knows the other speaker is using. The husband assumes that the wife is being cooperative even though she has violated the relevance principle. Remaining topical is a key function of the relevancy maxim and the wife has violated the expectation that conversationalists extend the topic. The conventional response to the husband's question would be a direct answer where the wife indicated some time frame in which she would be ready. This would be a conventional implicature with a literal answer to a literal question. But the husband assumes that she heard his question, that she believes that he was genuinely asking how long she would be, and that she is capable of indicating when she would be ready. The wife could lie about how long she will be and violate the quality maxim, but instead she chooses not to extend the topic by ignoring the relevancy maxim. The husband then searches for a plausible interpretation of her utterance and concludes that what she is *doing* is telling him that she is not going to offer a particular time, or doesn't know, but she will be long enough yet for him to have a drink. She may also be saying, "Relax, I'll be ready in plenty of time."

What is implicated in discourse is not logically entailed by the utterance so implicatures are an important solution to problems that cannot be solved by a semantic theory principally concerned with truth conditions and entailment. Implicatures have two defining features that make them particularly useful. First, they are cancelable. This means that attaching a clause or often even a word changes the meaning of an utterance. If two people are leaving a restaurant where they just paid an exorbitant bill and one says

10. That was inexpensive

he or she is obviously violating the maxim of quality (tell the truth). As we explained earlier, the hearer will use a conversational implicature to work out the meaning and discover that the utterance has ironic intent. But an added clause as in Sentence 11 changes the meaning and importance of the utterance.

11. That was inexpensive, I really thought it was going to be worse.

Nondetachability is a second feature of conversational implicatures. This means that the implicature does not change when the same thing is said in different words. For example,

12. Some cheap meal, eh.

calls for the same implicature as in Sentence 10.

Conversational implicatures and their features are powerful mechanisms for interpretation because they model the competence that speakers must have in order to accomplish meaning. It is a strength of Gricean implicatures that they allow speakers and hearers to code assumptions and background knowledge into their decisions about meaning. As such, these implicatures are central to the semantics of discourse. If we examine implicatures a little more closely we can see how the relationship between form and content tap into the subjective state of individual interpreters. A conversational implicature relies on three things for interpretation: the propositional content, the particular maxim that has been violated, and the nature of the implication (Grice, 1975). We have talked about propositional content elsewhere in this chapter. It is the coordination of lexical and syntactic choices responsible for the inherent meaning of an utterance, meaning that does not include extralinguistic or additional understandings. But the second thing that an individual must recognize is the relationship between the propositional content and the maxim.

Speakers must have an understanding about the general state of affairs to recognize that a conversational maxim has been violated. This means that inter-pretations about meaning and implicatures are based on a language user's cogni-tive models for general experience. To say that a speaker has violated a Gricean submaxim implies that the speaker has some subjective sense of what it means to be relevant, say just what is needed, say it clearly, and truthfully. There is an interaction, then, between propositional content and a speaker's cognitive models that produces the interpretation that a maxim has been violated (Sanders, 1987). Communicators assume common understandings and use these assumptions in decisions about meaning. Cicourel (1973) made important contributions to inter-pretive procedures by arguing that all language users have a "common scheme of reference" (p. 34), a set of interpretive procedures that are presupposed by everyone. One of these interpretive procedures is *reciprocity of perspectives* or that both parties to a communication are orienting toward the situation and the subject matter in the same way, a type of "common definition of the situation." This makes for a shared basis for knowing what attitudes, beliefs, and assumptions to use when interpreting an utterance. Perspectives on a situation are not completely reciprocal but sufficiently general to work out meaning. Interpreters who know one another very well have richer information than those who do not. But even complete strangers share membership in social, cultural, and linguistic groups such that they can apply common stereotypes. The exchange in Examples 13 and 14 demonstrates the relationship between propositional content and maxim violation.

13. You know, I could use some help moving on Saturday.
14. Saturday is my birthday.

The propositional content of Utterance 13 makes moving and all of the work related to moving salient. The fact that it is the hearer's birthday is irrelevant, but "sense" (cooperation) is restored when the speaker in Sentence 13 connects the belief that "one does not work on one's birthday, or has other plans" with the time and effort required to help someone move.

The content of the implicature is an interaction between the cognitive state of the individuals and the four submaxims stated earlier. For example, Sentence 16 violates the *quantity* submaxim because it is not informative enough.

15. I have some questions about a loan.
16. Here's a brochure.

Assuming Example 16 is a bank officer and is knowledgeable about loans, there are reasons why he is not more forthcoming with information. Given the assumptions of the context and some norms about officials in institutions the reply in Sentence 16 implicates that: (a) the person does not want to be bothered and the speaker should leave him alone, or (b) all questions can be answered by reading the brochure, or (c) read the brochure first and come back if you need additional information.

Other maxims or presumptions have been proposed as part of the reciprocal perspectives that communicators hold. These are assumed to generate inferences and interpretive procedures in the same way as Gricean maxims. Bach and Harnish (1979) suggested a "politeness maxim," a "morality maxim," and a "principle of charity." The politeness maxim invokes the speaker not to be rude, offensive, insulting, and the like. The morality maxim warns against communicating private or special information, requires the speaker not to do or say things that are forbidden, and so on. Finally, the principle of charity is a maxim that instructs hearers to assume that speakers do not violate very many maxims, and give the speaker the benefit of the doubt whenever possible. The strength of the presuppositional overlap between a communicator and an interpreter is the primary determinant of implications. When the overlap is strong and there are minimal differences between communicators and interpreters then the likelihood of errors, misjudgments, and mistakes is diminished. By the same token, differences between people attributable to culture, language, competencies, or skills increase the chances for errors and uncoordinated communication.

SCRIPT-BASED SEMANTICS

We have been making the argument and demonstrating how if semantics is going to explain actual language use (communication) it must invoke extra lexical information; that is, meanings and semantic properties that are not usually a part of lexicons. These meanings must come from some semantic source outside of the sentence or utterance. A source of information not available from words and the rules for combining them. Such information is necessary to interpret Sentences 17 and 18.

17. Joan saw a ladder and crossed the street.

18. Pete bought a station wagon and was now a member of the middle class.

One cannot comprehend Sentence 17 or 18 without knowledge of ladders and taboos about walking under them, or cultural stereotypes that indicate social class membership. And no dictionary is going to mention these things in their definitions of "ladders" or "station wagons."

Work in the area of contextual semantics has been progressing for many years. One of the first attempts to code contextual information into semantic interpretations came with *presupposition*. Presupposition was originally formulated in logical terms and defined as statements that were true and took place before the utterance of a certain sentence (Strawson, 1950). Lakoff (1971) broadened the term to include subjective beliefs, attitudes, and assumptions.

Raskin (1978, 1986) developed the notion of *semantic recursion* where meaning was a matter of sentence elements and (a) the degree of understanding from previous discourse, and (b) the amount of pertinent information a hearer possesses. In order for recursion to operate one must do three things. First, identify words that refer to something else (these are called *recursion triggers*); second, relate the sentences to previous sentences in a discourse that have been interpreted; and third, relate the sentence to information not in the previous discourse. Sentences, according to Raskin, form a scale from having no recursion triggers— meaning flows immediately from the lexical items—to sentences that cannot be comprehended without reference to a previous discourse that the speaker and hearer do not share. The sentence in Example 19 is an example of a nonrecursive sentence that can be understood from the lexical items and how they are combined, and Example 20 requires knowledge of a previous discourse for comprehension.

19. The book weighs two pounds.
20. There is a tide.

The meaning of Sentence 19 emanates from the words, which can be looked up in a dictionary, and the rudimentary syntax that instructs us how the words go together. The information necessary for comprehending the sentence is highly empirical and quantitative. Each lexical item refers to a specific and verifiable object. But the example in Sentence 20 is from Hirsch (1987) where he explained how the phrase is an allusion from Shakespeare's *Julius Caesar* and cannot be understood separate from that discourse. If a speaker or writer says "There is a tide" (meaning "Act now") and the hearer or reader has no way to connect the line to the passage in *Julius Caesar* for its meaning, then the meaning of the message has not been conveyed.

Presupposition, semantic recursion, speech acts, implicatures are all principles that a competent speaker must be able to operate with. Contextual cues and mutually shared background information have been cited as central to a full semantics of communication and discourse. However, none of these concepts has been incorporated into a formal semantic theory that is general enough to accommodate a range of data about extralexical information. But the one theory and attendant set of assumptions that makes the best effort at a formal theory is script-based semantic theory. We briefly outline script-based semantics in the next section. Raskin's contributions are very well documented in this area and I rely on his work for the material that follows. Complete treatments of script-based semantics appear in Raskin (1981, 1986).

Cognitive Scripts and Meaning

A *script* is an array of semantic information that is triggered by a word. It is "a cognitive structure internalized by the native speaker and it represents the native speaker's knowledge of a small part of the world" (Raskin, 1986, p. 42). All communicators have internalized a storehouse of "common sense" that represents typical ways of behaving, standardized routines, knowledge of how people think and behave in common situations. People also have subjective and individual scripts that results from their private experiences and they may or may not share these scripts with other people in families, organizations, and so on. A script has been called a *schema* or a *frame* and we do not make a distinction among these terms. The concept has been used very successfully in cognitive psychology (Freedle, 1977), sociology (Goffman, 1974), artificial intelligence (Schank & Abelson, 1977), and education (Hirsch, 1987).

Raskin (1986) explained that scripts are formally represented as having nodes and links between the nodes. He made his point with the following example (p. 44):

21. John tried to eat his hamburger with a spoon but did not succeed.
22. John tried to eat his hamburger with a knife and fork but did not succeed.

A native speaker will have no trouble understanding John's difficulty in Example 21 but will wonder why he had a problem in Example 22. The difference between the two sentences cannot be explained by dictionary definitions because the fact that a hamburger does not belong to the class of foods typically eaten with a spoon is not explained in any dictionary or lexicon of any type. But this is precisely what accounts for the difference between the two sentences. The script for spoon might look something like what is shown in Fig 5.1.

Spoon

Instrument	Instrument	Instrument
Eat (Liquid, Grains)	Measure	Stir
Knife Fork	Amount Matter	Mix activity
Utensil Cutlery		
Material	Material	Material
Wood, Metal, Plastic		
Type		
Serving, soup, dessert . . .		

FIG. 5.1.
Cognitive script for spoon.

Spoons serve a variety of functions (eating utensil, measuring instrument, serving instrument) and have a number of lexical items associated with them. There are also numerous subcategories pertaining to types of spoons, what they are made of, what utensils they are related to, and so on. These relationships are not part of the standard definition of a spoon. They are part of the script that language users apply to the situation to establish meaning. Portions and sections of scripts are evoked by other language so John's difficulty in Example 21 is understandable because hamburgers do not fit the category of liquid and grains typically eaten with spoons.

Each word in an utterance evokes a script and a series of combination rules (Raskin, 1986) combine the scripts into compatible combinations. A clear and unambiguous sentence will evoke a single script, and an ambiguous or vague sentence will call up two or more scripts. Raskin demonstrated this process with a sentence blended from earlier examples in linguistics. The sentence in Example 23 is an example of an ambiguous sentence treated according to the possible combination rules (Raskin, 1986, p. 47):

23. The paralyzed bachelor hit the colorful ball.

1. Disease	1. Marriage	1. Collision	1. Color	1. Object
2. Moral	2. Academe	2. Discovery	2. Evaluation	2. Assembly
	3. Knight			
	4. Seal			

The 12 scripts in Example 23 can make any combination of 64 possibilities: 11111, 11112, 11212, 11222, 12111, 12112, and so on. So script 11111 would be interpreted as "a never-married man who cannot move some of his limbs struck a colorful object." Script 21212 would be paraphrased as "a morally suspect man, who had never been married, discovered (found himself at) a dancing party with many bright colors." Language users do not, however, go through all of these possibilities. Example 23 and all of the script combinations are theoretical possibilities and the actual linguistic and contextual cues will prompt the listener to use the correct script. Nevertheless, the combination rules must be technically capable of producing all the possible interpretations.

Combination rules will also generate presuppositions and probable presuppositions. In Example 24 there are a number of presuppositions and inferences that can be made.

24. I logged off my computer and went out to lunch.

The combination rules will generate the presuppositions in Examples 25–28, and the probable presuppositions in Examples 29–32.

25. The speaker is a human.

26. The speaker is physically able to move.

27. The speaker is not a baby.

28. The speaker knows something about computers.

29. The speaker owns the computer.
30. The speaker did not have lunch in his home.
31. The speaker has worked on computers before.
32. The speaker will eat in the near future.

The combination rules of script-based semantics will also add the semantic interpretation from Example 24 to another storage area marked WORLD INFOR-MATION (Raskin, 1986). World information is generalized knowledge about the state of the world. If we knew, for example, that the speaker in Example 24 was on a raft out at sea, we would search for an alternative meaning.

CONCLUSION

The general principles that underlie cognitive scripts or schemata have been successfully applied to a variety of intellectual domains. Raskin's (1985) own work has focused on semantic mechanisms of humor and the role of script-based semantics in explaining humorous messages. If I remark to a friend, after taking my son to his music lesson, that "little David played Brahms today, Brahms lost" I am capitalizing on the incompatibility of two scripts to make my point in a humorous way. There are two scripts for "play" (PLAY MUSIC:PLAY SPORTS) and in the front part of the utterance I have called up the MUSIC script but then switched to a SPORTS script. The quip relies on the image of a small boy desperately trying to play Brahms's beautiful and complex music but producing shrill and tortured sounds in the process.

Another very interesting and creative application of the general concept of scripts and schemata is Hirsch's (1987) argument that cognitive schemata of various types are necessary for cultural literacy. Hirsch has written a popular book and showed how schemata and contextual information is necessary to understand words and sentences. He cited research in cognitive science and artificial intel-ligence, but applied the findings to a justification of educational practices in school systems. Hirsch argued that cultural literacy is dependent on background information and generalized knowledge in much the same way we have been discussing it in this chapter. An educated citizen who can communicate intel-ligently in oral or written form shares certain associations. "To participate in the literate national culture," according to Hirsch, "is to have acquired a sense of the information that is shared in that culture" (p. 59).

This chapter focused on semantic principles that are necessary to account for discourse. A good semantic theory must explain the mental operations underlying language that explain a speaker's performance and account for his intuitive judgments about communication, including the speaker's awareness of truth, context, appropriateness, and presuppositional knowledge. We have seen that speaker's must make decisions about lexical options and hearer's must interpret these decisions on the basis of propositional content, speech acts, implicatures, scripts, and contexts. Communicators must orient themselves to contexts and assume interpretive competencies on the part of others. In the next chapter we take a closer look at particular rules of discourse. We examine how the semantic theory discussed here informs the linguistic mechanisms discussed in the next chapter.

actual speech there will be from-below components comprised of language, phrases, sequential relations (and paraverbal cues) that are systematically related to the overall structure of the speech but not determinate of it. The structure from-above brackets the lower level units and makes them sensible. But the units from-below can be organized such that more general structure is inferred. In this chapter we take up the problem of general knowledge schemes and how they are utilized to make sense of interaction. In chapter 7 we examine the various issues and mechanisms that constitute local coherence, "from-below."

REPRESENTING ASSUMED KNOWLEDGE

We commonly assume that sentences acquire meaning as a result of their internal lexical components and syntactic relations. But it is also true that the meaning of a sentence can depend on assumed knowledge and a sequence of sentences as a whole. There is typically an underlying semantic structure to a sequence of sentences. They may be ordered according to actions, events, time, space, causality, and the like. It is important for a speaker or writer to discover a way to ensure that a listener or reader can establish these relations to ensure correct interpretation. So a discourse is not simply sentences but sentences (or phrase units) that are ordered according to some conventions. If a discourse is to be meaningful it must satisfy various conditions of coherence. Moreover, there is a relationship between the surface characteristics of a discourse and coherence. These surface features of text—namely, lexical choices, syntactic structures, mood, tense, adverbial expressions, reference devices—are typically termed *cohesion* devices and are the subject of the next chapter. And although we separate "coherence" from "cohesion" for clarity and analytical purposes, the two are never really independent entities. Most authors agree that coherence is concerned with "connectedness" and some sort of macroproposition, and cohesion with textual devices.

Global coherence is a macrostructural organizational scheme (van Dijk, 1980). Many utterances and phrases cannot be defined in terms of local linguistic mechanisms. We assume, therefore, that meaning in a discourse is influenced to a large degree by more general organizing schemes that are not immediately apparent from the linguistic building blocks of a discourse. Van Dijk (1985) explained:

> Thus a macrostructure is a theoretical reconstruction of intuitive notions such "topic" or "theme" of a discourse. It explains what is most relevant, important, or prominent in the semantic infernation of the discourse as a whole. At the same time, the macrostructure of a discourse defines its global coherence. Without such a global coherence, there would be no overall control upon the local connections and

continuations. Sentences might be connected appropriately according to the given local coherence criteria, but the sequence would simply go astray without some constraint on what it should be about globally. (pp. 115–116)

Van Dijk's approach to the macrostructure is propositional in that all text is about a proposition; or, that semantic units of a text are linked to some general overarching proposition. A proposition is a global representation of a conversation and it has a psychological counterpart. This psychological counterpart is a framework or schema that includes rules, plans, and representations of a text. The statements listed in Example 1 might be considered related but not globally coherent.

1. I had Chinese food for dinner last night.
   The restaurant is near my house.
   My house is near the city.
   Houses near the city are expensive.
   It is difficult to get a good mortgage.

Global coherence provides an overall unity and sense of order to a series of utterances. Sometimes texts provide explicit cues about global coherence in the forms of titles, thesis sentences, headlines, and the like. The headline of a newspaper story provides an interpretative frame for the series of sentences that constitute the story.

Research in this area has essentially focused on how we store knowledge. There is much that must be assumed in normal communication. If we are going to understand natural language as well as we do, then there must be a cognitive process of storing and retrieving information. The remainder of this section is devoted to the theories of how we handle the conventional knowledge that is essentially responsible for coherence. We focus on stored knowledge rather than on how we learn things. It may be that the two are quite related but that is not our concern here. We also pay particular attention to the work in artificial intelligence (AI) that focuses on scripts and schemes. There are a number of terms that have been employed to describe knowledge storage—*frames, scripts, schemes, mental models*—and some subtle differences between them, but all are essentially a metaphor for how knowledge is organized and activated in human memory.

Metaphors for Knowledge Processing

During the act of communication (speaking or reading), we are processing incoming language information and also applying general knowledge that we have available to us in memory. The computational model of language understanding is perhaps the most popular. From this computational metaphor—that is, understanding is literally computed by applying stable cognitive processes to incoming linguistic strings—has emerged the ideas of *top-down processing* and *bottom-up processing*. Bottom-up processing is inductive; it is when language users compute the meanings of words by disambiguating the vocabulary and syntax of sentences or utterances they are exposed to. The meanings of words and the rules of syntax are the primary components of the computational formula for bottom-up processing. Top-down processing is deductive; it is based on the assumption that contextual information and previous knowledge are necessary to compute the meaning of a sentence.

Most of the analytical work in these areas is from artificial intelligence that has blended the traditions of cognitive psychology with computer science. The primary goal of (AI) has been to teach computers to produce and recognize grammatical sentences (see chapter 3). Traditional linguistics has been primarily concerned with grammatical renderings of sentences. And, of course, the computer is essentially a bottom-up processor. The goal of a computer, which has been taught to recognize grammatically correct sentences, would be to reject the sentences in Example 2. A computer that was processing from the bottom-up would not be able to coordinate the lexical items because it could not make "sense" of the sentence structure.

2. A store are near the building. It finding confusing. People no longer knew well streets. I no knowing why.

Any AI computer program that tried to parse these "sentences" and rejected them as nonsense would be performing correctly. And any human language processor would also have difficulty with Example 2. But the human language processor, unlike the machine, would search for meaning. If you were engaged in an actual conversation in which Example 2 was the manner in which the other person was speaking, you would work hard to interpret what the person was trying to say. In fact, if you go back and look at Example 2 you can probably untangle enough of the language to make a pretty good guess at what the person is trying to communicate. A human language processor can make sense of these sentences because he or she is not only processing from the bottom up. It is true enough that we begin with words and use them as scaffolding upon which to build meaning. But it is also true that humans use a top-down strategy that has expectations about what things mean and how ideas should relate to one another. The storehouse of information and knowledge that humans carry around with them makes for tremendous predictive power. Top-down processing begins with expectations so that if information from actual linguistic output is either missing, flawed, or otherwise degraded the human language processor can "fill in" what is necessary. That is why it is possible for most people to make enough sense out of the passage in Example 2. Van Dijk (1988) explained how the headline of a news story serves to structure expectations about the story that follows the headline and thereby assists with interpretation and understanding.

One important question then is how top-down processing works and how knowledge and information are structured. We can accept for now that bottom-up processing works pretty much according to the rules of sequential syntax and lexical semantics (see chapters 3 and 4) but top-down processing poses a different sort of problem. It is an important problem because one form of coherence (global coherence) is very reliant on principles of top-down processing. Humans collect a large amount of general information about the world. When we begin to process a piece of discourse we do not treat it as though the discourse has no relation to anything else. On the contrary, we integrate it into our earlier discourses, or that body of knowledge we call *general background knowledge*. This general background knowledge is very implicit as argued by Berger and Luckmann (1966).

> It is important to stress, however, that the greater part of reality maintenance in conversation is implicit, not explicit. Most conversation does not in so many words define the nature of the world. Rather, it takes place against the background of a world that is silently taken for granted. . . . At the same time that the conversational apparatus ongoingly maintains reality, it ongoingly modifies it. Items are dropped and added, weakening some sectors of what is still being taken for granted and reinforcing others. (pp. 172–173)

During communication we activate one portion of this implicit knowledge, and how this implicit knowledge is organized and stored has been the subject of much research. A logical representation of sentence items and their relationships has met with some success in semantics (see chapter 4), but representing the sometimes amorphous state of background knowledge is more difficult. In chapter 5 we introduced the notion of scripts and script-based semantics as a model for capturing extralogical meaning. In this section we examine theoretical and research issues in more detail.

Any speaker or writer can assume some information. If I mention to a friend that I "taught my Monday afternoon class today" I can assume that certain information is available to that person. I would not have to explain that the classroom had desks, students, lights, blackboards, and the like. My friend could safely assume that certain communicative activities took place such as lecturing, discussion, questions, and answers. All of these things would be assumed without being mentioned. These things are organized as a package of stereotypical information in memory. It is assumed that this information is organized as a whole unit rather than as individual pieces of information that must be collected and assembled in some way. Artificial intelligence researchers treat understanding, which is semantically related to coherence, as dependent on memory. Understanding is a matter of taking what you know (stored in memory) and relating it to what you are trying to understand; it is placing what you do not know in the context of what you do know. Global coherence works in generally the same way. A framework of information is called up from memory and laid over a discourse so as to make relevant connections and explanations. One of the key research problems in this area has been to adequately describe the nature of this storage concept. What does it look like? How is it organized? What is in it? The computer programs that attempt to model these knowledge and memory processes are considered theoretical models of the mind. No one argues that the human mind actually computes meaning in the same way as the computer. But if we can teach the machine to perform certain tasks successfully then we can conclude that we understand the process.

When explaining communication and understanding we must deal with the apparent paradox that people obviously understand language but we have little adequate theory to explain how they do so. Moreover, we do not need elaborate tests and experiments to show that people understand that two expressions may refer to the same thing (e.g., the ball and *it*), or that humans can explain the reason why someone performs a certain action. Yet it is quite difficult to explain exactly how these judgments are made. But AI practitioners have argued that if the computer can simulate language understanding, then we will have specified the process. The computer program is a metaphoric representation of language understanding. The literature in AI is one of the best ways to understand global coherence because it has made good use of linguistics, psychology, philosophy, and computers to form a synthesis—cognitive science.

Scripts. The concept of script developed by Schank and Abelson (1977) has probably had the most impact on how we think about representing knowledge and understanding. A *script* is a theoretical knowledge structure that depicts a typical sequence of events for a common situation. Scripts are used to describe common situations like "going to work" or "getting dressed in the morning." The most quoted example of a script is Schank and Abelson's description of a RESTAURANT script where the script includes activities such as going to the restaurant, ordering, eating, paying, and objects such as menus, utensils, waiters and waitresses, plates, food, and so on. Each script has objects, roles, and activities. Schank (1973) began by trying to describe meaning as a network of conceptual dependencies. It became clear in the early AI work that there was a difference between representing the meaning of sentences as opposed to the meaning of longer narrative texts. It was possible to program a computer to parse a sentence and generate plausible representations of meaning. But it was necessary to infer causal connections between events if the computer were going to adequately represent the meaning of a text. Because it is impossible to determine relations between all the events necessary to understand a text by using only the language of the text, it was necessary to infer the existence of memories, scripts, plans, and goals. Understanding language is memory based because we interpret what we hear or read according to what we know, and we modify what we know according to new information. Everyday discourse is coherent because when we are engaged in communication we make sense of what the other person says by interpreting it according to knowledge patterns we have in memory. These knowledge structures (scripts) fill in details by providing information that we retrieve from our own experience.

The concept of scripts and script-based coherence began by developing what was referred to in the previous paragraph as conceptual dependencies. Conceptual dependencies are a network of semantic concepts that include information not available from the actual spoken or written text. This network of semantic relations can be quite elaborate (see Schank, 1973) but we simplify the process here. The text in Example 3 is dependent on the assumptions in Example 3a for understanding.

> 3. David painted the wall with a roller.
> 3a. David applied paint to a surface by using his arm to transfer paint from the roller to the wall.

Sentence 3a includes some information that is not in Sentence 3 but is still part of our understanding of Sentence 3. By developing these often complex networks of conceptual dependencies Schank was able to generate a conceptual version of understanding that cannot be accounted for by syntax and the lexicon alone.

Learning is part of global coherence. Scripts also contain expectations about what objects or events will be present. When we learn we formulate and refine scripts and then use them in the future. A natural language user would have no trouble understanding what should be in the X position in Example 4.

> 4. John ordered a steak.
> When it arrived he picked up his X to eat it.

The conceptual nature of our understanding means that X can take any number of realizations (*fork, silverware, knife and fork, cutlery, utensils*) and still be coherent. Schank and his associates stress that understanding is expectation-based. The language of a piece of text cues us to understand the text in a certain way as in the following example.

> 5a. David took my picture.
> 5b. It wasn't a very good one.

We know what it means to use a camera to snap a picture and not think that the picture was very flattering. If this text continued we would expect it to continue in this vein. But if we encounter Sentence 5c then our script for this text has been wrong and we will have to reconceptualize.

5c. But I didn't think he would steal it from my dresser.

Because scripts describe situations in standard sequences they have a more dynamic character. It is easy to move between and among scripts. It is probably true that much confusion and "miscommunication" results from misapplied scripts. To "take a picture" can call up a script that is composed of cameras, posing, quality photographs, or it can mean "to steal."

Another way that computers have been programmed to demonstrate the explanatory power of scripts is in understanding story narratives. The script is assumed to render the text as coherent if it can answer certain questions and provide a summary. A teacher in a classroom would make the same assumptions about a student's knowledge of an assignment. If a student were asked to read a story and then summarize it and respond to questions, we would accept the student's correct responses as "understanding." The story in Example 6 can be "understood" by the computer. It was processed by a program called PAM (Wilensky, 1981) and is reproduced here as it appears in Schank and Burstein (1985, p. 148). Note how PAM analyzes the story in terms of character goals and the plans used to achieve these goals.

6. (UNDERSTAND STORY 1)

John needed money. He got a gun and walked into a liquor store. He told the owner he wanted some money. The owner gave John the money and John left.

WHO SHOULD TELL THE STORY? John

I needed to get some dough. So I got a gun and walked down to the liquor store. I told the shopkeeper that if he didn't let me have the money then I would shoot him. So he handed it over. Then I left.

Q: Why did John get a gun?
JOHN HAD A WEAPON WHICH ENABLED HIM TO ROB THE LIQUOR STORE.
Q: Why did John threaten the shopkeeper?
BECAUSE HE NEEDED TO GET SOME MONEY.
Q: What were the consequences of John threatening the shopkeeper?
THE SHOPKEEPER DIDN'T WANT TO GET HURT, SO HE GAVE JOHN THE MONEY.

It is important to emphasize that although these answers seem quite simple, they are answers that cannot be generated by analyzing the vocabulary and syntax alone. It is not stated anywhere in the story, for example, that "the shopkeeper didn't want to get hurt so he gave John the money," or that John "robbed the liquor store." The computer used its general knowledge to draw these conclusions. This is a reasonable theory of how we understand things and use global scripts to make particular instances in a text cohere.

The most serious criticism of script theory is the same criticism of all attempts to model the general world knowledge that humans have access to. That is, you can easily end up in an infinite regress of conceptualizations. To really arrive at a complete conceptualization of Sentence 3, for example, we would have to include everything involved in David's moving the paint from the roller to the wall including his muscles, body, thoughts, and so forth. We would also have to represent all knowledge of rollers, painting, David, and walls including linguistic and stylistic conventions. On the one hand, this criticism is serious because it is probably impossible to account for all such background knowledge and stop an infinite regress. On the other hand, the criticism is not so troublesome because script theory is a *theoretical* model and, awesome as it may seem, we can and must assume that all this knowledge is available for understanding. We do not need to assume, however, that it is always activated. We can hypothesize an unlimited number of cognitive scripts that language users need for understanding and are available for processing. But we can avoid the infinite regress problem by assuming that only necessary portions of scripts are activated.

A second criticism of script theory is the problem of idiosyncratic scripts or scripts that are highly dependent on unique individual and social experiences. We all probably possess individual scripts that are central to our personal lives. This is a very interesting issue with respect to script theory and we address this problem in chapter 8.

Schema. The concept most related to scripts is schema. However there are some subtle but important differences. Moreover, the research utilizing schema theory has been applied to some different areas. We refer to schemata again in the section that follows when we discuss propositional analyses of story grammars. Schemata are higher level data structures for representing concepts in memory (Rumelhart, 1980). They are the basic memory structures for the interpretation of experience. At one extreme they are assumed to be perfectly predictable of how a language user will interpret experience. The case of racial prejudice is one interesting application of these principles. We can imagine an individual whose ideas about members of an ethnic group are so fixed that he or she is completely predisposed to interpreting the attributes of a group in a particular way. But a more plausible use of schemata is that they do not determine discourse, but provide background assumptions that lead us to expect certain interpretations. Schemata are useful for explaining how language users *construct* meaning; that is, people do not simply recall messages but use a message in conjunction with their existing knowledge to build a mental representation. Our accumulated knowledge is manageable because it is organized. Cognitive schemes are these organizing elements, and they are active and malleable enough to change. We can understand the role of schemata better from an example taken from van Dijk (1987). The fragment in Example 7 is of a prejudiced man (M) speaking to an interviewer (I).

7. M: Yes, you see them once in a while, you know, and then you say hello, and that's it.
    I: And other experiences with others foreigners or so?
    M: Well, never have trouble with Turks and Moroccans, but with Surinamese are concerned, yes plenty of trouble, yes.
    I: Could you tell something about, a story or so, about your experiences?
    M: Story, yes I once walked on Nieuwendijk (shopping street in central Amsterdam) with my cousin, still a free man, and well, then came uhh let's see four Surinamese boys. Well, they said something, funny remarks and all that. I said something back, and all that. That's how. So those guys I don't like at all, or course. So. Well, nothing against Surinamese, because my mother is married to a Surinamese man, so, but those young ones among them, that is, yes bragging and fighting and all that. So.
    I: Anything more you can tell.
    M: Well, as far as I am concerned they can all fuck off, in that respect. Then the good ones must suffer for the bad ones, but I never have such good experiences with them.
    I: With other, with other foreigners or so, you don't have
    M: No, never any problems, no because (???). Those Surinamese, that may fuck off. When you see what is happening. Are married, they are married, they divorce, women takes from welfare, and he has no job, but is moonlighting. We have have experienced that ourselves, in K* (neighborhood in Amsterdam), with my mother's friend . . .

The first two utterances of M establish that he has generalized assumptions about ethnic groups. The interviewer has activated his schema about ethnic groups and foreigners. Moreover, it is apparent that the evaluation that dominates M's schema is negative because although the interviewer's first utterance (request for experiences with foreigners) is neutral, it triggers only negative experiences ("never have trouble with . . ."). The cognitive schema for prejudiced individuals are marked for negativity such that they are predisposed to process only negative information. Also, part of M's schematic structure includes negative stereotypes about foreigners and Surinamese (they are violent, they carry knives, no job, welfare, uncommitted to family) and these are instantiated in stories. The telling of these stories is one way that the assumptions of the prejudiced schematic are reinforced and control how information is processed about minorities.

There is also an interaction between the negativity of the schemata and the narrative structure of the story. Typical narrative categories are: SETTING, ORIENTATION, COMPLICATION, RESOLUTION, EVALUATION, CONCLUSION. The man in the interview fills the narrative categories in the following way (see van Dijk, 1987, p. 276):

SETTING:	I once walked on Nieuwendijk with my cousin. My cousin is still a free man (i.e., not married).
ORIENTATION:	Four Surinamese boys came along. They made a funny (provocative?) remark. I said something (provocative?) back.
COMPLICATION:	We had a fight. (I was cut with a knife.)
RESOLUTION/ EVALUATION:	
CONCLUSION:	I do not like these Surinamese guys.

The resolution and evaluation categories are empty. In his study of prejudiced discourse, van Dijk (1987) found that resolution was absent in ethnic stories about 50% of the time. In a classic narrative structure the complication (fight) would have some sort of resolution. But because negativity is guiding the schemata, the goal of the storyteller is to communicate negative information about an ethnic group. This is easier when the listener is not presented with a resolution but is allowed to conclude that the storyteller was the victim in the incident. The essence of the story is simple and minimal. It is designed to substantiate the most general negative macroproposition about the ethnic group, and the succinct manner in which it is told is a very effective way to generate a negative evaluation/conclusion.

There is a developing body of research supporting schema theory with respect to global text structures (Gulich & Quasthoff, 1985) and text processing in general (Bower & Cirilo, 1985; Kintsch, 1985). The typical research strategy has been to use schema theory to make predictions about comprehension of either well-formed or malformed texts. One line of theorizing holds that recall of a text should correspond to the schema for that text. And usually the propositions of a scheme for a text are hierarchic such that some propositions are more important than others. Memory for a text, then, should begin at the top and move down to lower level propositions, which should be more difficult to recall. This is a very consistent finding. More general, important, and higher level propositions are recalled better than subordinate ones (Thorndyke, 1977). Schema theories help explain comprehension of well-formed texts with most people agreeing on the meaning and importance of different sentences. But if a text is poorly formed and violates schema expectations then the text should be difficult to comprehend. Most studies do, in fact, find that deviantly formed texts are difficult to understand (Thorndyke, 1977). The greater the deviation from more standard schematic organizations of texts the more difficult comprehension. And listeners or readers who are confronted with a poorly formed text will work to correct it. They will take the input from the textual language and try to make it conform to their expectations about what information should be present and what it should mean.

Schema theories can serve some very practical purposes in pedagogy and understanding the reading and writing process. Understanding a written discourse of any type involves a variety of complex inferences. The goal of a skilled writer, for example, is to help the reader follow the written material. A reader tries to impose a structure on written discourse and a writer tries to produce a passage that can be comprehended. Cognitive processing at the level of schema involves more complex and abstract knowledge than processing the lexical and syntactic relations in a text because a reader must go beyond the text and make judgments about the author's intentions. Understanding is significantly enhanced if there is convergence between the structure of a text and the reader's familiarity with the structure. For example, if an author has written a fable and the reader is familiar with fables then the story will be much easier to understand. This is because fables are constructed according to conventions. They are usually epigrammatic with animal, men, gods, and characters. The fable illustrates a moral and is usually explicitly stated at the end. If a reader does not have a schema to attach to the discourse he or she will initiate a bottom-up strategy by attaching meaning to lexical and syntactic forms. But if a reader or listener can apply interpretive schemes to the text then a top-down strategy will be used and he or she can begin to apply meaning to the propositions in the story. In the fable example, a reader can interpret events by relating the action of the characters to a more general lesson.

Language interpreters at the United Nations often report that they "interpret the man rather than the language." It is very difficult to simultaneously translate from one language to another because the meaning of a word is not self-contained. It is dependent on other words or the general "scheme" of the subject matter. Many United Nations interpreters prefer to restrict the subject matter and the people they translate so they can get to know them better. In other words, translators improve their ability as they develop cognitive schema that help them interrelate their knowledge of a subject and a person's communication patterns with the text to be interpreted.

The importance of schema for interpretation is underscored by research on cultural differences in understanding that are attributable to schema differences. Cultures probably have different assumptions for their texts. Comprehension should suffer if a text varies from the conventional schema of the culture. One study (Kintsch & Greene, 1978) tested the comprehension of Americans who read stories based on European cultures and compared these results to stories based on Apache Indian culture. Even though the authors found differences it was still difficult to conclude that their were cultural differences because no direct comparisons were made. Tannen (1984) also noted interesting cultural differences in the application of schemes for interpretation. She showed Greeks and Americans a film about picking pears from a tree. The film had sound but no dialogue. Spoken and written stories were then elicited from the individuals representing the two cultures. Tannen found that Greeks told better stories organized around a central theme and had eliminated needless details. The Americans, on the other hand, were wordier and more jargonistic by employing cinema language ("soundtrack," "camera angle"). Moreover, Americans seemed to be interpreting on the basis of a set of expectations (schemes) about how they "should" respond as participants in an experiment. The Greeks were more conversational. The differences in culture resulted in attention to different aspects of the interaction that influenced topical focus and elaboration. The subjects in the experiment were clearly using cultural schemas to respond to the film.

Schema theories have some of the same problems noted earlier with scripts. The selection of a schema for use in processing is an unresolved problem. It remains difficult to explain how a schema model can select a particular scheme, on a particular occasion, that plays the key role in the local interpretation of a text fragment. Moreover, interpretation involves the selection and application of multiple schemes and parts of schemes. Consider the following extension of Sentence 3.

8. David, who is a funny kid, was going to paint my house and asked if I liked Jackson Pollack.

Interpretation requires a scheme for "David," "funny," "paint (house paint)," "paint (fine art)," and "Jackson Pollack." It is necessary to activate all or part of these schemes and make decisions among endless numbers of interpretations. A human interpreter can control both stereotypical knowledge and unusual or strange interpretations. A system such as a computer, armed with interpretive schema, must understand the irony, contradictions, and humor in Sentence 8.

TOPICALITY

The term *topic* is important in the study of discourse. It is essential to notions of coherence and is perhaps the primary organizational principle of global coherence. Discourse topic has an intuitive appeal because all language users can recognize how what they say or write is related to a general topic; topics organize language. Textbooks that offer advice on the process of writing and speaking spend lots of time on the notion of topic. Principles of organization, relevance, and comprehensibility in oral or written discourse are all fundamentally related to the topic of the discourse. It is probably impossible to be precise about the nature of topicality, or to assume that we can formally specify the relationship between texts and topics, but the concept still has strong explanatory value.

The use of the term *topic* has a long history in linguistics and this history stems from a fundamental notion in communication. The basic elements of any communication is that the communication is "about" something. There is a subject or topic. And when humans communicate they not only say something "about" something, but they comment on it. The *topic–comment* distinction is elemental to the nature of communication; all communications are a "comment" on a "topic." Givon (1979) has shown how communicative topics and comments have been syntacticized into sentences as "subjects" and "predicates." The goal of any written sentence is to communicate so the linguistic tradition of writing has incorporated the topic–comment structure of speaking into the subject–predicate structure of writing. It is easy enough to see that the two are often the same, as in Example 9.

9. Bill / hit the ball.

But we are not concerned with sentence topics and comments. For our purposes in discourse topic is a more general notion about the theme or subject matter that is being talked or written about. And, more importantly, in discourse we are concerned with a speaker or writer's topic and not with the topic of a sentence. Discourse topicality is actually more complex than sentence topicality because it is more difficult to recognize and does more organizational work than the subject of a sentence.

The topic of a unified text is the issue of concern by speakers or writers. Most theorists assume that a single proposition reflects a discourse topic. This view is a little simple but it was given credence in some early studies by Bransford and Johnson (1973). They conducted experiments to show that understanding a text depended on contextual and topical level knowledge. Subjects had trouble with passages like the one in Example 10, until they were given a topic for the text.

10. The procedure is actually quite simple. First you arrange things into different groups. Of course, one pile may be sufficient depending on how much there is to do. If you have to go somewhere else due to lack of facilities that is the next step, otherwise you are pretty well set. It is important not to overdo things. That is, it is better to do too few things at once than too many. In the short run this may not seem important but complications can easily arise. A mistake can be expensive as well. At first the whole procedure will seem complicated. Soon, however, it will become just another facet of life. It is difficult to foresee any end to the necessity for this talk in the immediate future, but then one never can tell. After the procedure is completed one arranges the material into different groups again. Then they can be put into their appropriate places. Eventually they will be used once more and the whole cycle will then have to be repeated. However, that is part of life. (Bransford & Johnson, 1973, p. 400)

Subjects were better able to understand and remember aspects of this text when they were given a topic. If this text were titled "Washing the Clothes" it would make more sense. The various actions and activities can be easily related to the topic of the text. The text, however, is strange and does not represent "real" discourse. Even though the experiment confirmed the utility of topics for comprehension it did so with an experimental stimulus that lacked validity. The passage contains none of the normal lexical cues that one would expect if this were a real case of instructions for washing clothes. Moreover, we could have given the text any number of titles and facilitated a different understanding of the text.

Story Grammars

Perhaps one of the most popular approaches to the global aspects of meaning comes from the marriage of psycholinguistics and computers, and their offspring, namely, artificial intelligence. The story grammar approach to topicality suggests that stories, conversations, and texts should be analyzed according to the same principles as sentences. From this viewpoint, just as sentences can be understood according to rules of grammar that specify legitimate strings of words, so too can texts be analyzed with text grammars that indicate when texts are well formed. Lakoff (1972) proposed the idea that folktales could be examined according to

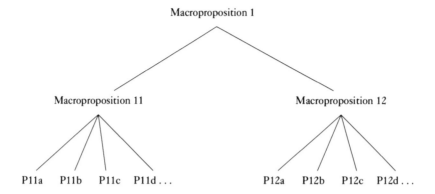

FIG. 6.1.

Schematic of hierarchical relationship of paragraphs to macropropositions.

principles of morphology, and Rumelhart (1975) and Thorndyke (1977) generated story grammars as a useful type of analysis for understanding texts.

The basic idea is that stories can be displayed according to a rewrite-rule
grammar and their structure can be captured by phrase structure rules, such as:

STORY >>>>> SETTING THEME PLOT RESOLUTION

The following example should clarify how the process works:

> (1) David was eating a cookie (2) when Alex bumped into him (3) and
> he dropped it. (4) The cookie fell to the floor, (5) and broke.
> (6) David yelled at Alex.

The numbered items are propositions or semantic units in the story. These
propositions correspond to morphological units of a sentence. They can be
arranged into a phrase structure tree such as in Fig. 6.1. We assume that story
grammars account for a number of findings. Some experimental findings report
that subjects omit details of a story. Story grammarians assume that subjects
remember the essence of a story from the story grammar. Subjects are more likely
to recall the nodes higher in the hierarchy (e.g., the episode) because they capture
more general information. In one study (Garnham, Oakhill, & Johnson-Laird,
(1982) researchers found that jumbled sentences of a story were more difficult to
interpret. Story grammarians assume that these mixed up sentences destroy the
structure of the story that is necessary for comprehension.

Propositions

Much work in the cognitive psychological tradition follows a bottom-up approach, whereby components of a text are analyzed into propositions. Most of the experimental work manipulates texts to test for a subject's ability to recall various aspects of the text. Success or failure to recall constituents of a text is used as evidence of overall text structure and its role in text comprehension. The domain of semantics is required to specify the functional relationship between sentences and a macrostructure even though this function is not linguistically or structurally apparent in the sentences. Van Dijk (1980, 1985) extended the work of story grammarians and has been successful at explaining how it is possible to map sequences of a text into coherent macropropositions. His work suffers from the shortcomings of all propositional approaches to topicality, but his theoretical contributions are rich nonetheless.

These mapping processes or transformations must be capable of taking the sentences of a discourse and logically transforming them into more general global propositions. These operations have been called "macrorules" by van Dijk. Their job is to select and map meanings from sentences into more general abstractions. Macrorules collect and organize the meanings of sentences into higher level topics and themes. It is possible to generate a hierarchic structure with specified propositional meaning at the bottom of the structure and global theme at the top. Macrorules are powerful because they are a way to formally connect language with world knowledge. Macropropositions are also important for predictability. The bottom-up nature of propositional analysis is not predictive. They are therefore required to be combined with macropropositions in order to be predictive. Accounting for the general knowledge assumptions that a speaker brings to a conversation is perhaps one of the most difficult challenges that face communication theorists and linguists. We can only subsume information such as "I took a shower, got dressed, went downstairs, had breakfast . . . ," under the macrostructure "getting ready in the morning" if the details and information relevant to the macrostructure are known to the communicator. The point is that macrorules do not operate only on texts but also knowledge of the world. Three macrorules that generate global structures and thereby help render a discourse as sensible were proposed by van Dijk.

The first is the *deletion–selection* rule. This rule holds that some propositions are included in the macrostructure and others are deleted; very simply, this means that the rule must capture and highlight information necessary for the interpretation of other information. And it must delete nonrelevant propositions. So in the above "getting ready in the morning" macrostructure the rule can delete certain irrelevant details such as the fact that one shoelace was longer than the other while tying my shoes, but the rule must select other information that is necessary for understanding the discourse.

A second rule proposed by van Dijk (1980) is *generalization*. This rule is responsible for taking several aspects of the local information and generalizing it to a thematic group; or, lower level propositions are organized into higher macro-propositions. There is always more than one higher order concept that can organize the propositions so the rule must be sensitive to contexts and people. Thus, for example, one might praise the work of Bill, Bob, and Harry and have "faculty" as a macrotheme, but not "men," or "Connecticut citizens," or "people over 40."

Construction is the third rule and it states that a macroproposition must include the usual conditions, components, sequences, and consequences that a macro-proposition denotes. Technically it must be possible to replace the macroproposi-tion with a typical sequence of micropropositions. "Getting ready in the morning" denotes a complex of events such as dressing, showering, and eating. Ventola (1987) described an interesting application of these rules in her description of service encounters. She explained how a "service encounter" is a macroproposi-tion denoting greeting, giving, offering, informing, questioning, and so on. The previous sequence is appropriate for a conventional service encounter and can be explained by a specific macrorule. But if the clerk and the customer know one another and are also making plans for the weekend then a new macroproposition would have to be constructed.

Macrostructures are abstractions and although they employ some formal ter-minology and rules they are really quite subjective. Because the knowledge, beliefs, attitudes, and assumptions of language users can vary, it means that different macrostructures can be assigned to the same discourse because individ-uals have different criteria for relevance and importance. This has certain disad-vantages because meanings are assigned by people who can construct their own macrostructures. Individuals will select and focus on different aspects of a text and we can therefore expect different interpretative strategies. Nevertheless, there seems to be enough overlap and shared social convention to ensure success-ful communication.

A different explanation than the one held by story grammarians for why people have a better memory for higher level propositions has been proposed by van Dijk and Kintsch (1983), and it is a general theory of hierarchical structure. This theory is elaborated in Kintsch (1985) and van Dijk (1985), and is assumed to have psychological reality. Kintsch and van Dijk assume that a set of propositions can be extracted from a text according to the rules just discussed. But it is not the position of a proposition in the hierarchic structure that is so important to memory; rather, it is the fact that information from propositions is integrated in cycles. They offer a more dynamic reformulation of how semantic prin-ciples are applied to propositions. The more a proposition is integrated the more likely it is to be remembered. Moreover, theorists increasingly realize that discourses do not "contain" meanings; participants assign meanings (on the basis of macrostructure rules) as the discourse unfolds. Interpretation is an activity that is accomplished during the moment-to-moment interaction. So language users hold relevant general information in permanent short-term memory in order to semantically link a turn to a previous turn, and to acquire the necessary information to make future turns sensible. Higher level phrase structure nodes assist with this process and are thereby easier to recall.

Problems With Propositional Analyses. There is a basic methodological problem with propositional analyses that makes them difficult to interpret and apply. A discourse analyst must be able to decompose a text into its constituent propositions. But there is no algorithm to guide this process. There is no systematic way to identify propositions and different analysts will arrive at different propositions. Even though the theory of propositional analysis is strong and appears rigorous, the actual analysis of propositions is subjective. This means that one analysts set of propositions cannot be tested effectively because they represent only one interpretation. Kintsch's solution is to state propositions first and then see if they can be logically related to the sentences in a text. But this argument is terribly circular.

Moreover, it is probably true that there is no such thing as a single proposition that is a semantically correct representation of a text. A proposition is a representation of what one wishes to communicate and therefore dependent on the individual, his or her background, and communicative goals. A particular sentence cannot be treated as having a single proposition as in Sentence 11.

11. I am leaving.

The utterance in Sentence 11, expressed by a husband going to work in the morning, expresses a different proposition than if said by a wife who is in the middle of a fight with her husband. Identifying the propositions of a sentence requires knowledge of the speaker's intentions and the context of the utterance, and is clearly an interpretation on the part of the discourse analyst. And computing the intended meaning and intentions of a speaker involves much more information than is available in a text. If an analyst uses knowledge of background and context then he or she must be able to make this knowledge explicit and state how it was arrived at, which is typically difficult and subjective. Story grammarians and propositional analysts are also interested in computer models of textual understanding. Those working in artificial intelligence, which attempts to model understanding, have found it impractical to attempt to "teach" the computer everything required to produce a set of correct propositions.

Topic Scheme

The concept of topic is attractive because it is a primary organizing principle for either oral or written communication. It is especially important to the discourse theorist because it organizes a collection of sentences or utterances into a coherent whole. The concept of topic is also a very practical means of distinguishing intelligible and coherent discourse from incoherent and even "disturbed" discourse. The following, taken from Johnston (1985, pp. 85–86), is an example of discourse that has topic maintenance and management as the primary skill problem associated with a disturbed child. It is a portion of a conversation between a mother and her 9-year-old son (Peter) who has been diagnosed as language disordered with an accompanying affective disturbance.

12. P: Sam XXX, meet some new people quiz. Sam—
    M: You met some new people?
    P: Yeah! Sam says, "Wake up you pumpernickel." [laugh]
    M: What?
    P: Jumps up and down, on the bed, and says, after he says, "Wake up."
       Sam says,
       "Bobby and Peter" and says, "You're acting dead, wake up."
    M: Oh.
    P: And says, "Do it again."
    M: Is Sam a little boy or a big boy?
    P: No, big teenager.
    M: Oh. He's a teenager. Does he live at the cottage?
    P: Yea, that's where he lives.
    M: I see. Is he a friend of Mike's?
    P: Mike's friend go home.
    M: I think I met him, Peter.
       You played ball with him, I think, one time when we left.
       Did he come in and wake you up?
    P: Uh, yes.
    M: Saying "Wake up, Peter"
    M: Boy, there's a lot of traffic today, I guess cause it's Friday. Peter, did you
       get that I sent you?
    P: Yes.
    M: Do you remember what color it was?
    P: I can't turn it on.
    M: Don't bother about it, it's all right. Peter, I'm so glad you're coming
       home today. I've been looking forward to seeing you today. I woke up
       this morning and I said, "Go get Peter."

P: You no need these Froot Loops?

M: Did I what

P: Rice Krispies and Froot Loops, one of these box is full of Rice Krispies and Froot Loops, one of these box is full of Kellogg's.

M: What boxes?

P: Froot Loops and some Rice Krispies. There—one of these box is full of Kellogg's Rice Krispies and Kellogg's Froot Loops, one of these box is full of Kellogg's.

M: OK, where did you see the boxes you're telling me

P: Tucie. You know name is? It's a Tu-can bird. It's a Tucan bird.

Even a casual reading of the text suggests that Peter is having trouble maintaining the topic and, even more subtly, adjusting to topic shifts and alterations. Johnston categorized Dialogue 12 for topic-maintenance properties and reported that 45% of Peter's turns fail to maintain the topic, and that 64% of those turns that can be categorized as topically relevant are responses to questions. Moreover, on those occasions when one speaker is unclear and needs additional information interactional partners must cooperate on discovering and providing the necessary information. The mother fails at each attempt to enlist Peter's cooperation at providing mutual reference so that she can track the changes in topical movement. In the first six turn sequences in Dialogue 12 the mother is having trouble establishing the discourse topic and initiates efforts to clarify. (Her turns: "You met some people?" and "What"). Given Peter's failure to cooperate she gives up and lowers her expectations for specificity. A number of theorists (e.g., Labov & Fanshel, 1977; Rochester & Martin, 1979) have described disturbed and schizophrenic speakers in terms of various structural mechanisms in discourse (e.g., anaphora, lexical ties) and concluded that these features were unrelated to topic. The concept of "topic" is what defines the differences between coherent "normal" interaction and the language of disordered or clinical speakers.

One of the problems with the analysis of topic is how a topic is assigned to a discourse, how someone determines which is the correct topic determination. This problem is confounded by the fact that most conversations, for example, are composed of a variety of topics but the individuals in these conversations can name and identify these topics with consistency. The conversation in Dialogue 13 is an example of "small talk" (Schneider, 1988, pp. 324–325) and illustrates the variety and organization of topics even in simple settings.

13. A: You're here on holiday at the moment, are you?

B: Yes, that's right.

A: Good, super.

B: Mhm.

A: What country do you come from? Germany, or . . . ?
B: Germany, yea, right.
A: Yea.
B: Mhm.
A: Whereabouts in Germany? north? Northwest?
B: Yes, that's right.
A: From the coast, are you?
B: Yes, I am.
A: Yeah.
B: I am from Hamburg, actually.
A: From Hamburg?
B: Yeah.
A: Very nice.
B: Mhm.
A: My brother used to work near Hamburg.
B: Oh did he?
A: Yea, I went over once or twice myself, to visit him.
B: Great! super!
A: Mhm. It's very nice countryside.
B: Yes, it is quite nice, I suppose.
A: Is this the first time you are here?
B: Yes, it is actually.
A: Great.
B: yeah.
A: So where did you come in from today?
B: From Glasgow.

The conversation in Dialogue 13 may be labeled SMALL TALK but there are many additional topics that might also apply. It could be labeled GETTING TO KNOW SOMEONE and there are many subtopics dealing with RESIDENCE, LOCATION, HOME, FAMILY, and TRAVEL.

Both Schneider (1988) and Planalp and Tracy (1980) reported that language users are aware of topics and competent at identifying topics and topic boundaries. Planalp and Tracy asked 60 subjects to segment a conversation into various topics. One group used a transcript only and another group used videotapes and read transcripts. The subjects were extremely reliable at segmenting the conversation into topics and the video contributed little or nothing to their accuracy. A strong explanatory concept of topic must allow all reasonable expressions of a topic to be included in the judgment of "what a discourse is about." For that reason I suggest the term *topic scheme* as an expression of how interactants recognize what is appropriate and "topical" in a discourse.

In 1932 Bartlett introduced the concept of "scheme" to describe the cognitive organization of events and experiences. Schank and Abelson (1977) elaborated on this concept and proposed that cognitive structures are available for interpreting information. A scheme is a framework that contains information about stereotypical sequences and events. A topic scheme is an array of topics and subtopics that go together. It is an open ended set of events and objects that are required to interpret what the speaker is talking about. So a genre of communication called SMALL TALK is composed of a set that includes topics such as RESIDENCE, LOCATION, HOME, FAMILY, WEATHER, etc. Whenever interactants recognize a topic they *impose* the topic scheme on the text such that subtopics are identified whenever possible, and topics in the scheme but not in the text are assumed to be appropriate.

One reason subjects in experiments can identify topics so competently is that topic schemes are part of the stock of world knowledge that we carry around. We learn the patterns of communication from experience and formulate over time what Venneman (1975) called a *presuppositional pool*; that is, a body of information collected from general knowledge that is sensitive to situations. People proceed as if everyone draws from the same pool so that individuals behave as if certain things can be assumed and taken for granted. Topic schemes contain a set of subjects because participants assume that these subjects are shared and do not need to be established explicitly in a discourse text. So the set of topics included in SMALL TALK is large and may contain any subset of topics deemed trivial or unimportant. As a discourse proceeds, however, some topics are expressed and some are not. The content of the topic scheme determines how a text will develop but it is first necessary to activate some entry in the topic scheme. What is relevant in the discourse will be determined by what is activated in the topic scheme. The interplay between the abstract topic scheme and what is "uttered in text" facilitates comprehension. For example, if one joins a conversation in the middle one typically asks "what is being talked about," and "what was said up to this point" in an effort to make sense of the current interaction.

The topic scheme is also instrumental in determining conversational relevance. Grice's (1975) cooperative principle holds that participants in an interaction conform to certain principles, one of which is relevance. Participants in communication are obliged to be relevant in their contributions or they will suffer negative judgments about their communicative competence. It is the topic scheme that determines relevance. A communicator is relevant when his or her contribution to a discourse is integrated into the topic scheme. The most typical pattern is for each participant to extend or elaborate on a previous utterance as in Dialogue 14.

14. A: Where do you want to go for dinner?
    B: Don't know, haven't thought about it.
    A: Do you want pizza, subs, what?
    B: A sub sandwich sounds good.
    A: How about South Whitney.
    B: Oh, they are too slow and they never get it right.
    A: Lena's then.
    B: Yea, good.

Speaking on a topic, and making each contribution relevant to the general topic, is a feature of everyday conversation.

Topic Management

We must not lose sight of the fact that conversation is dynamic. It is a process whereby participants integrate their presuppositional pools to negotiate topics and topic changes. During the course of almost any conversation the topic will move from one subject to another and perhaps back again. Competent communicators must learn to recognize and manage the fluid nature of topic changes. We saw earlier that participants in conversation are quite proficient at locating topic changes (Planalp & Tracy, 1980). There are generally two tasks that communicators must accomplish in order to manage topicality during interaction. The first is that a speaker must influence the interpretation of an utterance, and indicate the main topic, by making some information prominent. The speaker must organize his or her conversational contribution such that one element or idea is foregrounded and taken as the point of departure. Second, interactants must recognize cues that signal topic shifts.

Focus and Foregrounding. Not everything uttered in a text is equally easy to refer to or focus on. When people are talking, some information is prominent and in the foreground of the interaction, and other information is in the background. A piece of information is *foregrounded* when it is established in the foreground of consciousness and other information remains in the background. Consider a passage used in a study by Tyler and Marslen-Wilson (1982):

15a. The little puppy trod on a wasp.
15b. The puppy was very upset.

The "puppy" is foregrounded in example 15a and 15b. The second line of the passage makes the puppy the main theme of the exchange. The effect of foregrounding can be seen by what happens if we continue this passage as in Example 16.

16a. The little puppy trod on a wasp.
16b. The puppy was very upset.
16c. It started to buzz furiously.

Line 16c appears awkward because it is responsive to information that is not foregrounded. The topic of the text is the puppy and if Line 16c had been uttered there would have been momentary confusion as the participants shifted topic emphasis. But any theory of discourse and how participants comprehend text must explain how topics come in and out of the foreground. There are at least two ways this occurs.

First, there is a distinction between *explicit focus* and *implicit focus* (Sanford & Garrod, 1981). Information that is explicitly focused is clearly foregrounded by being mentioned in the text. These items are clear to all participants in the interaction and can usually be clearly referred to with a pronoun as in Example 17.

17. The book was really very good. *It* was well written.

Comprehension in Example 17 is quite simple because "book" is foregrounded and the referent for the pronoun is clear. Implicit focus, on the other hand, is when the foregrounded information implies other information that is logical or assumed by the topic but that information is not clearly stated. Therefore, participants can hear Example 18 and still easily comprehend and integrate the information in the text because authorship of a book is implied and implicitly focused.

18. The book was really very good. The author is very skilled.

A second very important way that information is either foregrounded or back-grounded pertains to the way people use their knowledge about the world and its general patterns to interpret a text. The different entering assumptions and information that people bring with them to a piece of text is perhaps most responsible for either clarity or confusions. A very interesting study by Anderson, Garrod, and Sanford (1983) demonstrated how people use their experiential knowledge about typical episodes to understand a text by foregrounding some information and backgrounding other information. An episode is an identifiable collection and sequence of behaviors that go together in some way. Subjects in the Anderson et al. study read passages such as the following:

19a. The children were all enjoying the birthday party.
19b. There was an entertainer to amuse them.
19c. No expense was spared to make the party a success.
19d. One hour later energies flagged.

or

Five hours later energies flagged.

The theory is that experiential knowledge of typical episodes would predict that the party would still be in progress one hour later but probably over after five hours. And the children are the foregrounded information in Example 19. The text was continued with either Sentence 20 or 21.

20. Playing the games had exhausted them.
21. Organizing the games had exhausted him.

The continuation in Sentence 20 was easily read and interpreted whether subjects read the 1 hour or 5 hour Line 19d because Sentence 20 extends foregrounded information, and the children could be tired after either 1 hour or 5 hours. But the continuation in Line 21 makes a pronominal reference to information that is not foregrounded, that is, to the entertainer rather than the children. There was more confusion and difficulty in understanding Sentence 21 when it was read in the 1-hour experimental condition rather than the 5-hour condition because of the assumption that the party was still in progress and the children are foregrounded. Continuation 21 was read more quickly and there was less of an interpretive problem in the 5-hour condition because it was beyond the expected bounds of the birthday party episode. Subjects processed the fact that 5 hours had passed, and with that information the children slipped further into the background.

Topic Shift Signals. When two discourses or segments of a discourse have different topics there should be a marker that distinguishes one topic from another, and indicates the shift from one topic to another. We said earlier that participants in interaction were pretty good at identifying the various topics in a discourse. So there must be some structural basis on which interactants are able to characterize topics and topic shifts.

One of the most blatant and efficient topic cues is the *bold marker*. This is when someone says something like "speaking of X," or "I want to tell you about X," or "That reminds me of something . . . ," and so on. These topic indicators are very direct and make it easy for the hearer to follow the topic and prepare to process information. The hearer will relate all of the ensuing information to the "X" topic indicated. Moreover the speaker can then use a series of pronominal references to keep the topic in focus. Jefferson (1978) divided these bold markers into even more distinct classes. She called the phrase "speaking of X," a *marked repeat* because somebody has already mentioned X and the speaker is repeating what has already been referred to. And "I want to tell you about X," is a *disjunctive* marker because it is apparently unrelated to anything previous.

Other than explicit topic changes and introductions, there are certain words that cue a new topic. These words indicate that a shift in topic is forthcoming. This shift can be subtle or more dramatic. A word like "well" can signal a shift to a new but related topic as in Example 22.

22. A: I just think the environment is an important issue.
    B: Not me, I think it's a middle-class issue and less important than feeding people.
    A: *Well*, how do you feel about the Alaskan oil spill?

Other words such as "anyway," "incidentally," "so," and "now" can cue topic changes. The "well" in A's second utterance indicates that the speaker is no longer going to pursue the matter of the environment in general, but going to move to a specific incident or application.

Tracy's work on topic shifts and continuations has helped explain the structure and relevance of passages such as in Example 22. Her conclusions support the global coherence hypothesis that states that the best way to be relevant in a discourse is to make your contribution related to the general topic or issue under consideration. Tracy (1982), drawing on Reichman's (1978) work, labels the conversation in Example 22 as a distinction between *issues* and *events*. An issue is "a general statement of principle, feeling, or belief and an event is a particular instance or episode that occurred in the past" (Tracy, 1983, p. 321). The issue in Example 22 would be a general statement such as "the importance of environmental concerns" and the event would be "the Alaskan oil spill." Tracy (1982) was interested in whether people use global notions of coherence (respond to the main or general point) to maintain relevance, or whether they rely more on local coherence (respond to the immediate prior utterance). She found clear evidence for issue extensions: That is, when a discourse has an issue–event structure, an extension that continues the issue is preferred. Extending an issue rather than an event is seen as more relevant. This is termed *the relevance rule*.

A follow-up study (Tracy, 1983) confirmed this finding but searched for some limits on the relevance rule. Tracy measured message comprehensibility and message importance on extension preferences. She found that the preference for issue extension was lessened when the message was less comprehensible. In other words, when a conversation was difficult to understand issue extensions were less competent than event extensions. Low comprehensibility makes it difficult for people to even infer an issue so extensions are considered odd and out of place. Tracy also assessed the impact of message importance by arguing that it is safer to extend a topic that is less relevant when the message topic is not particularly important to a speaker. The argument here is that an uninvolved speaker cares less about how his message is extended. But this argument was not supported. If a message is clear speakers treat a topic seriously. In a third study, Tracy (1984) replicated the message comprehensibility finding and also found that extending an issue conveyed communicative attentiveness, which is an important component of competent conversational behavior.

Formal Topic Structure

There is one additional way in which topicality contributes to the need for coherence in interpreting discourse. In the previous discussion we concentrated mainly on topic content as it is expressed in propositions, schemes, lexical items, issues and events, and so on. In this section we briefly consider the *form* of topicality; that is, how one structures a message in discourse so that the reader or hearer are able to use visual and aural cues to keep track of the topic and thereby render a discourse coherent. Topicality is certainly the most important aspect of global coherence. And, as we have seen, interactants can successfully identify the topic shifts in a discourse. But there are also structural bases for how language users can mark topics and their changes.

In written language, the paragraph is the most identifiable demarcation of a topic. The standard definition of a paragraph is as a unified idea unit that makes a particular point. The paragraph in written discourse serves as one type of structural topic indicator. There is a strong visual component to all written language and paragraphs in particular. They have clearly identifiable beginnings and endings and utilize visual features such as indentifiable beginnings and endings and utilize visual features such as indentations and spacing. Readers use paragraphs to cue themselves about topics and what is being communicated. Brown and Yule (1983) discussed paragraphs as structural markers of topic and explain how the partitioning of text into paragraphs is often responsive to stylistic concerns or visual appeal. In other words, a paragraph cannot be defined neatly as a single semantic unit. Some writers tell a story that has a unified semantic theme, but take many orthographic paragraphs to do it.

A newspaper story is a good example of how paragraphs signal topicality. The journalistic format is one form of written discourse that makes use of paragraphing to signal subject matter and ease interpretation. Journalistic writing tries to produce a narrative that distinguishes changes in time, place, people, events, and so on. The subject matter of a story is of course instrumental to these distinctions but the paragraph structure also plays a central role. The reader of a newspaper report must use the linguistic and structural cues in the report to relate details of the story and infer topics. Van Dijk (1988) considered news topics to be semantic macrostructures; that is, topics are propositions that contain the gist, upshot, or most important information about a story. Paragraphs contain propositions that are hierarchically organized into more general macropropositons. The diagram in Fig. 6.1 schematically represents this arrangement. Paragraphs build propositions into macrostructures and these macrostructures can be hierarchically related to even more abstract or general macrostructures. A portion of a report from the *Hartford Courant* (January 10, 1990) about the death toll after the American invasion of Panama illustrates this.

220 CIVILIANS DIED IN PANAMA, PENTAGON SAYS
Combined Wire Services

WASHINGTON—The Pentagon, in its first accounting of non-military casualties in last month's U.S. invasion in Panama, said Tuesday that about 220 Panamanian civilians were killed in the fighting.

At the same time, the Pentagon estimated that 314 members of the Panamanian Defense Forces were killed.

The estimate of civilian deaths suggests that almost 10 Panamanian civilians died for each of the 23 U.S. servicemen who were killed.

Pentagon spokesman Robert Hall disputed estimates that have placed the number of Panamanian civilians killed as high as 1,200. He noted that the American estimate of 220 was slightly higher than the 203 estimated by the Panamanian institute for legal Medicine, which records and investigates all suspicious or violent deaths in the country.

Both the U.S. and the institute's estimates included people who may have been looters, out-of-uniform Defense Forces soldiers or members of Manuel Antonio Noreiga's armed Dignity Battalions.

"We cannot guarantee to you that they were all civilians," said spokes-woman Margaret Tutwiler of the Department of State. "If it was a [Defense Forces] member in civilian clothes . . . that has not been sorted out."

Meanwhile, Peru said Tuesday it granted diplomatic asylum to a top Noriega associate who is on the U.S. most-wanted list and to 11 others who took refuge in the Peruvian ambassador's residence in Panama City. U.S. troops have ringed the residence since Monday afternoon.

Peru Foreign Ministry spokesman Jose Torres said the 12 would be allowed to enter Peru if they wished, but no such discussions had taken place.

There are eight paragraphs in this portion of the story. The most general topic or macroproposition that is necessary to understand this story has to do with the invasion of Panama by the American military. Such a macrostructure (United States invades Panama) is assumed (and probably safely so) because the invasion was a significant news event that had been in the papers and on the news for a

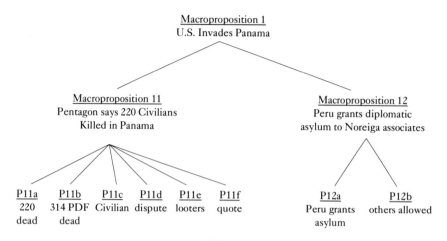

FIG. 6.2.

Representation of topic structure of Panama story.

number of days. The main topic of the story is summarized in the headline and the paragraphs are divided in such a way as to provide specific information. The headline would correspond to Macroproposition 1 in Fig. 6.1. In order for the reader to derive this information from the text, and to read the text as related to the headline, the paragraphs must be partitioned according to events that relate to the headline. The first paragraph is little more than a slight elaboration of the headline. The second reports Panamanian Defense Force deaths. The remaining four paragraphs add some detail and relate the main point of the story to other issues and incidents such as civilian deaths, comparing casualty estimates, distinguishing between soldiers and civilians, and a quote from a government official. Each of these issues have been divided into separate paragraphs for processing ease. Newspapers often make use of single sentence paragraphs. Four of the first six paragraphs (Paragraphs 1, 2, 3, and 5) are only one sentence long. So the notion that a paragraph is a developed and unified idea is routinely violated in journalistic writing. The second macroproposition is introduced in Paragraph 7 when the story switches from casualty counts to Peru granting diplomatic asylum to Noreiga's associates. Figure 6.2 is a schematic representation of the topic structure of the story.

One of the most common ways of sectioning content into paragraphs, especially in journalistic writing is to use adverbial expressions that signal temporal sequence. Longacre (1979) suggested that some of the more typical adverbial expressions that begin a sentence should be considered topic shifters. Words such as "generally," "also," "then," and "next," signal changes in time in a narrative and are often used to begin new paragraphs. In the Panama story the distinction between Panamanian Defense Force casualties and American casualties is highlighted by separating these issues into separate paragraphs and beginning the second paragraph with "At the same time." The shift to a second macroproposition (Peruvian asylum) is accomplished with the adverbial "meanwhile."

The combination of an indented line, spacing on the page, and linguistic markers such as adverbial expressions is how a writer communicates that he or she is beginning a new topic. But paragraph structure remains a subjective choice on the part of the writer. One reason for this is that topics cannot be approached only in a formally linguistic way such that they are properties of texts. In the same way that meaning is assigned to a text by a language user, and therefore has a subjective component, topic structure can be subjectively related to both the writer and the reader. After all, different individuals place more or less emphasis on certain topics and vary with respect to their assumptions of importance. This makes the linguistic signals of topicality even more important. The writer of a paragraph must work to assist a reader with how he or she assigns a topic to a piece of text. In journalism this is done with adverbial expressions and paragraph divisions that represent small details of a story. In the future it would be interesting to pursue the norms of paragraph structure and topic shifts in other genres such as philosophy, cookbooks, technical manuals, academics texts, and the like.

There is an interesting extension on the notion of structural markers of topicality in written discourse. Brown (1977) and Brown and Yule (1983) discuss structural markers of topic shifts in spoken discourse, and refer to these as speech

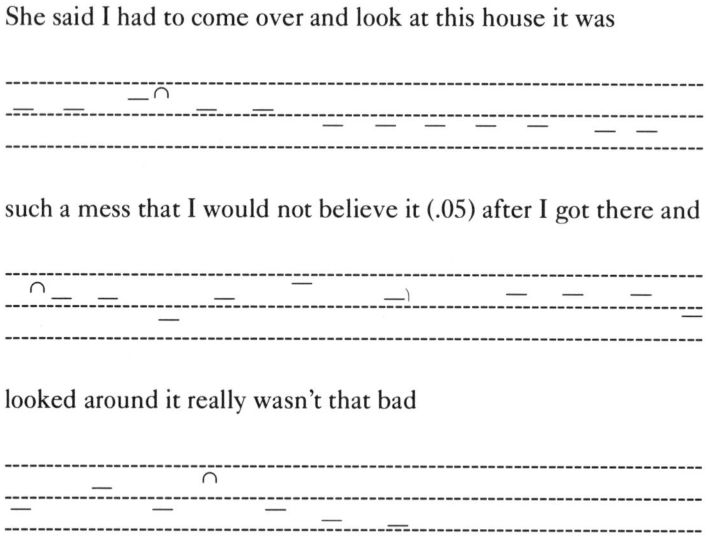

She said I had to come over and look at this house it was

such a mess that I would not believe it (.05) after I got there and

looked around it really wasn't that bad

FIG. 6.3.
Illustration of a paratone.

paragraphs or *paratones*. We only consider these briefly as a point of comparison to written paragraphs, but Brown (1977) found considerable support for the fact that people phonologically mark the boundaries of speech paragraphs.

When people read written text aloud they identify the beginning of a new paragraph with intonational cues. There is evidence (Brown, 1977) that they do the same thing to the flow of naturalistic speech. When interactants begin talking they highlight the topic phonologically and often make the entire beginning of an utterance higher in pitch. And, as Sacks, Schegloff, and Jefferson (1974) have demonstrated, the end of a conversational turn is typically marked with lower intonation and less stress on lexical items. Figure 6.3 is a pictorial illustration of a paratone. The three-line stave represents the top, mid, and low points in the pitch range.

We can see that this paratone begins in a high pitch range and then ends in a lower one as the speaker completes his utterance. The combination of phonological emphasis and pauses that bound the beginning and end are the formal markers of the paratone. There are of course internal variations of pitch that serve as semantic cohesive devices, but these are not part of the paratone unit. For example, the high pitch emphasis on *such* serves as a semantic contrast to the emphasis on *really* at the end. The speaker is characterizing what someone else said, and prefers the hearer to think that the person was exaggerating. "Such" is an adjective that is often used for semantic emphasis so it makes sense that it would be phonologically emphasized. The speaker wants to communicate that the exaggeration was uncalled for and uses "such" to establish this expectation. He can then say that it was not *really* that bad. The relationship between these two pitch levels helps serve the speaker's communicative purpose. There are numerous functions of intonation but we can safely say that speakers mark their topics with paratones. The particular way speaker's mark topics is subject to variety, but it is clear that failure to organize the stream of interaction in this way will further burden the interpretive responsibilities of the listener. In any case, the pragmatic use of phonological prominence is more related to issues in local coherence and is taken up in the next chapter.

7

Coherence and Local Organization

In the last chapter we were primarily concerned with the global semantic coherence of a text. Global coherence is essentially a cognitive-psychological perspective where the goal is to identify a macrosemantic interpretation of an instantiated text. In van Dijk's (1985) terms, global coherence presupposes the existence of a semantic macrostructure that is a theoretical reconstitution of ideas such as topic, theme, gist, or goal of discourse. It concentrates on what is most central or prominent about a discourse and acts as an overall executive manager on local language, acts, and sequences. Local coherence, on the other hand, is concerned with the pragmatic relations among actual components of a text. At its rawest level a text is an unbroken string of surface expressions—words, phrases, and speech acts. Local coherence is "from-below" or "bottom-up" and focuses on how meanings in a text are linked up to form and contribute to more general and complex meanings.

In this chapter we explore how more microlevel structures contribute to the interpretive act. Interpretation is of various kinds but primarily concerned with assigning meaning of the type IF X then ASSIGN Y. An X is usually a morphemic or syntactic form and Y is the interpretation or meaning of the expression. The various types of contributions to local coherence and interpretation is the subject of this chapter. We begin this chapter with a brief description of Halliday and

Hasan's (1976) work on cohesion because it is the most comprehensive and formal treatment of local coherence, and has become a standard reference. From there we build up to more extensional types of meaning by examining speech acts or utterances where the hearer understands the intentions of the speaker. And finally, the chapter examines the exchange structure between two communicators and the various sequence mechanisms that constitute some fundamental organizational structures at the local level.

COHESION

We begin by examining some of the formal linguistic features that are available to a speaker or writer to signal a hearer or reader about how a text is supposed to be organized and thereby interpreted. We pay particular attention to the reference system in discourse. Up until now we have used the term *text* in a general sense to refer to functional language use or, according to Brown and Yule (1983), "the verbal record of a communicative event" (p.6). But a more specific treatment of text is concerned with the internal linguistic mechanisms that hold a text together and contribute to its sense of being a unified whole. That is, how parts of the text are interconnected according to principles of binding and connectivity that require an interpretation. A number of authors have worked to address these issues in local organization of discourse (e.g., de Beaugrande & Dressler, 1981) but by far the most complete, technical, and comprehensive treatment of the problem is that offered by Halliday and Hasan (1976).

Cohesion and Text

Halliday and Hasan are concerned with cohesion that "occurs where the INTER-PRETATION of some element in the discourse is dependent on that of another" (Halliday & Hasan, 1976, p. 4). *Cohesion* has to do with relations among surface linguistic forms where *coherence* refers to more general organizational patterns that lend order to a discourse. The dependency relation is key to cohesion. When one element of a discourse presupposes another, and this other element cannot be understood without referring to what presupposes it, then a cohesive relation has been established. Another way to think about cohesion is as a tie between two linguistic forms that assists a text with its sense of wholeness as in Example 1.

  1. Bundle the papers with string. Then place them on the curb.

The relationship between *them* and *papers* is a cohesive tie. The function of *them* is to refer to *papers* and the cohesive tie makes it possible to interpret the two sentences as related. The term *them* presupposes *papers* and makes no sense without that presupposition. These principles of cohesion are part of the language system. The possibilities for cohesive relations among linguistic features are built into the language system. It is the semantic relationship among these features that is important because the term *them* is only cohesive if it is semantically linked to something previous in the text. All texts (oral or written) rely on cohesion for their own creation. A text becomes a structural unit when its elements cohere with each other. This means that cohesion in a text is reliant on a system of relationships that promote cohesion. These relationships are local because they are properties of the text as such and not of some larger structure. Cohesion creates the continuity between one part of a text and another. This continuity is not, however, the whole of a text because general themes and patterns of coherence are also responsible for texture. But this continuity is essential for the reader or hearer of a text to supply all the necessary information and assumptions that are required for interpretation. Halliday and Hasan identified five types of cohesion—reference, substitution, ellipsis, conjunction, and lexical cohesion—but pay particular attention to reference, substitution, and ellipsis. The descriptions and critique here are necessarily brief.

Reference. All texts have some elements that refer to something else for interpretation. These elements are not directly semantically interpreted but rely on reference to something else for semantic interpretation. The *them* in Example 1 is an example. There is a further distinction between endophoric and exophoric reference. *Endophoric* reference is when a cohesive tie relies on some element within the text for interpretation: When a tie must go to something back in the text it is called an *anaphoric reference*, and when it must wait for something forward in the text it is called a *cataphoric reference*. An anaphoric relationship says "look backward in the text for an interpretation," and a cataphoric relationship says, "look forward." An *exophoric* reference instructs the listener to go to the context of the environment for interpretation and not to some other place in the text. These types of reference are illustrated in Example 2:

  2a. Exophoric reference: I'll have that [person pointing to a sandwich].
  2b. Endophoric reference:
    (i) Anaphoric: I'll take this sandwich. It looks tasty [*it* refers back to *sandwich*].
    (ii) Cataphoric: That looks good, the sandwich [*that* refers forward to *sandwich*].

The pronomial system in a language does much of the work of cohesive reference. Halliday and Hasan explained how the most prevalent types of referential ties are personal pronouns (e.g., *he, she, it, they, him, her, theirs*, etc.) and demonstratives (e.g., *this, that, those, these, there,* etc.). Another type of reference is comparative where a likeness is expressed between two things. Likeness is referential because a thing must be "like something." Expressions such as *same, identical, similar, different,* and a variety of adjectives and superlatives all express comparative relations of some sort. All of these types of cohesive references are endophoric in that they refer to internal semantic relations within the text.

Substitution. The difference between substitution and reference is that substitution is a difference in "wording rather than in meaning" (Halliday & Hasan, 1976, p. 88). It is important to underscore the fact that all distinctions in types of cohesion are not clear-cut. There are instances of cohesive ties that cannot be distinguished clearly as one type or another. This is sometimes the case when considering the differences between reference and substitution. Whereas reference is a distinction between semantic forms and meaning, substitution is a distinction between linguistic items. A substitution is a relation between two vocabulary items or a vocabulary item and a phrase. The cohesion in Example 1 lies in the semantic identity between *papers* and *them.* Pronouns are structural markers that instruct one to look elsewhere for meaning. Substitution, on the other hand, implies a repetition of a particular vocabulary item. So in Examples 3 and 4:

3a. Nice tattoo.
3b. Thanks, I am thinkin' of getting a new one.

4a. Is he sick today.
4b. I think so.

one and *so* are substitutes; *one* substitutes for *tattoo,* and *so* for *he is sick today.* Substitutes can literally take the place of what precedes them. Examples 3 and 4 point up two of the three types of substitutions discussed by Halliday and Hasan. In Example 3b the substitution is nominal in that *one* is a noun substituting for a head noun (*tattoo*), and in Example 4b the substitution is clausal because *so* presupposes the entire clause *he is sick today.* The third type of substitution is verbal where the term operates at the head of a verb group as in Example 5. The *do* in Example 5b substitutes for the verbal clause *turn the soil today.*

5a. We need to turn the soil today.
5b. I have no time for that, and neither do you.

Ellipsis. A third form of cohesion is ellipsis where something is left unsaid. Actually, substitution and ellipsis utilize the same principle of relationship between words but in the case of ellipsis there is zero substitution or no lexicogrammatical unit. The reference that is necessary to make a text cohesive is missing but "understood" as in Examples 6 and 7.

6a. Do you like blue corn tortilla chips.
6b. Yea.
7. David hit the ball, and the ball me.

There is a "slot" in Example 6b that is left blank but presupposes the phrase *I like blue corn tortilla chips*. And the second clause in Example 7 can only be interpreted as the ball *hit* me. Ellipsis is not the fact that a speaker must apply information from his or her own background to interpret an utterance because that is always true and is of marginal help when explaining cohesion. Rather, ellipsis is when there is a structural place that presupposes some item that provides necessary information. The space after *yea* in Example 6b is a structural slot that gets filled by a clause from the preceding utterance. This is the same as substitution except that in substitution a lexical item marks what is to be presupposed, and in ellipsis nothing is in the slot. Ellipsis can also be nominal, verbal, or clausal as in examples 8, 9, and 10 respectively.

8. The test will have essay questions and multiple-choice questions. The multiple choice are least important. (slot for *questions*)
9a. Where are you going?
9b. To class. (slot for *I am going*)
10a. Larry was on his way over but someone called and held him up.
10b. Who? (slot for *called and held him up*)

Conjunction. Conjunctive relations are the fourth type of grammatical cohesion discussed by Halliday and Hasan. Conjunctive ties are not primarily instructions for where to look in a text for meaning, rather they are expressive of semantic relations that are presupposed in the text. Reference, substitution, and ellipses are relatively straightforward because they are primarily directions for interpreting elements in the textual environment. An interpreter is told to either "refer back" to some element in the text (reference), "substitute" one lexical item for another (substitution), or "fill in" a blank slot with a noun, verb, or clause, from somewhere else in the text (ellipses). Conjunctions, on the other hand, specify how information at one point in a text is related to what has preceded it. This relationship is semantic rather than structural. So the word *later* in Example 11 is a conjunctive expression that achieves cohesion through the semantic relationship of time succession. The time sequence is the only thing that relates the two events. Examples 12, 13, and 14 relate the two events through structural relations of various types.

11. Bob finished work. Later, he had a drink.
12. Bob had a drink after work.
13. After work Bob had a drink.
14. Bob followed work with a drink.

There are a number of common conjunctive elements the simplest of which is "and." Others are *but, yet, so*, and *then*. These are simple adverbs or coordinating conjunctions. There are other compound adverbs (e.g., *furthermore, nevertheless, consequently*), and prepositional phrases (e.g., *on the contrary, as a result, in spite of that, in addition*) all of which are common conjunctives in the language system. These various conjunctive elements in the language system can be used to establish particular types of conjunctive relationships. Halliday and Hasan (1976) described four particular types of conjunctives they call additive, adversative, causal, and temporal. An example of each is in Example 15.

15. I spent the entire night working on my class project.
    a. *And* it was really difficult. (additive)
    b. *Yet* I am not very tired. (adversative)
    c. *So* I am almost finished. (causal)
    d. *Then*, in the early morning, I fell asleep. (temporal)

Conjunctions depend on meanings or sentences and on the generalized types of relations that we recognize. An *additive* conjuncture relationship annexes information to the propositional content of a sentence. Such a conjunction typically links information along a series of points in an effort to contribute to a main proposition. *Adversative* conjunctions communicate information that is contrary to expectations established by a previous piece of text. The expectations can result from the content of the text or from something in the speaker–hearer relationship. The *causal* conjunction communicates that some information or state is the result of the condition just prior to it. These too can be links along a series of points that support a main proposition. Finally, when two successive utterances or sentences are related by sequence of time, then the conjunction is *temporal* as in Example 15d. Temporal conjunctions express a subsequent occurrence that is not necessarily causal, additional, or counter to expectations.

Lexical Cohesion. The final type of cohesive relationship discussed by Halliday and Hasan is lexical cohesion, which is when cohesion is achieved by vocabulary selection. Lexical cohesion is perhaps the most complicated because a particular linguistic item does necessarily perform a cohesive function. The word *she*, for example, necessarily calls for particular information that must be extracted from some other place in either the text or the environment. But things are not so direct with lexical cohesion because every lexical item can potentially enter into a cohesive relationship. A vocabulary item contributes to cohesion when it is synonymous or near synonymous with another vocabulary item, or when one term has a superordinate relation with another such as in Examples 16, 17, and 18 respectively.

16. The book was very important. It was a rare volume of poetry.
17. He saddled his horse and rode the great steed into battle.
18. Roger bought a new bat. He just loved baseball.

In Example 16 *book* and *volume* are synonymous. In Example 17 *horse* and *steed* are near synonymous. And in Example 18 *baseball* implies a more general class of objects that includes a *bat*. Each of these are cohesive because one lexical item refers to another. Again, *bat*, or *volume*, or *steed* are not cohesive unto themselves but stand in semantic relation (reiterate) to the vocabulary terms that precede them. These lexical devices allow for continuity of meaning. They may occur in conjunction with referential relations but are not dependent on them. The semantic system of a language, and the patterns of use that recur over time, determine what words are related to what other words. These relationships are central to the linguistic system even if they can only be stated as inclinations and propensities, and not as rules.

Cohesion and Communication

Halliday and Hasan's (1976) work with textual cohesion is significant because it offers close analysis of organizational levels beyond the sentence. The most impressive successes in the study of language have been in phonology, morphology, and syntax. But these disciplines are confined to the internal structure of the sentence. Most efforts to examine relations beyond the sentence level—into the connections that produce well-formed sequences and allow longer stretches of discourse to be understood as sensible or relevant—have been tripped up by the need to apply principles of rhetoric, pragmatics, and communication all of which have less tenable theoretical foundations. Surely Prague school linguists and scholars such as Levi-Strauss and Dell Hymes have conducted broad based textual analysis. But there is very little work that relates issues in textual cohesion to more social and strategic levels of human interaction. Communication by its nature occurs at a number of levels (e.g., cultural, institutional, functional) but a concern with message strategy and effectiveness is at the core of communication.

Communication involves constructing messages that direct a listener or reader to a selected portion of reality. Communication is a strategic act (Sanders, 1987). It is listener adapted and reliant on the ability of the communicator to take the perspective of the other and adapt his or her message accordingly. Language users learn to identify some of the relevant characteristics of listeners and, in the most successful cases, adapt their messages to these listener characteristics. Part of becoming communicatively competent (in the social and strategic sense) is learning the relevance of certain characteristics to the listener. Highly skilled communicators are able to make intelligent decisions about their messages and control the communicative code well enough for successful outcomes. Sanders (1987) explained how the first problem for communicators is to control as well as possible how they are understood; they do this by formulating messages according to conventions of language and the audience that will maximize the possibility of being understood in the desired manner. Communicators must then be concerned with their effects on the behavior of others. They must make estimates about how what they say will constrain future messages from the speaker or the listener. Now cohesion plays an important role in this process because in order to achieve understanding, communicators must signal a listener as to their intended meaning. There are any number of conventions for achieving this, but the cohesion devices discussed earlier are some of the most significant. In this vein, some scholars have tried to correlate cohesive devices with the general coherence or clarity of a text (Bolinger, 1979; Mosenthal & Tierney, 1984). It appears that analysis of cohesive devices in interaction can, in part, offer clues to underlying coherence relations and reveal important qualities of individual speakers, their cognitive processes, and some interpersonal qualities of dyadic interaction.

Communicators are typically not very reflective about the use of cohesive devices; references, conjunctions, and so on are not under a lot of conscious control by people. But research does indicate that cohesive devices vary systematically with constraints on their use (Murphy, 1985; Sag & Hankamer, 1984). Ellipsis and substitution, for example, are oriented more toward the immediate context of interaction and used to focus on information that is currently under consideration but will dissipate soon. It is easier for individuals to use devices such as ellipsis and substitution. Pronominal reference, on the other hand, requires more effort from the communicators. They are more difficult because speakers must have a firmer sense of how the other person has been interpreting messages thus far so that speakers can feel confident that they will be understood. This process requires the speaker to take the perspective of the other and subjectively calculate the level and specificity of understanding by the other person before the speaker can make a choice about language. Various cohesive devices are also affected by whether they refer to the internal structure of a speaker or to the utterances of a hearer (De Stefano, 1984). We can presume, perhaps, that communicators who are particularly adept at tying their own utterances to those of others might be responsible for more integrated, smooth, and coherent conversation than those communicators who concentrate on their own messages only.

Research by Villaume and Cegala (1988) offers one interesting application of these ideas. Villaume and Cegala reasoned that the nature of a speaker's interaction with an interlocutor can be understood in part by how they tie utterances. And they argued that an interactant's interpretive processes are revealed by the cohesive devices that help interactants with the burden of establishing meaning. Villaume and Cegala analyzed type of cohesive device, and the interactional direction of the device, that is, whether the device referred to the speaker's own turn or the turn of the listener. They also reasoned that interactional involvement (Cegala, 1981), or the extent to which a speaker is sensitive to and participates in the flow of interaction, would be correlated with the patterned use of various cohesive devices. In their study, Villaume and Cegala found that dyads where both members had tested low on interaction involvement did rely more on interactive ellipsis and fewer within-utterance references. That is to say their linguistic ties to each others utterances were not explicit but reliant on the other person "filling in" missing information. And low-involved participants tend not to assist with the interpretive burden of the other as evidenced by a lack of within utterance cohesive ties. Interestingly, when low-involved speakers are communicating with a high-involved partner they elaborate their utterances and increase their use of within-utterance ties; that is, they adapt to the high-involved speakers. This finding demonstrates that patterned use of cohesive ties is sensitive to speaker characteristics and dyad types, and is consistent with Cappella's (1990) claim that convergence is a fundamental property of interaction.

The cohesive devices discussed earlier are central to the local organization of discourse. They are some of the basic machinery of the text. But some important questions remain. First, is cohesion as explicated by Halliday and Hasan a sufficient determinate of text? And second, are the features of cohesion necessary to achieve texture or that sense of semantic unity with the environment that characterizes texts. Halliday and Hasan suggest that cohesion is "necessary . . . but not the whole story" (p. 324). It is important to draw one distinction more clearly than Halliday and Hasan have, and that is the distinction between semantic relations and the textual expression of those semantic relations. Halliday and Hasan overemphasized the textual constituents of cohesion when, in fact, few would deny that cohesion is the result of semantic relations within the text. Cohesion depends more on underlying meaning relations than on the elements of the verbal record. There are any number of examples of texts that are easy enough to interpret but display no specific cohesive devices such as in Example 19.

19a. Please pass the salt.
19b. What a beautiful table.

In this example, and in many other situations, there is not an explicit tie between a and b. But most people will assume that this example is textual and that the sequences are sensible enough from some perspective to assume that b is related to a. What makes the sequence here sensible is the semantic relationship between a and b. This relationship draws on principles of global coherence rather than local co-interpretation mechanisms for meaning. But it still is constitutive of a text; it remains the case that texture can be achieved (at least in simpler examples) without resorting to explicit cohesive ties.

Another way to look at this issue is to ask whether or not formal cohesion ties will guarantee texture. How easy would it be for a language user who was confronted with a text to understand the text on the basis of formal cohesive ties only. One interesting test of this is to jumble the organizational pattern of a text, thereby offering no global coherence clues and losing the impact of known semantic relations, and testing how well a text can be understood. Consider the passage in Example 20.

20. [1]124 was spiteful. [2] soon as two tiny hand prints appeared in the cake (that was it for Howard). [3] Full of a baby's venom. [4] Neither boy waited to see more; [5] soda crackers crumbled and strewn in a line next to the door-still. [6] The women in the house knew it and so did the children. [7] The grandmother, Baby Suggs, was dead, and the sons, Howard and Buglar, had run away by the time they were thirteen years old—as soon as merely looking in a mirror shattered it (that was the signal for Buglar). [8] another kettleful of chickpeas smoking in a heap on the floor; [9] For years each put up with the spite in his own way, but by 1873 Sethe and her daughter Denver were its only victims.

This passage is the opening paragraph from Toni Morrison's novel *Beloved*; we need to say little more about how cohesion will not necessarily produce a passage that is immediately identifiable as a text. Comparing this passage with the correct sequence (1, 3, 6, 9, 7, 2, 4, 8, 5) demonstrates how difficult, if not impossible, it is to capture the meaning of a passage using textual connections only. A reader will use some of the verbal devices in the passage but is more likely to construct a general scenario that fits the events. Example 1 in chapter 6 shows how a sequence of sentences can "appear" cohesive but are really inadequate. There is the assumption that contiguous sentences that display cohesive ties form a coherent text, but this assumption can be dangerous. There is research that indicates that meaning, other than the most blatant, escapes interpreters unless they have more general organizational schemes for a text. The telegraphic language of children, some messages, and advertisements is another example of coherent texts that are without explicit cohesive devices. The meaning of Example 21 is clear enough even though there are no textual cohesion devices.

21. Arrive Thursday, Bradley, flight #371 American. Call if late.

A study by Ellis, Hamilton, and Aho (1983) asked subjects to take a randomly ordered conversation and resequence the conversation in what they thought was the correct order. The conversation appears in Dialogue 22.

22. 1 A: Ah, I know what I wanted to tell you.
    2 B: What?
    3 A: What are you doing Saturday night?
    4 B: Going to dinner and then a show.
    5 A: Well, what time do you get done because there is a party which you are invited to.
    6 B: Another party, I got invited to Bill's party too.
    7 A: Really, he didn't invite me.
    8 B: I guess I shouldn't have said anything.
    9 A: I talked to Bill the other day.
   10 B: Well, I was going to go after the show.
   11 A: Maybe I wasn't invited because he knows I was already going to a party.
   12 B: Mmm. I believe . . .
   13 A: It's Sara's party and it should be fun.
   14 B: Yea, where's it at?
   15 A: Somewhere over on MAC.
   16 B: This side of Saginaw?
   17 A: I am not sure. Pete's going to find out this afternoon.
   18 B: Yea, well the thing is the show gets out pretty late and . . .
   19 A: I'll see Pete this afternoon and then let you know exactly where it is.
   20 B: Well, we'll see.

This was a case of a complete conversation that was clear and simple to understand for the two people involved in the conversation. The subjects in the experiment, however, were confronted with nothing but the text and cohesive devices as cues for how to understand the text. The subjects clearly had difficulty making much sense out of even this simple conversation. Except for a few contiguous pairs of utterances, they were not very successful at resequencing the conversation. Pairs 1 and 2, 3 and 4, 4 and 5, 6 and 7, and 7 and 8 were easily recognized by the subjects. Sequence 1–2, for example, capitalizes on the power of ellipsis to signal contiguity between the two utterances. The "what?" in Utterance 2 is only sensible if it follows Utterance 1 and competent interpreters will use ellipsis to tie the utterance to the one preceding it. Simple adjacency pairs (discussed later) are also easily identifiable by subjects because of a strong local organization (e.g., 3–4). They are the type of pair where one utterance creates a slot for a particular second utterance.

But except for some highly prescribed relationships, explicit cohesive tries are only moderately successful in creating texture and a sense of full understanding about a discourse. The participants in Dialogue 22 are an important source of coherence in the text. In a sense, they bring necessary information that is outside the text and cannot be ascertained by a close line-by-line reading of the text. It is important, then, to distinguish between the formal verbal record of cohesion, as described by Halliday and Hasan, and the underlying semantic relations that "tie" propositions in a text. Language users do *not* rely heavily on explicit cohesion for interpretation. (See also Hobbs, 1982; Mosenthal & Tierney, 1984). Texts are determined by those taking part in the communication process. Fragments and contiguous sequences of utterances or lines of print are treated by participants in communication as textual, and as such they make every effort to interpret coherently. There seems to be no advantage to arguing that certain formal textual devices are necessary for cohesion. It is important to reiterate, however, that Halliday and Hasan were not concerned with on-line processing of the meaning of text. Rather, they were interested in detailing the linguistic devices in the grammatical system that are available to mark cohesion. And although these devices are not sufficient to establish textuality, this does not detract from the compelling and heuristic nature of Halliday and Hasan's work.

SPEECH ACTS

The formal ties available to a speaker or writer are important for the creation of coherent messages. But participants in interaction are also performing some *action* (see chapter 5). The language-in-use occurs in a context and has real effects. If I say that "I promise to mow your lawn" I am using language in our interaction to perform action—the act of promising. The distinction between the propositional nature of an utterance and its functional nature is important. *Propositional structure* refers to the content, subject matter, or ideas of a communication. The *functional* or *actional structure* of an utterance is concerned with what the utterance *does*. The example just given functions as a *promise*, and its propositional content involves *mowing a lawn* as opposed to a promise to do something else.

The British philosopher J. L. Austin (1962) was the first to make very explicit the different functions of language. He showed how many utterances are not just statements about some information, but are actions. If, in the appropriate context, a speaker says something like:

23. I'll *bet* you $5 on the Laker game tonight; or,

24. I *promise* to mow your lawn; or,

25. I *apologize* for what I said yesterday,

then the speaker is doing more than making statements about betting, promising, or apologizing. He or she *is* betting, promising, or apologizing. The utterance of these acts constitutes their performance. Each of the three examples are composed of sounds with conventional vocabulary and syntax; and each refers to some idea or subject matter. But each is also, as described by Austin, and *illocutionary* act that produces an effect on the hearer; each makes the speaker's intentions known. Another way to understand illlocutionary force of the utterance is to imagine each uttered in isolation. A speaker could utter any of the examples while alone but they would have no effect and produce no action. But in the context of another person each of the examples has a strong influence on the listener.

Austin called statements "constatives" and argued that they have no privileged position as a language function because even though it is possible to simply describe the world, that is not what people do most of the time. Illocutionary acts have intent and perform action, and their force is achieved when a hearer understands what the speaker was trying to do when the speaker said X. Statements have their propositional content as the main concern of the statement. In the case of statements, the question of truth or falsity is a legitimate question. But performatives perform action and it makes no sense to talk about truth or falsity. It makes no sense for me to respond to statement 23 with "That is not true." In Sentence 25 the apology is performed simply by its statement. It would be possible for me to say "I am sorry for what I said yesterday" and not mean it. The word "sorry" is not a performative verb, rather it is a description of my feelings and therefore subject to a test of truth of falsity. It would be possible to question whether or not I am truly in a state of sorrow. However, if I say "I apologize" then the act itself is an apology.

Speech acts begin to play an important role in communication and local coherence in a variety of ways. One way is by the choices that a hearer has when responding to an act. A friend of mine might say:

26. You should buy cattle futures.

I might respond with:

27. I don't think that would be a good investment.

The response in Sentence 27 would refer to the content of Sentence 26. If I interpret 26 as a statement then it is subject to matters of truth or falsity. The anaphoric *that* refers to the content of the utterance. We could imagine the discourse continuing as a discussion about investment opportunities and strategies. But rather than the response in Sentence 27 what if I said:

28. You are always giving me advice.

Then I am responding to the speech act performed (advice) and not to the propositional content. Now we might imagine the conversation evolving into an argument about our relationship. So speech acts can relate to textual cohesion by the way participants in communication refer to utterances.

Austin realized that his distinction between constative and performative was not entirely clear, and that the same utterance can contain both. A speaker could use the performative verb and restate Sentence 26 as:

29. [I state that] you should buy cattle futures.

Then one could both question the truth or falsity of the claim and recognize that the person has performed a speech act—*stating*. Austin responded to this problem by developing a more general theory that included three types of acts. An utterance is at one level *locutionary*, which means that it is made up of sounds with sense and reference. Traditional linguistics has been predominantly concerned with this level of analysis. Second, utterances have *illocutionary* force as described earlier. This is when a hearer understands the intent of an utterance and recognizes what the speaker is trying to accomplish. The third level is the *perlocutionary* act or the effect that an utterance has on a hearer. This has been the traditional domain of rhetoric. The distinction between illocution and perlocution has not always been easy to draw. A number of illocutionary acts (e.g., requests) have effects on hearers as part of their goals.

Identifying Speech Acts

If speakers were always explicit about what they were doing, in the sense that they were clear about the illocutionary force of their utterances, then speech act theory would offer the most powerful account of communication. But speakers are often unclear about what they are doing; they are typically indirect, multifunctional, and vague about the purpose of their utterance. A speaker's utterance does not always have a clear indicator of what its function is, and even the use of a simple performative verb does not guarantee the illocutionary force of an utterance. Most of Austin's examples of speech acts were from highly prescribed and ritualistic contexts. When the preacher says "I pronounce you husband and wife" or a defendant utters "I plead guilty" then these are clear cases where the function and inevitability of the utterance is clear. The illocutionary force of a speech act is easiest to identify in highly conventional contexts such as wedding ceremonies, courts of law, and games.

But what about all the other cases where the purpose and context of an utterance are less clear. Most scholars have worked to classify illocutionary acts in terms of the recognizable intent of the speaker. This recognizable intent is an effectiveness criterion because illocutionary force is achieved when the hearer recognizes what the speaker intended to say or do. The hearer does not have to understand, agree with, or be affected by the utterance; the hearer must simply understand the speaker's purpose in uttering X. Bach and Harnish (1979) argued for the communicative nature of illocutionary acts by suggesting a set of speech acts where the speaker expresses his or her intent to influence the hearer in some way as well as expressing an attitude about the subject matter of the utterance. So to *suggest* is not only to make some information or course of action available, but also make the hearer believe that the speaker is knowledgeable. It is not important that the hearer accept the suggestion just that he treat it as one. Bach and Harnish suggested four categories of illocutionary acts that are communicative in nature. The first is *constatives*, acts that reveal the speakers beliefs or knowledge state, and have the hearer accepting these beliefs or knowledge states as their main intention. Suggesting, describing, informing, and predicting are examples of constatives. In each case the speaker is trying to put the hearer in the same knowledge state as himself.

When a speaker is trying to induce a hearer to action, and provides motivation for the action, then the speaker is using *directive* speech acts. Directives include advice, prohibitions, and suggestions. The speaker wants the hearer to do something and is providing reasons, information, or motivation for the action.

The third type of communicative illocutionary act proposed by Bach and Harnish are *commissives*. These are when the speaker is agreeing or obligating himself to do something for the hearer in the future. Promises and offers are examples of commissives. The speaker is by uttering the act committing himself to some future action.

The last category is termed *acknowledgments* and these include acts such as thanking, congratulating, and apologizing. Acknowledgments are when the speaker is communicating emotions or feelings that he or she wants the hearer to understand.

There is still difficulty with the relationship between utterances (actual language use) and the actions these utterances are supposed to perform. In other words, it is still possible to misassign a speech act or experience confusion about what function it is performing. When we are engaged in normal conversation we must use the local lexical and syntactical forms to assign meaning to an utterance and, unfortunately, there is no way to map the language of an utterance onto specific speech act functions. Searle (1969) worked to specify as completely as possible the criteria involved in identifying a speech act and the situation in which that act "counts" as performing a function. He began by stating that normal communication conditions must occur, that is, the speaker and hearer must share a common language, both must be able to hear, and so on. From these basic assumptions, Searle extracted what he called constitutive rules for the performance of a particular speech act. The following is an example of the necessary conditions for the act of "warning."

Preparatory condition	Hearer has reasons to believe the event will occur and is not in the hearer's interest.
	It is not obvious to both speaker and hearer that event will occur.
Sincerity condition	Speaker believes the event will occur and is not in the hearers best interest.
Essential condition	Counts as an undertaking to the effect that event is not in hearer's best interest.

A speaker might say, for example, "If you don't organize your expense receipts, then you will have trouble at tax time." This utterance would count as a warning because it meets the three conditions just stated. The hearer believes that he or she will have trouble at tax time and that this is undesirable. Both the speaker and hearer recognize that trouble at tax time is not obvious and can be avoided (preparatory condition). The speaker genuinely believes that trouble at tax time is not in the hearer's best interest (sincerity condition). And if trouble at tax time is not in the hearer's best interest then the utterance counts as a warning (essential condition). The essential condition is most important because it is what distinguishes a "warning" from "advice." An event that is not in the hearer's interest is a warning but if the event is in the hearer's interest than the speech act counts as advice. If the speaker said "Organize your expense receipts and things will be easy at tax time," then an "easy tax time" is in the speaker's interest and the utterance would count as "advice."

But Gazdar (1981) has been critical of attempts to assign speech acts to functions. He continued to ask how we know what a speaker is doing when he utters something, and how we know which functions are indicated by which utterances. One problem is that different speech acts can have the same illocutionary force. So the mapping process must be complex and incomplete indeed if numerous utterances can have the same illocutionary force; thus, the three speech acts presented here can all be classified as "promises" even though they are very different utterances.

30. I'll drop it by after dinner.
31. I'll get it to you by the 15th.
32. I'll always love you.

Gazdar has also pointed out how the same utterance can perform more than one function. Statement 33 may be either a question or an inquiry.

  33. Would you care if we went to Assagios for dinner.

Searle (1969) explained how statements such as the one just given have a literal meaning and form of expression and a nonliteral one, and that is why the utterance can perform more than one function. Levinson (1981) extended some of Gazdar's criticisms by faulting Searle and the principles of constitutive rules and claiming that speech act theory is too *ad hoc* and unable to explain how one act can perform more than one function. Levinson's example of "Would you like another drink" can be either a question or an offer and the hearer's response ("yes" or "no") does not solve the problem. Levinson claimed that there is an indefinite number of possible act interpretations for certain utterances. He continued his criticism of speech act theory by questioning its reliance on speaker intentions that are not observable.

The criticisms of Gazdar and Levinson notwithstanding hearers do interpret speech acts and recognize illocutionary force. Levinson's claim that speech act theory must yield a finite set of categories and a set of interpretive procedures is exaggerated. Speech act theory is essentially a pragmatic theory in that it must rely on assumed properties of contexts, metaphorical extension, interpersonal relations, and the sociology of language for interpretation. Language users correctly infer the illocutionary force of an utterance because they bring knowledge not only of language and grammatical mood but of speakers and hearers, personal relations, paraverbal behaviors that condition language, knowledge about communication patterns, relevant macrostructure propositions, and presuppositional knowledge. When all of these are brought to bear on an utterance a hearer typically has little trouble working out the intent of the speaker. The interpretation of speech acts is a local coherence property in part because of the variety of channels of information available to interactants is necessary for their interpretation. The search for a fully specified analytical scheme that assigns functions to speech acts is probably misdirected. Although some illocutionary acts are literal and easily classifiable because they are expressed directly in a highly conventionalized context, most do not correspond to any literal reading. A fuller understanding of how communicators interpret illocutionary force requires reference to pragmatic rules that a listener can use to infer the illocutionary force of a speaker.

Speech Acts as Interactive Accomplishments

Much of the data for speech act analysis is contrived. It is made up to demonstrate how certain principles apply. There is nothing wrong with these invented pieces of data because they are examples of actual utterances performed by native speakers and thereby subject to analysis. But in practice hearers often do not have a lot of help from the surface features of an utterance for interpreting illocutionary force. Moreover, speakers in "real" interaction have the advantage of interaction history and pragmatic knowledge about the subject matter, context, and other person. A number of theorists have been suggesting that the interpretation of illocutionary force is not so easy as we move from one situation to another. We must ask whether the interpretation of a speech act from one context to another, or one relationship to another, is as unproblematic as Searle suggested. Is an "apology" or a piece of "advice" the same among government officials, families, friends, parental relationships, colleagues, and the like? Are they based on identical constitutive rules? Speech acts are a fundamental communication phenomenon but their meaning and function are determined locally and perhaps not completely according to constitutive rules that are translatable across contexts. Edmondson (1981), for example, has argued that speech act theory lacks a hearer orientation, or an orientation that is more communicative in nature by taking the perspective of the other. Actual language produced in communicative situations is hearer responsive rather than speaker responsive. A hearer is concerned with how a speaker's utterance is integrated into his or her own action, and the hearer's judgment about the function of a particular speech act is relationally dependent. The issue of whether or not speech act theory has slighted important cultural and situational constraints on language, and failed to account enough for interactively produced meaning, can be pursued from a number of perspectives, namely, interpersonal, cultural, pragmatic, and psychological.

One of the basic claims of speech act theory has been that constitutive rules of illocutionary acts are a semantic base underlying language, and that different people rely on the same constitutive rules (Searle, 1969). This is open to some doubt because it is possible to demonstrate that interpersonal relationships condition the interpretation of speech acts. In a quite comprehensive study of discourse in families Kreckel (1981) argued that she has provided empirical evidence for the contention that constitutive rules vary according to the subcodes that they form. Kreckel used the term *subcode* to describe systems of meaning that are characteristic of highly specific communicative contexts (see chapter 8). Groups of people who have very similar interaction histories and share much presuppositional knowledge about one another and certain situations communicate, according to Kreckel, through subcodes. These codes are most typical in familial, ethnic, occupational, and specified cultural contexts. Homodynamic subcodes involve tendencies to choose the same forms of expressions and concepts and result in meaning convergence through similar interaction experiences. Heterodynamic subcodes are when people acquire patterns of interaction in different contexts and through different communication media. In Kreckel's studies of family interaction she assumed that family members would develop strong homodynamic subcodes. She had access to data from a film crew that lived with and recorded a family for 6 months (Kreckel, 1981, p. 5). Kreckel used this empirical data to examine two questions about illocutionary acts.

One question that can be asked is whether or not different language users use illocutionary acts according to the same rules. In one investigation, members of different families were asked to generate common sense definitions of more than 100 speech acts. Each member of the different families stated what situations were relevant for an utterance to count as a warning, advice, and so on. Each family member discussed in detail what was meant by various illocutionary acts. This procedure allowed for comparisons within and between families as well as comparisons of subcode specific rules with Searle's rules. Kreckel reported that comparisons of definitions for illocutionary acts shows powerful consistency within families and marked differences between families. For example, one comparison was for the illocutionary act of "warning." Searle (1969, p. 67) suggested that warnings do not include the necessity of taking evasive action, but Kreckel's data indicates that an attempt to get a hearer to take evasive action is an essential feature of "warning" as used by members of this particular homodynamic subcode. In another family a warning was more associated with a speaker's attempt to get a hearer to do something than with an influence attempt.

A second issue concerns the degree of convergence between speakers and hearers as to what utterances correspond to what illocutionary acts. In other words, it is fair to ask whether or not speakers and hearers recognize various types of illocutionary acts when they hear them and do they agree on their definition. Searle's classifications become problematic if speakers and hearers cannot consistently identify speech acts, especially because most speech acts are not typically uttered in the highly ritualized contexts that speech act theorists use as examples. Kreckel (1981) had her subjects go through an elaborate procedure of classifying messages. She took a sample of interaction and had subjects categorize various segments of the message into classes of communicative concepts such as "warning," "threatening," "asserting," "suggesting," and so on (Kreckel, 1981, pp. 131–137). Kreckel found that homodynamic subcode users (family members) had much higher classification agreement than those outside the code. The understanding of messages and their illocutionary force is greater among common code users than not, and this is especially true in communicative situations where there is considerable shared experience and understanding. Sharing a subcode even increases the level of understanding of messages that are designed for heterodynamic conditions such as public speeches and presentation. It appears that native speakers who share a history of experience and language use draw on their linguistic and extralinguistic knowledge to interpret various speech acts, and they do this according to "constitutive rules" that vary from the ideal grid of speech act theorists.

It is possible to question whether or not the rules for illocutionary force in particular relationships (families) depart from the paradigm case of Searle enough to warrant a new approach or seriously question Searle's constitutive rules. We would expect differences to dissipate at more abstract levels of analysis. Moreover, differences in families are hardly surprising; any commonly used terminology will vary at least slightly in meaning as it is used in one situation or another. But it is also true that speech acts are not the same as words. Speech acts do not exist in the general case and they acquire their meaning in concrete interaction. Also, the nature of the rules that speakers and hearers *use* to communicate illocutionary force are empirical issues that must be subject to investigation. Searle's argument that the constitutive rules of speech acts are analogous to the rules of a game is misleading. The rules of a game such as chess are far more fixed and rigid than the rules of social acts like warning or advising. Game rules can be more capriciously adjusted and are not subject to experiential influences of cultural practices. Speech act theory fails to consider action as a consequence of human social forms where meanings are interactively produced and not the achievements of autonomous individuals.

This debate can be extended by arguing and demonstrating that acts of speech are not asocial and translatable across cultural contexts. As I have been arguing, speech act theorists are rightly concerned with communicative intentions, but have described speech acts as the accomplishments of individuals who are not influenced by their relationships or local interaction practices. A cultural perspective on speech act theory holds that language is not a resource to represent the world (such that the individual can assert, promise, warn) but that words are relevant to relationships and how people come to understand the world. Rosaldo (1982) complemented Kreckel's work with her ethnolinguistic study of the Ilongots of the Northern Luzon in the Philippines. Rosaldo explained how speech acts in Searle's and Austin's work focuses on the inner nature of the speaker. Austin (1962) was concentrating on conventional acts in ritualized contexts such as marriage ceremonies and the like. When Searle elaborated on this and used the act of promising as an exemplar he directed attention to the inner life of individuals and how a set of rules (constitutive) can logically transform the inner life of a speaker into a public statement of action. Searle forgot that promises are offered only in certain situations to certain kinds of people; that a promise to or from a wife, colleague, neighbor, political figure, or child are different things indeed because meaning is not, according to our cultural stereotype, located only in people. Rather meanings are shaped by culturally particular acts, beliefs, relationships, and practices.

The Ilongot's employ verbal action that cannot be separated from issues in social order and ways of speaking. Rosaldo explained, for example, that Ilongots do not use "propositions" (e.g., assertions, statements, argument, claims) to state something true or false about the world. Although Ilongots have some similar speech acts (words to "explain," "tell," "advise"), they are typically used in the beginning of an utterance and are concerned with the formulation of relationships and the establishment of individual character. The Ilongots are less concerned with statements of fact than with who holds knowledge and the speaker's relationship to the holder of knowledge. The Ilongots use directives as do English speakers but overt directives ("Go get the garbage") are "not considered as harsh or impolite" (p. 216). This is because directives have less to do with speaker wishes and demands and are more to do with affirming social relationships. Directives for the Ilongots are typically acknowledged and rather than being characterized by a structured speaker prerogative, they are one pair part in an adjacency pair (Sacks, 1973). Directives are answered with agreements, acknowledgments, denials, and so forth. The power of directives rests not in their ability to match speakers wants with a social act, but in their place in the unfolding discourse between two individuals (Rosaldo, 1982, p. 217). Rosaldo's Ilongot data are an important attempt to modify, not reject, Searle's categorizations and explanations of speech acts by making them more sensitive to sociological and interactional constraints (see also Labov & Fanshel, 1977; Bach & Harnish, 1979).

There is a third way to understand speech acts as interactively produced and embedded into the flow of language *in situ*. Sequencing models of local coherence cannot capture many of the utterances that can rightfully constitute a coherent reply. A speech act does not necessarily establish any conditional relevance; in other words, the acts of "promising," or "warning," or "advising" do not place any obvious conditions on what may follow. Jacobs and Jackson (1983) explain how social actors use speech acts coherently not because these acts are part of an established and predictable pattern of exchange, but because the particular speech acts in an interaction are locally defined ways to achieve communicative goals. Jacobs and Jackson's rational model of conversational coherence is reliant on a theory of practical reasoning constrained by locally defined ways of achieving goals.

The essence of the rational model of local organization of discourse is that people perform illocutionary acts to influence the communicative situation in the direction of some goal, that is, speech acts affect what people in the interaction think and align the speaker with the actions of the other and the social system (see Craig, 1986). People respond primarily to the goals of the interaction and not to specific speech acts per se. The unfolding discourse has a sense of coherence because each utterance is interpreted as a contribution to the general purpose of the interaction. The reasoning process that connects goals to utterances is practical; that is, when a speaker believes that an act will produce a desired effect (e.g., belief, want, information). It is the interaction of the local language-in-use with the rational goals of the communication system that accounts for coherence. Consider the indirect response in Example 34b.

34a. What time is it?
34b. Kelly's class just let out.

The reply in Example 34b is indirect and does not express what is called for. But it can be interpreted as sensible and coherent because it is the result of practical reasoning, a process that takes the shared knowledge of the speaker and hearer (the hour that Kelly's class lets out) and uses the cooperative principle to associate the utterance with the shared knowledge. Sanders (1986) made a related case for the fact that speech acts are not necessarily a function of structural features of an utterance and a context, but the result of overall efforts to produce a rational conversation. An act, according to Sanders, can have illocutionary force where the felicity conditions were established antecedently. The second response in Example 35 is a warning. The goal is to keep the speaker in 35a from going to Katy's house. The "warning" was produced interactively as a pragmatic response to the speaker's goal.

35a. I am going over to Katy's house.
35b. They haven't shoveled their walk yet.

Finally, it is interesting to compare the classificatory nature and structure of speech acts proposed by speech act theorists to those investigated by social psychologists. These researchers are trying to uncover the understandings that naive language users have about speech acts. Wish, D'Andrade, and Goodnow (1980) performed an interesting experiment designed to explain communicative actions as realized psychologically in conversation by social actors. Wish et al. began by having subjects in an experiment code the interaction on a television program using assertions, evaluations, reactions, questions, and requests as categories. Each of these five categories were consistent with those of speech act theorists (e.g., Bach & Harnish, 1979), and were coded for additional communicative intent. For example, assertions were identified by type (simple statement to assertion based on complex conclusion), and by force (subtle suggestion to strong attempt to persuade). These data were then factor analyzed to see how individuals perceived the categories; to see if the coding organizes for naive language users in the same way they were grouped by speech act theorists. The results were quite interesting. The first factor, *asking versus informing*, contained one pole defined by elements of questions and requests, and the other pole was all about assertions and reactions. The second factors was *initiatory versus reactive*; the third was *dissension versus approval*; the forth was *forceful versus forceless*; and the fifth was *judgmental versus nonjudgmental*.

The results from these data indicate clearly that the examples from the categories did not load very consistently onto the superordinate categories based on the expected performative verbs proposed by speech act theorists. True, it is unfair to directly compare Wish's procedures with those of speech act theorists, but this social psychological study does underscore the fluid nature of these categories. It is also evidence that the perception of these performative verbs that presumably have illocutionary force is *relational* in nature. It is further evidence of Edmondson's (1981) claim that speech act categories need to be more hearer oriented, that the force and function of speech acts are more dependent on relational and interactional implications than previously imagined. Hearers are more concerned that the utterance of a speaker be integrated and consistent with the flow of the interaction than in whether or not the illocutionary intent is clear. The study by Wish et al. highlights the importance of conversationally realized speech acts; that people "hear" evaluation when the speaker is making an assertion; that communicators express "force" and "authority" in some nonobvious ways. In general, categories of speech acts are important and useful but probably do not capture some of the more fundamental and subtle communicative actions that are produced in interaction.

SEQUENTIAL ANALYSIS AND SEQUENCES

The work on speech act analysis in linguistics and philosophy is primarily responsible for advancing the view that utterances can be analyzed as social action. Yet the speech act analysis perspective still concentrates on the isolated utterances and is preoccupied with the semantic and syntactic features of an utterance which are considered independently from communicative exchanges. So speech acts are in the troubling position of being at once considered in isolation—searching for literal meaning and constitutive rules—and then examined as a set of variations resulting from the complexities and multifunctional realities of actual communication. One of the significant criticisms of speech act theory is that its supporters fail to understand that "utterances are *in the first instance* contextually understood by reference to their placement and participation within sequences of actions" (Heritage & Atkinson, 1984, p. 5). Therefore sequences, not isolated sentences or utterances, are the primary units of analysis. Sequential analysis research recognizes that a current utterance in an interaction provides a communicative context for the interpretation of subsequent interaction. The prototypical example is when one turn at talk projects or implies the next turn. Such organization at the local utterance by utterance level is termed *conditional relevance* by Schegloff (1972), and a conceptually related term is *sequential implicativeness* (Schegloff & Sacks, 1973). This form of interaction recognizes that some first action occasions a second, and this second action is understood as related to the first. If the second action does not occur then its absence is an identifiable event. The *adjacency pair* is the strongest expression of conditional relevance where the second part of a two-act exchange is literally defined by the first part. So a "question" creates a slot and an interpretative frame for an "answer;" "greetings" occasion "greetings;" and "offers" implicate "acceptances" or "rejections" (see later).

But virtually all utterances occur at some structural position in interaction. Although adjacency pairs are prototypical examples of conditional relevance and structure, *any* utterance can be made coherent by a prior utterance and establish a context for subsequent turns. Just as no word or sentence is fully interpretable in isolation, no utterance occurs outside the boundaries of a sequence. As we began to explore in the previous section, the illocutionary force of an utterance can be profitably understood according to how it functions in relationship to a prior utterance. The analysis of sequences is an excellent entry into the highly context-bound nature of interaction-in-use. For our purposes here we define an *exchange* as an initiation that has no restrictions on possibilities, where what follows is more predictable (see Stubbs, 1983). A *sequential exchange* can be considered a single propositional unit where the frame is established by the initiation (e.g., adjacency pair). The following is an attempt to be more precise about statements such as "utterances are in the first instance contextually understood by reference to their placement and participation within sequences of actions." I rely on some work in linguistics, discourse analysis, and communication to achieve increased precision. Some of these proposals are advancements and modifications of principles treated in Coulthard and Montgomery (1981), Stubbs (1983), and Coulthard (1985).

Form and Structure in Conversation

The tradition of linguistics, which we have alluded to quite often in this volume, has worked out issues in phonology and syntax fairly well. There are concepts in linguistics of structure, well-formedness, and predictability that serve as criteria for evaluating the acceptability of words or sentences. In fact, many of these concepts have been established in considerable detail. Each of these criteria apply equally to discourse, which is the search for order beyond the level of the sentence, but as I demonstrate here there are some important variations and shortcomings. I also concentrate below on *sequential structure* as opposed to many other issues in the general analysis of discourse. Stubbs (1983) and Coulthard (1985) provided discussions of linguistic approaches to discourse. In these discussions they extend the linguistic tradition of rank scale where one level of analysis has a "consists of" relationship with the smaller units that combine to form the larger ones. Thus, a sentence is composed of clauses, and these are composed of smaller groups including words, morphemes, and phonemes. Some time ago discourse analysts (e.g., Coulthard 1985; Sinclair & Coulthard, 1975) proposed a new rank level of discourse with its own scale that is realized at the level of grammar. For example, the following *directive* can be realized by the four clause types—imperative, interrogative, declarative, and moodless (see Coulthard, 1985, p. 122).

36.   shut the door
                           can you shut the door
         I wonder if you can shut the door
              I want you to shut the door
                       let's shut the door

The form of the verb is the same in each sentence from Example 36 but each is marked for varying unclassifiable degrees of politeness. The utterances in Example 36 are important from a communicative perspective because of the relationship implications and the "added" meaning of each utterance. What the speaker is requesting is unproblematic but each utterance says something about the context, speaker–hearer relationship, and other sociolinguistic phenomena.

To understand the organizational role of sequential interaction in establishing local meaning we must turn to a few basic concepts that characterize discourse sequence. The first is *structure*, or the constraints on linear sequence. There is structure in a sequence anytime one utterance presupposes or constrains the predictability of what can follow. A related concept borrowed from linguistics is *well-formedness*: The extent to which a sequence can be considered coherent or not. As I stated earlier these concepts are fairly straightforward when applied to phonology or syntax, but much more restricted when applied to utterance sequences. Discourse is surely not random (see Kellermann, 1991). And people when confronted with random sentences or utterances are able to recognize them as random. The principles that underlie this recognition are the subject of discourse analysis in general, and sequential structure in particular. There is the claim in discourse that "anything can follow anything" and therefore concepts such as structure and well-formedness are not applicable (Stubbs, 1983). But this conclusion is too hasty for two reasons: one, structure and predictability for phonology and syntax are more problematic than is often admitted because analyses in these areas rely on highly idealized data. And second, it is possible to demonstrate the importance and well-formedness of sequential structure in discourse.

The concept of the phoneme in phonology is highly abstract and analyses of structure and well-formedness typically use phonemic data. Some phonologists (Brown, 1977) claim that it is impossible to render "actual" language use into a formal phonemic transcript. Phonological descriptions routinely ignore various accents, styles, borrowed words, and types of speech. The same is true for grammaticality. It is easy enough to state simple and clear-cut cases of grammatical sentences (e.g., "John hit the ball") but what counts as ungrammatical is less clear. There is a difference between being ungrammatical and nonsense. Chomsky's use of grammaticality was borrowed from mathematics so it is very structural in nature. His often quoted grammatical but meaningless sentence ("Colorless green ideas sleep furiously") cannot be interpreted but relies on a restrictive use of the term grammatical. There are reasons to argue that grammaticality is not an "either-or" decision but a continuum. Halliday (1978) has taken the strong position that there should be no distinction between what is grammatical and what is acceptable.

Much of the same can be said about the predictability and well-formedness of discourse sequences. We can make judgments about the structure and well-formedness of discourse but these judgments lie on a continuum. Just as the words of a sentence establish predictions about what will follow, so it is with discourse sequences. This is certainly true with respect to propositional content (see Kellermann, Broetzman, Lim, & Kitao, 1989). If a speaker says something about a topic then it is highly predictable that what follows will be topical and relevant (Grice, 1975). The most fundamental structural rule in discourse is stated as follows. It is the rule of *contingency relevance*.

> **Contingency-relevance rule:** Whenever two utterances, words, phrases, or sentences occur next to or contingent with one another, then hearers or readers will assume they are related. The first will be used as a discourse frame for the second.

This is true in all discourse and accounts for the humor of the exchange in Example 37, which is adapted from an example in chapter 5.

37a. David played Brahms today.
37b. Yeah, who won.

The humor is appreciated through the realization that Example 37a frames the discourse as "musical performance" but 37b is a response based on the use of the word "play" for athletic competition. The contingency-relevance rule makes the "musical performance" interpretation preferred, but the humor is the result of a departure from this interpretive preference. It is easy enough to provide many other demonstrations of the structural and predictive power of the contingency relevance rules. Consider those situations where we hear only one person in a conversation (e.g., telephone, person in next room, etc.) and how well we are able to predict what the other person is saying.

But are the structural relations described here truly powerful and capable of more formalization, as in phonology and syntax, or are they simply organized according to the conventions of propositional content and typical patterns and activities in the world. Structure and predictability are probably the most important concepts in discourse and communication. We see here that it is possible to formulate sequential models of discourse that are something more than simple nonlinguistic contingency relations. This is true because of the presence of sequential rules that dictate certain structural relations that are fundamental to the production of meaning in interaction.

Even though it is sometimes argued that anything can follow anything in human interaction and hence sequences are not very binding, the fact that we can recognize incoherence is evidence that coherence is structurally preferred. Nevertheless, discourse structure is likely to be somewhat less deterministic because it is constructed by two different language users, which is not true of the linguistic system in general. One person can never absolutely constrain what another person says. That is why discourse structure is most easily responsive to maxims of cooperation (Grice, 1975). Given that what B says will be interpreted within the framework of A's contribution, it is possible to talk about discourse structure. Sequential relations control much of the meaning in discourse. Sanders (1987) has argued that explaining the contribution of a communicator by reference to attitudes, personality, or knowledge of subject matter is secondary to other considerations. Structural relations control meaning in discourse by classifying certain utterances. It is possible to show that the syntax and semantics of a speaker's utterance are often insufficient to account for meaning, and the utterance's position in a sequence is more important. It would be difficult to retrieve the meaning of the utterance in Example 38 if it occurred in isolation.

38. The rare chair.

But if steaks were being served and a speaker had previously said "where should I sit" then the meaning of Utterance 38 would be clear, and the discourse structure controlled the meaning. Communication is by definition strategic and for this reason the disposition to say something, and the nature of the propositional content, are secondary to (a) whether the utterance is relevant and sensible at a particular point in the unfolding interaction, and (b) which subsequent messages are possible if a contribution is made at a juncture (Sanders, 1987).

Exchange Structure

The general structure of sequential exchange in discourse has received its most complete treatment from Sinclair and Coulthard (1975) and Coulthard and Brazil (1981). They begin by describing initiation and response as fundamental and complementary elements of the discourse exchange. An initiation is constraining on the next move in the exchange and the response is considered retrospectively within the frame of the initiation. The two central criteria that characterize and distinguish these elements of the exchange structure are (a) whether or not initiations produce predictions about what will follow, and (b) whether a response is explained by what preceded it. There is the possibility of a third move that is a follow-up but it is neither predicting or predicted. Thus:

	Predicting	Predicted
1. Initiation	Yes	No
2. Response	No	Yes
3. Follow-up	No	No
4. Resp/Init	Yes	Yes

So an initiating utterance "predicts" that something will follow, and a responding utterance was "predicted" by something that preceded it. A follow-up to this basic structure is either not obligatory or terminal and therefore not predicting or predicted. There is the possibility of a fourth element (Resp/Init) that is both predicted and predicting. There are some responses that are looking for a follow-up as in the following example from Coulthard (1985, p. 135).

39. Teacher: can anyone tell me what this means
    Pupil: does it mean danger men at work
    Teacher: yes . . .

The pupil's statement is predicted by the teacher's initiation and is predicting of a response: In short, it is a response to the preceding element and initiatory with respect to the subsequent statement.

This theoretical set of combinations classifies each utterance in terms of structural prediction, which is the defining characteristic of exchange. The minimal exchange structure is

$$\begin{array}{cc} \rightarrow & \leftarrow \\ [\ I & R\ ] \end{array}$$

where the $\rightarrow$ arrow indicates that the element predicts a following utterance, and the $\leftarrow$ arrow indicates that the element is predicted by the preceding item. Other researchers have offered theoretical formulations that are comparable to this type of exchange structure. Schegloff (1972) extended on Sacks' work and explains the *adjacency pair* as a two-turn structure. Goffman (1971) used the term *interchange* to describe sequential structure. And Fisher and Hawes (1971) introduced the *interact* as a fundamental exchange structure.

Given the features of exchange structure it is possible to expand the implications for types of exchanges. A feature can be ± predicting or ± predicted. So if an initial utterance is + predicting, meaning that it predicts a response, then it is – terminal, or cannot be a terminal utterance. The same is true for a + predicted utterance, that is, it cannot be an initial utterance because something must have preceded it (therefore, – initial). Some strings are impossible such as [I F] and [I R/I] because it is impossible to have a follow-up to an initial utterance, or a response-initiation to an initial utterance. (The [] brackets indicate the boundaries of the exchange, and () indicate optional elements.) Other possible exchanges can also be predicted such as the following. A follow-up F is optional in both strings.

$$[\text{I R (F)}]$$
$$[\text{I R/I R (F)}]$$

The [I R/I R] string is what describes the exchange in Example 39. Coulthard and Brazil (1981) explained how this pattern is descriptive of the teacher–student exchange because the teacher is not asking a genuine question. The teacher knows the answer to the question and is prompting the students. The pupil's response and initiation (R/I) is a genuine question. The R/I move can be distinguished from the R by its high termination and interrogative syntax. Termination is the decision to end the utterance in a high pitch which is characteristic of questioning. The response by the teacher is in a key that is appropriate for the exchange. Other types of questions, which are simple [I R] would be indicated by lower termination by the teacher and the pupil as in Example 40 from Coulthard (1985).

40. Teacher: What's the capital of France?
    Pupil: Paris.

AB Events. Labov and Fanshel (1977) were very interested in exchange patterns that could be understood according to discourse predictions. Sometimes the surface grammatical features of an utterance will predict what follows (e.g., question–answer) but there are many instances where this is not true. And there are rarely obligatory sequences between utterances even though there is between actions. The particular linguistic form of an initiation does not demand the linguistic form response but there are actional and coherence demands. Conversants use language to perform some action, and initiations and responses are coherently related in this manner. Labov and Fanshel (1977) worked with therapeutic discourse and were seeking a way to identify acts that represent some state of affairs. The set of events known to and drawn from the biography of the speaker are known as A-events, known to Person A and not necessarily to anyone else. Person A has access to these states of affairs and can speak them without fear of contradiction. Particular information or statements such as *I am hungry* or *I don't know* are examples and are not open to question or correction. B-events are known to the hearer and have the same status as privileged information. A speaker, then, cannot make statements about B-events such as *You are hungry* unless A has unmitigated authority over B. AB-events are knowledge shared by both A and B.

O-events are known to everyone and D-events are disputable. These classifications are about social acts that are generally agreed on by all present. Labov and Fanshel used these classifications to identify typical sequences in therapeutic discourse. They state, for example, the confirmation rule that *If A makes a statement about B-events, then it is heard as a request for confirmation.* This rule indicates that A can make a statement about a B-event but that it cannot be confirmed without B. So the utterance in Example 41 functions as a request for confirmation because A is making a statement about a B-event. B could respond with a simple *no* or a surprising or explanatory *yes*.

41. And you never thought he would do it.

Because Labov and Fanshel were interested in formulating additional interactional consequences of different types of statements they are able to classify a variety of typical sequences. So if A makes a statement about a B-event the response is one of *confirmation*; if A makes a statement about an A-event the response is one of *acknowledgment;* if A makes a statement about a D-event then the response is evaluation. The principle issue here is that elements of the exchange structure can be classified according to predictions about discourse structure.

SEQUENCE MECHANISMS AND COMMUNICATION

We have examined some issues in sequential structure and concluded that the exchange is the basic structure of interaction. We now turn to some specific sequences that perform certain "work" in communication; that is, a series of elements of exchanges that taken together comprise a coherent and orderly series of messages, which have internal structure, and are designed to perform some desired action in conversation. Some of these sequences elaborate on adjacency pair structure and others are designed to prevent or repair the negative social status that often accompanies violations of social rules. Other sequential aspects of communication discussed below are included to demonstrate the range of strategic choices available to communicators. Individuals often do not have much voluntary control over certain patterns of interaction, or are simply not very reflective about them (e.g., turn taking), but the variety of sequences discussed below can be used to understand and improve communication. They can be used consciously to increase the likelihood of achieving some interactional goal, or bettering one's strategic position.

Turn-Taking. The most basic fact of oral communication is that speakers and hearers trade off the roles of speaking and listening, and they do it quite competently. Sacks, Schegloff, and Jefferson (1974) explained that the rule of one speaker at a time means that the communication system must adopt techniques for exchanging turns at talk. If two people are talking at once then they begin to remedy the situation by having one yield the floor—even perhaps as a result of aggressive talking over by another—or, if the problem is silence there is pressure to fill it. So communicators try to accomplish turns smoothly without silences or overlaps.

A speaker controls the turn-taking system by exercising certain types of influence over the next turn. One, the speaker can simply direct who speaks next by naming the next speaker. An introduction—*It's my pleasure to introduce Robert Bently*—is one way to name the next speaker or asking a question directly to someone—*What do you think Bill?* The second choice is to manipulate who will be the next speaker but not select the person. Making a statement that is topically relevant to only one person would be an example. And the third choice is to select no one and have other participants select themselves. Sacks et al. note that these three options are responsive to individual utterances and that there is an ordering preference. If one speaker selects a next speaker and somehow that selection is interfered with then the right of the selected speaker is preserved:

42. Bill: [to Tom] How'd you like the movie?
    Pete: Oh, I thought it was . . .
    Bill: I was talking to Tom.

An even more interesting aspect of the turn-taking sequence is how a listener knows that the speaker is finished and it is time for the listener to become a speaker. Sacks et al. explain that it is impossible to be absolutely sure that a speaker is finished because he or she can always continue, but there are points of possible completion. Learning how to use these possible completion points is part of developmental communication. Language users acquire the technical capacity to recognize completion points and begin a turn at talk. In one case listeners can predict the ending of a phrase or utterance and complete it for the speaker.

43a. My friend Roger is a fine musician
43b.   [jerk   ]

Or, at the completion of a sentence two speakers may begin simultaneously and produce overlap that must be remedied. In this case the rule that the person who first began has the floor is sufficient remedy for the overlap.

In a series of studies Duncan (1973, 1974) discovered that cues for speaker change can be grammatical, paralinguistic, or kinesic. A speaker provides a *turn signal* that indicates a completion point. He claimed that all smooth turn exchanges in his data were the results of turn uptakes that followed one of the cues listed here. All confusions and difficulties resulted when a speaker tried to capture a turn when no cues were displayed.

1. Intonation: The use of pitch level and termination.
2. Paralanguage: A drawl on the final syllable or the stressed syllable of the phonemic clause.
3. Body motion: Termination of a hand position or relaxation of a body position.
4. Terminal expression: The use of stereotypical expressions such as "ya know" which indicate the completion of an idea.
5. Paralanguage: A drop in pitch or loudness in conjunction with a terminal expression.
6. Syntax: The completion of a grammatical clause involving a subject and predicate combination.

These rules change for different communication exchange systems. Conversation is the most common exchange system and it uses a rule structure where the turns are allocated as described above. But debates, court proceedings, and discussion groups often alter the rules, especially debates and court proceedings where turns are pre-allocated; who speaks when is not decided on a moment by moment basis as is casual conversation, but is pre-determined by an individual or the rules of a procedure. Pre-allocated exchange systems have the advantage of no interruptions and agreement on who has the right to speak. The turns on the floor are typically longer because of prepared and pre-arranged messages, and because there is little pressure on others to speak, which is not true of conversation.

Initiations. Although language users develop technical competence at turn-taking they also learn many other discourse sequences. The two most typical sequences in an interaction, which all communicators must master, is how to initiate and close a conversation. There are probably three basic behaviors common to conversation initiation. Schiffrin (1977) describes these as *recognition* where two people first realize who it is they are talking to and categorize them in some way. They recognize each other as "friends," or "old acquaintances," or "colleagues," and so on. They also use this introductory moment to apply biographical information that distinguishes the person from others. Following this immediate cognitive recognition there are *identification displays* where each employ certain behavior cues that indicate recognitions. A smile, arm wave, or widened eyes are typical examples. These identification displays are behavioral but still function as recognition symbols for the other person. Finally, there is *social recognition* that involves actual communication. These are greetings, exchanges, and references to previous interactions all of which escalate the sense of involvement with the other person. Schiffrin used these opening sequences as prototypical and able to explain the consequences of various departures. If one person deletes one of the sequences then this can create an embarrassing moment or a snub. Person A might display identification cues but if Person B ignores them then the initiation process has been fractured and Person A will take offense. In a related study Krivonos and Knapp (1975) concluded that the most observed initiation sequence was: mutual glance, head gesture, smile, verbal salute, reference to other, personal inquiry, external reference, topic initiation. This sequence can be compressed, elongated, or truncated on the basis of relationship, situation, or frequency of encounter.

A related concept to conversation initiation is Nofsinger's (1975) *demand ticket*. This is a verbal device that forces a speaker to have the floor. It is used when the initial opening sequence has been performed or compressed. The demand ticket is almost coercive in its power to obligate someone to speak. It is not necessarily a way to initiate a topic as much as it is a way to get the floor. The first utterance by A in Example 44 is a demand ticket because it forces B to grant A the floor and attend to A's message.

44. A: Guess what?
    B: What?
    A: Last night Judy . . .

Nofsinger posited what he called a pertinence maxim that is related to a Gricean relevance maxim in that it states speakers should not say what is "pointless or spurious." The should be relevant and consider their contributions important. The demand ticket works because hearers assume that a speaker who utters a demand ticket will not violate the maxim. The data reported by Ellis, Hamilton, and Aho (1983) in Example 22 included a demand ticket in the first utterance of Example 22. The subjects in the experiment were significantly likely to pair the first two utterances in that example because the demand ticket is highly recognizable and obligatory.

Telephone conversations are an example of variations on the initiation sequence. Schegloff (1968) stated that a person may say "hello" when he or she answers the phone, but this is an answer to a summons. It is not a greeting or any form of social recognition. Given that now a channel of communication is open there is often a greeting that begins the conversation, assuming that the caller is talking to the preferred person. But answering the telephone is analogous to a second-pair part of an adjacency pair—*summons-answer*. Yet with the telephone a complete summons-answer exchange only results when the subject matter of the initiation is broached. No genuine phone conversation looks like Exchange 45, and movies or mystery books that capitalize on patterns such as those in Example 45 do so because they realize the power of such a deviation.

45.	Ring-ring	Summons
	Hello	Answer
	(silence)	

Hopper (1989) wrote about an interesting variation of an initiation that has become more relevant because of the advent of certain new technologies. Hopper's analysis is an interesting extension of Schegloff's (1968) work on initiations because Hopper described a type of initiation that can take place any time during an on-going conversation. Telephone technology now offers subscriptions to "call-waiting" such that if one subscribes it makes a particular situation possible: At any time during a phone conversation a "beep" on the subscriber's phone will indicate that some unknown caller is seeking access to your line. To take the unknown call the subscriber must momentarily terminate the present conversation and initiate the new one. The beep serves as a demand ticket summoning the subscriber to respond. The beep serves the same function as a telephone ring (summons) with the subscriber answering. The summons–answer structure is maintained during this unique communicative context as is the recognition sequence, exchange of greetings, and initial inquires. But after the initial inquiry the subscriber reports that he or she is on the other line and then Hopper explained the various trajectories that are available in this context. The following sequence is prototypical:

46.	Partner:	And you know that . . .
	SUMMONS:	Beep
	Subscriber:	Hang on I have a call on the other line
	Partner:	Okay
	(switches lines)	
	Subscriber:	Hello
	Caller:	Bill
	Subscriber:	Yeah
	Caller:	Diane
	Subscriber:	Oh, high
	Caller:	How are ya
	Subscriber:	Fine, hey I am on the other line
	Caller:	Oh

The initiation sequence is the same up to when the caller says "How are ya." Rather than responding to this initial inquiry the subscriber states the call-waiting problem. The terminal "oh" from the caller signifies a transformation in the situation (Heritage, 1984). Even with the unique communication opportunities presented by new technologies verbal initiations are built by language users on the scaffolding of conventional sequences.

Terminations. Interactants are also able to produce sequences that close or terminate a conversation. When finishing a conversation there are three functions that the verbal and nonverbal communication must fulfill (see Knapp, Hart, Friederich, & Shulman 1973). The first is to indicate that the interaction is coming to an end and that contact between the two people will cease. This can be accomplished by a statement of appreciation such as "Well, I've enjoyed this" and nonverbal behaviors that signal decreased access such as a backward or leaning orientation. The second function is to state a basis or opportunity for future contact. Eye contact and some statement such as "See you later" are adequate for this function. Summarizing and restating what the encounter has meant is the third function described by Knapp et al. Some of these processes are altered according to how well the interactants know one another however their basic functions remain unchanged. Partners who are less acquainted and have more status differential are less likely to reinforce one another. And low status members of dyads say less during the termination process. In dyads where the individuals are acquainted they are more likely to express concern for the welfare of the other.

The telephone has been a source of research for interaction terminations as well as initiations. Schegloff and Sacks (1973) suggest that the first thing to accomplish when terminating a phone coversation is to indicate that there is nothing more to say. Terms like "So:oo" and "Well" signal the end of the topic and declining interest in continuing the conversation. In an investigation by Clark and French (1981) they suggest the following sequence: First, the subject matter of the communication is terminated as the interactants signal the completion of the talk; next is leave taking where both parties make statements about each other, the conversation, and future contact; finally, the parties say good-bye and the conversation is terminated.

Terminating an interaction is a cooperative activity. If the two parties are uncoordinated with respect to when to close an interaction then the person who wanted to continue but was shut off will experience negative social and personal status. In conversation both parties are expected to jointly and adroitly move toward termination. They must agree that all has been said and both are willing to discontinue. The use of terms such as "well" indicate the end of the conversation and if there is an attempt to bring up an additional topic then a subroutine must be initiated. Something like "Oh, one other thing" will return the parties to conversation.

Preface–Follow. Earlier we examined the various social and behavioral indicators that accompany the initiation of communicative contact. Another common sequence is the *preface–follow* that functions to introduce subject matter of some type. An individual preface is an utterance-initial statement that signals the parties in an interaction that certain propositional content will follow. There are many classes of utterance-initial preferences such as jokes ("Did you hear the one about . . . ," or "I heard a joke the other day . . ."), stories ("There is something I wanted to tell you"), or topic markers ("You mentioned yesterday that . . . ," or "Speaking of . . ."). Prefaces can also be individual acts but they become part of a sequence when they are followed by a contingent utterance. When a speaker uses a particular marker such as "well," or "now," or "by the way" to indicate a topic shift or some change in the utterance-by-utterance coherence they are signaling the hearer that what follows is a deviation from previous utterances.

Full presequences (Jefferson, 1972) express the most complete form and function of prefaces. *Presequences* such as the one in Example 47 are a sequence of speech acts where the interpretation is based on a sequence yet to come. The presequence serves as a preface for what will follow. Typically the presequence is psychologically motivated so as to avoid the loss of face that might accompany a dispreferred response.

47. A: What are you doing this weekend?
    B: Nothing much, why?
    A: Do you want to go out?
    B: Yea, sure.

Presequences are prefatory in nature. Person A was able to establish that B was available to go out. If B had said "I am busy, why" then A could have said "Oh, no reason just wondering" and spared himself the loss of face and difficulty associated with a dispreferred response. Prefatory sequences are responsive to the structural preference for agreement (Levinson, 1983; Pomerantz, 1978, 1984). As we have seen, adjacency pairs have second pair parts that are preferred (e.g., an answer is the preferred response to a question; acceptance is the preferred response to an invitation), but on occasion dispreferred second-pair parts occur. Presequences and prefaces in general are a way to mitigate dispreferred second-pair parts.

Pre-requests work the same way. They provide a preface to a question that will take place later in the sequence. In the following dialogue, A requests information before asking for what he wants.

48. A: Do you sell backyard furniture?
    B: Yes.
    A: Do you have wicker chairs?

The pre-request saves the speaker from risking face. It is structurally possible for A to go directly to his request for wicker chairs, but a "no" answer is dispreferred and can be avoided if A can determine the possibility of the store having the chairs.

Compliments are another sequence organized around preference. Pomerantz (1978) demonstrated how compliments and their responses can be explained within an adjacency pair framework where some responses to a compliment are preferred (acceptance agreement) and some are dispreferred (disagreement). The following exchange would be a prototypical compliment with a preferred response.

49. A: That was an excellent paper you wrote.
    B: Yes it was excellent.

But Pomerantz pointed out that there is another social constraint that conflicts with the preferred form of accepting a compliment: The social taboo against accepting self praise. Responses such as the one just stated by B are seldom encountered—if ever—and look unacceptable because they are not responsive to the constraint prohibiting self praise. Actually compliment sequences are organized according to a sensitivity to the competing demands of accepting compliments but avoiding self praise. Language users solve the problem of these competing injunctions by adopting one of four strategies. They can downgrade the compliment, qualify it, reassign credit, or return the compliment. Examples of each of these are in the following example:

50. B: Oh, it isn't really that good.   (downgraded)
    B: Yea, but it still needs work.   (qualified)
    B: It is only because of your help.   (reassigned credit)
    B: Your paper was excellent too.   (return)

Insertion Sequences. Most of the structures described so far have had one pair or pair-part followed by another; it is also possible to embed a sequence where one pair occurs inside another. Schegloff (1972b) referred to these as insertion sequences where one or more pairs is inserted in the middle of another pair. Insertion sequences occur because the speaker who is responding to a first pair-part is unsure of something or requires additional information, so rather than uttering a second pair part the speaker begins an inserted sequence with a new first pair part. For example, Dialogue 51 is a prototypical question–answer adjacency pair:

    51. A: Are you going to the party Saturday night?
          B: Yes/No

but Dialogue 52 contains an insertion sequence where the answer to the question does not appear in Turn 2 but in Turn 4. The adjacency pair in Example 51 is expanded to include another sequence that adds information before the answer is supplied.

    52. A: Are you going to the party Saturday night?
      ⎡ B: Why do you ask?
      ⎣ A: I dunno, just thought it would be fun.
         B: Yes I am going/or No I am not going.

The bracketed B–A exchange is an adjacency pair within another. Schegloff explained that the first statement of A makes some answer conditionally relevant. And if B does not supply the second pair-part then its absence is noticed in the same way as if there were no insertion sequence. The interaction is not "complete" until the second pair-part of the initial utterance is produced. Insertions can of course expand adjacency pairs indefinitely, bounded only by pragmatic limits.

CONCLUSION

Chapters 6 and 7 have concentrated on the central problem of using language communicatively and that is the problem of coherence. Global coherence discussed in chapter 6 is principally a matter of the general cultural and social knowledge structures that make the language and ideas of a text sensible. Local coherence discussed in this chapter focuses on the pragmatics of actual components of a text. These include the linguistic ties that are primarily responsible for cohesion; speech acts or the action performed by various types of utterances; and the typical structural and sequential mechanisms that perform much of the work of influencing the local interpretation of meaning.

These two chapters form an important cornerstone in this volume because coherence, and how it is achieved, is fundamental to communication. It is impossible to separate issues in coherence and the orderly and meaningful ways that people connect ideas from communication. Moreover, the investigation of the specific techniques of coherence mirrors the systematic study of communication because both are reliant on form and strategy; both depend on pragmatic and semantic relevance (Planalp, Graham, & Paulson, 1987). I argued earlier in this chapter that Halliday and Hasan could be criticized for relying too heavily on explicit textual ties for cohesion, and that coherence was more determined by the shared knowledge that characterizes the communication process. Both coherence and communication rely on form—from subtle linguistic choices to sequential exchange structures—and strategy, or that communicators use language, patterns, and rules in a tactical manner to accomplish goals. This interplay between form and strategy, pragmatics and semantics is what drives the communication process. The next and final chapter in this volume describes how individuals integrate the linguistic, cognitive, and strategic resources into a code that is necessary to accomplish communication. We see that this concept of a code is necessary to explain how individuals are able to both perform standard communicative routines and interactively produce meaning that is responsive to personal and situational peculiarities.

8

Communication Codes

The purpose of this chapter is to outline a theory of codes that addresses how communication gets accomplished. More specifically, I demonstrate that an individual's communication is strongly influenced by his or her organization of experience—particularly linguistic experience. I term this a *code* perspective on language and communication. The central thesis is that meaning results from the interplay of an individual's organization of cognitive categories and real-time communication. A communication code is a cognitive system composed of elements, and these elements are semiotic signs that acquire significance through human experience and their relations with other signs. These codes can take on various levels of specificity, in accordance with social experiences, and are activated in "lived" interaction. After explicating the bases for codes, the chapter explains the theoretical and empirical existence of two particular codes termed the *pragmatic code* and the *syntactic code*.

As we have seen throughout this volume the communicative situation is an intricate network of information sources, of which the verbal context is one of these sources of information. All of the sources of information in a communicative context contribute to the interpretive act. The two most significant sources of indeterminacy of communication—other than the natural features of language—

are those expressive behaviors communicated by the paraverbal channels, and all the sources of information located in the participants shared experience. The variation introduced by different participant experiences is probably the most dramatic. An individual can extract and interpret information during communication from the immediate experiences that accumulate with such density during actual interaction, or from history or memory that draws on the range of personal, social, and cultural experience. As these interlocking worlds of experience unfold they determine what is said and unsaid, and generate the stream of elliptical verbal behaviors that characterize communication. This communication confirms and recreates individual identities and intermingles the past with the present.

Indeterminacy is why individuals must construct their own internal texts, and these texts vary with individual experience. These internal constructions of meaning are not only a matter of comprehension, but are also a consequence of reflecting on earlier communication. When individuals draw on previous experience to weave it into the present, they immediately tap into different communicative contexts that externalize the experiences and meld them into a more concrete social reality. A full and principled explanation of communication has always required reference to concepts such as context, background, perspective, or assumptions. When Betrand Russell wrote that logical systems must be self-consistent and operate from a single perspective he established the power of deductive logic, but he also removed it as an analytical instrument for describing human communication. Givon (1989) classified language and communication as a *pragmatic* science; that is, they rely on contextual meaning, metaphoric extension, cultural relativity, and the sociology of language to provide explanations. Language and mind regularly violate Russell's prescriptions for logical systems. Human language, and its attendant cognitive activities, is always reorganizing and readjusting itself; it is always shifting logical perspectives and changing its frame of reference. And this tendency is not because the language system is "weak" or prone to "error;" rather it is inherent and natural to the human organism. Givon (1989) wrote:

> This propensity of consciousness is neither an aberration nor an accident. Rather, it is a necessary, adaptively motivated capacity; it stands at the very core of our perceptual and cognitive processing mechanisms. It is a precondition for the mind's ability to **select**, evaluate, file, contextualize and respond appropriately to mountains of information. (p.4)

The mind must make a judgment as it encounters this mountain of information. It must process information and make decisions about relevance, urgency, meaning, and appropriateness, and it must do this under restrictions for time and storage capacity.

Givon (1983) demonstrated and concluded in a series of linguistic studies that the less predictable and accessible the information contained in a communication is, the more isomorphic the sign relationships must be with their designates. There is a clear correlation between the predictability of information and the amount of mental effort required to process the information (McKoon & Ratcliff, 1980). And as Givon (1989) stated, "The more mental effort is used in processing information, the more coding material will be used in representing the information in language" (p. 106). This evidence stipulates a systematic structural relation between an expressed linguistic unit (e.g., a word or picture) and what it designates, even if what it designates is an abstract mental process. Just as there are more isomorphic points between an icon and its designate than there are between a symbol and its designate, there is more linguistic isomorphism between language and difficult or unpredictable information than there is between language and more accessible and easier to process information. The logic here is that difficult information requires more coding or more effort to reach it. The listener's attention must be seized and focused in order to communicate information that is less expected or accessible. This is true within all aspects of the linguistic system. For instance, lexical morphemes (e.g., nouns, verbs) carry more information than do grammatical morphemes (e.g., "and," "a") and they are usually phonologically and morphotactically larger. And informational novelty, which is less predictable, is typically signaled in communication by a dramatic use of intonation that is perceptually more prominent (Bolinger, 1984).

Semiotic signs are the elements of codes. When the relationship between a sign (signifier) and what it designates (signified) is direct and one of resemblance then the sign is an *iconic* sign. A photograph is the most obvious example because it resembles that person or object. An icon displays isomorphism with what it designates; it bears similarity to it. Verbal signs that compose human code systems are not very iconic, although they still retain iconicity. High iconicity is equated with interpretability. A picture of someone engenders recognition more quickly than reading the person's name. Givon (1989) suggested the *iconic imperative* that, "All other things being equal, a coded experience is easier to store, retrieve, and communicate if the code is maximally isomorphic to the experience" (p. 97). Humans try to package language in a manner that is easiest for storage and communication. There is a sort of "pressure toward iconicity" as humans try to impose nonarbitrariness, and there is linguistic and communicative evidence of this pressure. Semiotic elements on the other side of the iconicity continuum are symbolic and indexical. These signs go beyond what they depict and indicate meaning that is not immediate or obviously signified. Figure 8.1 is an application of the process in the creation of a corporate logo (Manning, 1980). The notion of "flight" is only hinted at by the bottom symbol on the continuum. Nevertheless, the scant and arbitrary nature of the highly symbolic logo allows for other conceptualizations that are of value to the user of the logo. The nonliteral nature of the symbol decreases the possibility of communicating certain information, but its ambiguity allows the viewer to "read" more into the symbol such as "strength," "simplicity," or "technological efficiency."

It is possible to show a pragmatic relationship between all sorts of linguistic and cognitive phenomena thereby demonstrating that there is an iconic relationship between language and mind, and that Chomsky's (1957) preoccupation with an abstract description of human grammar was misguided. Rather, even the subtle and highly technical aspects of a grammatical system are responsive to pragmatic or communicative needs. Word order in a sentence, for example, has been shown

FIG. 8.1.
Iconicity continuum (Manning, 1980).

to be related to topic importance such that more important information tends to be fronted in a sentence because of its urgency and the importance of understanding the information correctly and immediately. (See, e.g., Fox, 1983; Givon, 1983) A correlative principle is that when two ideas are semantically related they tend to be in linear proximity in actual language. Passive constructions are another example of a pragmatic sign relation between a grammatical feature and conceptual categories. The passive voice changes the topic of a sentence (object becomes topic of a clause), it depersonalizes the communication as the agent becomes less important—and, incidentally, is moved to the rear of the sentence—and makes the event in the sentence more static. Therefore, the issues of communicative importance in a sentence are isomorphic with the conceptual and mental importance of certain information.

The most pivotal conclusion that emerges from the work discussed earlier is that we can demonstrate a correlation between a point along a linguistic dimension and one along a nonlinguistic dimension. The phonology, morphology, and syntax of natural languages is related to the pragmatic conceptual considerations of relevance, information, predictability, and importance of messages. These norms of language turn out to be socioculturally determined. This means that the cultural and contextual requirements of communication are apparent in the linguistic dimension. And the converse is also true, that the conceptual categories of the sociocultural environment are indicated by close analysis of the linguistic dimension. The various codes I posit here rely on this assumption. These codes also draw on the argument and empirical demonstrations that show the evolution of language has been along the iconicity continuum toward increasingly abstract or symbolic communication.

CONCEPTS AND CODES

Individual communicators acquire and carry with them organized knowledge that is composed of concepts. Knowledge is distinct from experience in that knowledge is communicable; it has been established in contact with others and can be used, even in the loosest sense, reliably. Communication is primarily concerned with the sense or concept of a word. The *sense* of a word is the concept associated with it, as opposed to reference which is extensional and refers to the truth value of a word, or its denotative meaning. Concepts of a word are typically associated with definitions, although the acquisition of concepts is a thorny issue. There are the inductive and deductive perspectives on knowledge acquisition of Lock and Kant, but these positions have been criticized and need not be mutually exclusive (Bolton, 1977). And of course Piaget's (1947) provocative work showed that concepts are formed by the reciprocal interaction between cognitive states and the environment. Concepts are quite consistent with the organic properties of the

communication system as we have been discussing it. A concept is an "organization in the experience of reality which is achieved through the utilization of rules
of relation and to which can be given a name" (Bolton 1977, p. 23). Concepts do
not only denote specific physical objects or spatial relations because that would
limit them to a very restricted range of representation. Their arbitrariness makes
the flexibility and versatility of language possible.

Codes rely on a system of concepts. To acquire a concept is to increase the
cognitive structures available to one, and at the same time improve one's comprehension of the environment related to the concept. This quality of concept
formation is central to code systems because it requires the interchange between
stable and changeable features. The concepts that signs designate are at once
static entities based on past experience, and then dynamic entities as they evolve
to accommodate new experience and knowledge (see Rosch, 1977). We saw
earlier that language was an adaptive human mechanism that was capable of
reorganizing and orienting itself, and that this was an organic quality of human
nature. The iconicity of sign relations is regularly being modified by the developmental processes of diachronic change and learning. The accretion of codes
results from this process. Just as developing concepts by adapting the environment to pre-existing perceptual processing of experience is a natural occurrence
in the biological scenario, so too do sign relations vary to suit contexts, individuals,
historical developments, and cultural variation.

The modulating nature of signs and concepts, and the supposition that concepts and sign relations are formed through reciprocal interaction, seems to imply
that no two individuals would ever be the same. This conclusion is logical but
certainly does not lead to fatal solipsism. The fact that so much communication
is routinized and successful is evidence of strong convergences in concept formation. It is quite likely, for example, that two people growing up during the same
time and with similar circumstances will have a similar concept of say "book." If
these two people have read books, seen them in school, and checked them out of
the library their sense of the word "book" will be congruent. In contrast, someone
who is nonliterate or dislikes reading intensely will have a different sense of
"book." Knowledge becomes *shared* and the quality of communication improves
to the extent that two people have had corresponding interaction experiences in
the past. When two people have some common experiences they can use these
experiences to create some co-reality.

Work in contextual semantics (Raskin, 1986; also see chapter 5) helps solve the
problem of how there can be a difference between what two people cognitively
store about a word (e.g., "book") but both use the term to refer to the same object.
The crucial issue here is to explain how language users "understand" a word or
phrase by invoking extra logical information; that is, meanings and refined
understandings that are not part of the lexicon and cannot be determined by
lexical and syntactic operations on the actual utterance. The sentence "Pete

bought a station wagon and is now a member of the middle class" is dependent on knowledge of cultural stereotypes for interpretation. No dictionary will mention a station wagon as an index of social class. Concepts that make up codes are embedded in semantic scripts. Every word of a sentence evokes a semantic script with nodes and relationships among nodes. The information needed to interpret *station wagon* is available to the language user in a cognitive script that includes a small domain devoted to station wagons as a symbol of class membership. The complete script for station wagon would be quite complex—including nodes such as FUNCTIONS, ACTIVITIES, OBJECTS, DRIVE, MOVEMENT, DESIGN, MATERIAL, PARTS, COST, DANGER, TYPES, QUALITY, LABOR, STATUS, and so on—but the full meaning for how the word is used results from the accumulation of knowledge from previous communicative experience with the term.

Raskin (1986) explains how a set of combinatorial rules combine scripts evoked by expressed interaction to disambiguate a sentence. Given no interactional clues to the contrary, the combinatorial rules will assume a bona fide communication mode—no lying, acting, joking, and so on (cf. Grice, 1975; Searle, 1969)—and evoke an unmarked script (e.g., the most frequent interpretation). If this does not work a marked script will be foregrounded. As individuals encounter new experiences and engage new forms of communication they develop new scripts and remark old ones. To understand the reference to station wagon in the paragraph earlier, a language user would use the reference to "middle class" to activate the class membership and social status nodes associated with automobiles.

Although contextual semantics offers a workable model of the cognitive processes involved in disambiguating signs, it does not specify how systems of signs develop that reflect the language user as a member of society and various social experiences. It follows that individual's establish a set of concepts in accordance with principles that organize experience and knowledge about reality. When a concept and its attendant sign relation is formed, and when this sign relation takes its place within a *system* of sign relations, we can begin to talk about a code. In a very general sense a code can be understood as a perspective that is arranged according to its relationship to other signs and perspectives. The meanings of words bump up against one another and where the meaning of one word leaves off, another one begins; the limits of one word must be understood in terms of the limits of another. To understand the meaning of a sign requires knowledge of the entire field of signs that the particular one refers to. And so it is with codes.

The term *code* has often been used in linguistics to denote grammatical relations. And traditional linguistics has neglected the social functions of speech and uses code to refer to the referential qualities of language. Moreover, the term *code* has often assumed a one-to-one relationship between a signifier and a signified as in Morse code or various computer codes. But the very opposite is closer to true because the same expressive sign can designate different concepts. Codes are anything but simple one-to-one relations between signs and concepts because the basic semiotic relationship is variable and reliant on multiple uses for the same sign. Codes, then, are:

> A collection of signs arranged and organized according to pragmatic principles including context, appropriateness, feasibility, genres, and other situational features. Codes are particularly sensitive to the developmental and cognitive consequences of experiences with language. They are a system of sign relations that regulate meaning and are invoked in actual interaction. Some codes are sign systems that are highly responsive to context and group experiences where the expressive units mark specific nonlinguistic social categories.

Those codes that are responsive to particular group experiences have been called subcodes by Kreckel (1981). These subcodes are really little more than particular theoretical applications of codes so I do not use the term. I do, however, refer to general and specific codes where specific codes express specialized group meaning such as those found in the patterns of talk used by groups such as doctors, criminals, tattoo enthusiasts, and the like. The line distinguishing general and specific codes cannot be drawn explicitly, just as the nature of sign relations and meaning make it impossible for any two codes to be completely independent. The codes described here reflect a broader based history of experience with language (distinguished as we see here by literacy), whereas some of the specific examples are determined by the interaction priorities resulting from group-specific goals, relationships, practices, and forms of expression. A general code is more like a "system of systems" that a speaker develops as a member of the larger society. Its principles and properties are available in all aspects of the culture but are typically displayed in public forums. Some applications of codes are much more context dependent and developed in the shared language and knowledge of a group. A researcher who studies the "reality" of some group such as criminals, schools, corporate cultures, hospitals, working-class boys, journalists, and so forth, is interested in discovering specific codes. These are of more practical interest because they are even more enmeshed in used language. Specific codes are the sign systems that make it possible to express subjective reality; and, perhaps more importantly, to create and sustain reality, what Halliday (1978) called "a social conception of information."

Codes are pretty fluid and flexible. People are able to move in and out of them as experience and need dictates. Codes are forms of social knowledge that emerge from practices and beliefs but are not laid down in any statute. Their patterns of meaning vary from time to time so that "experience" with the code is more important than anything else. Experience does not imply a private subjective reality because people can converge on the meaning of an experience, but the benefits of living a code rather than mere exposure to it are substantial. Garfinkel's (1967) Agnes is a good illustration: After a sex-change operation (from male to female) Agnes found that she could not successfully communicate a female identity. Her task was to subordinate her male code and learn a female code. Interestingly, beliefs and ideas from many sources about how to "pass" as a female were not successful. Only after Agnes immersed herself in communication with other females, and learned to use (both linguistically and cognitively) the idiolect of females, did she successfully pass as a female.

Codes can be situated along a sort of psychological–sociological continuum. Although my purpose is to demonstrate the efficacy of both sets of assumptions, it is important to underscore that although codes are essentially cognitive models they cannot be separated from real-time social interaction. There is an ontological commitment to the theoretical reality of codes in the same way as there is to concepts such as scripts (Raskin, 1986; Schank & Abelson, 1977), constructs (Delia, O'Keefe, & O'Keefe, 1982), Gricean maxims (Grice, 1975), and related psychological concepts such as goals, plans, attitudes, and the like. A code is a representation that explains part of how language users accomplish their meaning and communication in social situations. A psychological, more accurately *psycholinguistic*, orientation toward codes focuses on the inner qualities of integrated networks of abstract constructs. These constructs are composed of the semiotic relationships discussed earlier. From this theoretical standpoint understanding language and communication requires reference to internal mental representations of how things are or might be. At its most extreme this psycholinguistic orientation makes the individual responsible for the initiation and termination of communication, and assumes that causative variables exist before interaction and are predictive of messages and meaning (see Sigman, 1987; Thomas, 1980).

But a purely psycholinguistic orientation to codes is inadequate and must be supplanted by a sociolinguistic orientation that focuses on the interplay between the cognitive aspects of a code (semiotic constructs) and actual interaction. This is true for two reasons. First, and most important, codes are formed, altered, and refined in interaction. Sanders (1987) makes a cogent argument for the fluidity of specific interpretations in interaction. A strong psychological perspective on codes fails to account for interactively produced meaning. If codes exist and operate only "within" individuals then there is no place for the role of real-time interaction, and communication becomes little more than an attempt to match psychological systems. Communicators use the rules and conventions of the code to produce a message that will be interpreted properly, but those rules and conventions can only entail an array of possible interpretations (Sanders, 1987). A code and its attendant cognitive structures can account well enough for the propositional content and illocutionary force of a message. But an utterance also takes place within the context of an unfolding dialogue, and a *specific* interpretation results from connecting the utterance to its antecedents and projecting interpretive consequences. The actual meaning that a language user attaches to a real-time utterance is dependent on how that utterance contributes to the unfolding discourse.

The notion that expressions are constrained in accordance with how they fit into unfolding discourse helps explain one way in which codes can be powerfully contextually sensitive. The specific lexical and syntactical form of an utterance makes its relationship to other utterances in an interaction either more or less explicit, and therefore influences the nature of the interpretation. Moreover, this utterance narrows or widens what can be said subsequently. In another study, Sanders (1984) deomonstrated how this notion that communicators are constrained at each juncture in unfolding interaction explains variations in style by showing that vocabulary choices could be accounted for by antecedent utterances and did not require a lot of psychological baggage. If a communicator makes a quasi-desicion at each juncture in an interaction, then his or her psychological dispositions become secondary to concerns for relevance and projections about future interpretations. Real-time interaction activates coded interpretations. The presence or absence of a code makes a set of lexical and syntactical choices available, but does not determine them. What is actually uttered by a speaker can be accounted for by an antecedent utterance and the speaker's ability to interpret the antecedent utterance according to the code.

A second reason that a psycholinguistic orientation is limited concerns the social nature of communication. The social level of analysis recognizes patterns of behavior that transcend individual biographies, yet help to organize and account for individual communication. Social norms and practices constitute a large system of communication and individual communicative behavior can be situated within that system. A significant amount of cognitive development results from the internalization of interpersonal communicative processes (Blumer, 1969).

This aspect of codes is consistent with Bernstein's (1975) essential *social* theory, which is that forms of social organization and interpersonal behavior among members of a social system are internalized to reflect shared experiences and conceptualizations. And, as Bernstein argues, these modes of social organization are not only internalized but generated and sustained in language. Moreover, I affirm Bernstein's basic sociolinguistic principle: namely, that language used in one context must also be analyzed in relation to language used in the other contexts in which one habitually communicates. Bernstein's mistake, however, was twofold: First Bernstein maintained that codes were the sediment of class values; he therefore directed attention away from how linguistic qualities are sensitive to situational and personal demands and made it difficult, if not impossible, for his conception of codes to accommodate the same individual's varying experiences. Such accommodation must be considered central to any communication-oriented concept of codes. Second, Bernstein failed to consider the nature and role of a genuine cognitive process in communication (see Applegate &

Delia, 1980). Bernstein, like Mead, acknowledged the development of the social self but Bernstein neglected the individual self. And even after Bernstein shifted to more semantic and pragmatic concerns (Adlam, Turner, & Lineker, 1977; Bernstein, 1981) his emphasis on culturally determined identity obscured other possibilities. The essence of listener and situation-adapted communication is the ability to produce messages that are appropriate for one listener or situation but not another. Bernstein failed to account for this fundamental communicative concern because his theory is really a version of a radical Whorfian hypothesis that sees language as a deteminate of cognition.

SYNTACTIC AND PRAGMATIC CODES

In recent years the study of language and linguistic processes has shifted some-what from a perspective that assumed that all languages were of equal complexity to an evolutionary perspective (Berlin, 1971; Swadesh, 1971). The authors who supported an evolutionary perspective argue that languages develop in a manner consistent with the orthogenic principle, or the notion that development proceeds from globality to increased differentiation and articulation. Linguistic evolution is *from* an unspecialized global language dependent on shared knowl-edge of social relations *to* an autonomous system of specialized, explicit, and highly differentiated communication. Some recent theorizing and research (Ellis & Armstrong, 1989; Ellis & Hamilton, 1985) has followed this theoretical trail and demonstrated the existence and utility of two general codes termed the syntactic code and the pragmatic code. There are strands of literature that provide the assumptive base for the two codes, and the following discussion is designed to demonstrate the implications of these assumptions and show how the two codes are theoretically and empirically predictable from the theory of signs. Members of a literate culture, as McLuhan has often observed, interiorize natural speech and reshape it according to the norms of writing. Natural speech is unrehearsed and discontinuous; writing is planned and internally coherent. As this argument unfolds we see how the two codes emerge: One system of signs is organized in accordance with principles and research from the tradition of literacy and planned language use—the *syntactic code*; the other code is consistent with the traditions of oral and unrehearsed language use—the *pragmatic code*.

The interaction in Dialogue 1 is an example of specific pragmatic code usage. You see from the ensuing explanation that understanding is highly reliant on group-specific interpretation that a language user "brings" to the situation.

   1a. Gene: Nice work.
    b. Jesse: Thanks, got it done not too long ago.
    c. Gene: Not at some chop shop, eh.

    d. Jesse: Naw, a custom studio.
    e. Gene: Nice, the guy was an artist.
    f. Jesse: Yeah, I'm thinkin' 'bout getting some new ink.
    g. Gene: Where you gonna put it?
    h. Jesse: Don't know yet, but I've got some clean spots.
    i. Gene: Lookin' good, see ya.

This conversation is between two tattoo enthusiasts in a tattoo shop. There is a tattoo subculture with strong affiliational consequences such that their marks identify them as belonging to a special group (see Sanders, 1988). They were unfamiliar with one another but both members of a fairly well defined subgroup that has developed its identity through mutual interaction and the acquisition of a particular code based on shared knowledge and identity.

The interaction can be analyzed as symptomatic of the pragmatic code from a number of perspectives. First, the signs are highly dependent on other signs in the code for their value, and they fulfill social functions. A correct interpretation of this conversation is very dependent on both shared knowledge and the conditions it which the conversation took place. For example, the phrase "clean spots" acquires its meaning from the practice of marking the body and the attendant notion that "clean spots" are places on the body with no tattoos. "Clean" is not used in oppositon with "dirty" in this particular sign system, as it would be if we were talking about a laundry detergent that "cleaned" clothes. Moreover, those portions of the conversation that can be partitioned into communicative acts are also dependent on the code sign system for interpretation. A communicative act is a single speech act that expresses a concept. It is analogous to "conveying information" (Chafe, 1970). These acts cannot be treated in isolation because they have distinct properties within a code and can differ between codes. A communicative act can acquire its value in two ways: one is by the phonological stress that determines the focus of the information, and the other is by the position of the act in a sequence, or its syntagmatic relationship with other acts (Quirk & Greenbaum, 1973). The first act ("nice work") functions to both initiate the conversation, and to compliment the other person on his tattoos. The stress is on NICE indicating the predominantly complimentary function of the act. The act, by its initial position in the interaction, is a generalized compliment of Jesse's tattoos and overall appearance. Had the same act appeared in some other sequential position it may assume a different function such as the sarcasm in the following dialogue:

    2. Ron: This one's beginning to fade.
      Curt: Who did that?
      Ron: Some guy at a boutique in Providence.
      Curt: Nice work.

This corresponds to our everyday understanding that utterances change meaning as they change positions in a sequence of interaction (Sanders, 1987; Sigman, 1987).

The pragmatic impact of code usage can also be understood by the effect of the particular code on nonusers. There are two strategic disadvantages to those outside the code. First, because outsiders are not familiar with the entering assumptions and previous interactions they cannot distinguish between what is given and new information (Clark & Haviland, 1977), or what information is "stressed" in the interaction. In Line 1h there is a vocal stress on "some" ("SOME clean spots"), which was said with irony. Jesse takes pride in his tattoos and realizes that they mark him as different from "straight" society. The fact that he has at least SOME "clean" spots implies that although he is a member of a select out-group, he is not completely stigmatized. The given–new strategy is a way of deciding what a speaker is referring to, or what is being focused on in an utterance. The statement "John threw the *BALL*" has given–new structure that some information is assumed (given) and other information is new:

Given Information: John threw something (X)
New Information: John threw a *ball* (X = ball)

But the level of given and new information is not discrete; rather each is a continuum. Given information can be logically inferred with no hesitation or suggested as in a conventional implicature (see Danes, 1974). And new information can be completely new or, on the other hand, foregrounded or emphasized information. I suggest that the subtlety of new and assumed information is particularly salient in personal code interaction. Moreover, the information value of new and given information is highly specified for users of a particular code because they can only rely on their common knowledge and interpretation schemes. In Line 1c there is phonological stress on "not" ("NOT at some chop shop, eh"). The given information is that "chop shops," which do poor work, exist and that these shops are responsible for low quality work. The new information is that Jesse's tattoo was NOT acquired at one of these shops and that accounts for its attractiveness. It is also a way for Gene to compliment Jesse. The interaction in Dialogue 1 is smooth, coordinated, and effective because the participants share knowledge of concepts like "chop shops" and the kind of reputation they have. Their experience with the code enables them to display a variety of knowledge related to "chop shops," and their oppositions "custom studios," and "artists."

Second, outsiders to the code must rely on the finite boundaries of the text for information and interpretation. They do not carry much assumed knowledge. The knowledgeable code user can bridge assumptions spurred by the text with his or her knowledge of the code. An outsider to the code must use common knowledge or knowledge derived from codes of a similar nature. Kreckel (1981) conducted an exhaustive study of the role of shared knowledge in family discourse, part of which included an analysis of outsiders versus insiders' interpretation of messages. She found the insiders were significantly better at understanding messages. And, more interestingly, even public communication by family members was less understood by outsiders indicating that common knowledge is insufficient even for situations such as public interviews and messages not designed for the family. Individual code users rely on a coherent intersubjective system of interpretation. Their chances for understanding are increased even in the face of idiosyncratic variation because the code provides coordinate practices that contextualize such idiosyncrasies.

In another form of data collection and analysis Ellis and Hamilton (1985) and Ellis and Armstrong (1989) used the theoretical elements of codes to make predictions about language use in particular contexts, namely, marital relationship types and media portrayals of language. These studies organized linguistic indicators around four general themes that were theoretically related to pragmatic or syntactic code usage. The themes were structural complexity, verb complexity, elaboration, and personal reference. The study of marital relations (Ellis & Hamilton, 1985) correlated marital relationship types (traditionals and independents) with the linguistic code indicators. For example, one relationship type was termed *traditional* (Fitzpatrick & Indvik, 1982). These couples were highly interdependent in that their expressions of control were complementary. In other words, issues of control in the relationship were well worked out such that each person was comfortable with his or her position in relation to the other. Traditionals have well-defined roles that are distinct but dependent on one another (e.g., one dominant, one submissive). The authors predicted that traditionals would engender a symbolic environment compatible with the pragmatic code because the interaction is based on relatively clear role prescriptions. The couples had well-developed knowledge of one another and thereby shared assumptions. Language does more "work" in the pragmatic code; a word or a clause does the work of a complete sentence because the interactants share more presuppositons. A logical extension of this was that if talk within the pragmatic code does more "work," then the entire discourse should be paratactic. That is, it should display loose coordination with few explicit cohesion references because such references are simply unnecessary. The opposite should be true of the other relationship type termed *independents*. They utilize a syntactic code that is hypotactic or comprised of tighter internal conjunction. Independents rely more on equality in a relationship characterized by individuality and less clearly defined roles. The independents were involved in a greater variety of interaction and spent more time negotiating relationship issues. Consider two examples of interaction drawn from traditionals and independents respectively:

3. Allice: Shouldn't let 'em talk back.
    Edgar: He sez too much.
    Allice: There's still a fear of you comin' down on 'em.
    Edgar: It's these schools.
    Allice: It's not like before.

This is an example of the complete treatment of a particular issue by a traditional relationship. Allice began with a new topic (their son talking back) and the discussion ended with Allice's final comment. The code differences become more apparent if the previous dialogue is compared to a sample of the independents:

4. Larry: I have this strong feeling that there are people in nursing homes, and no one comes to see them.
    Michelle: Well, that's because nursing homes are depressing.
    Larry: Look at my situation, speaking of nursing homes, my grandmother is in one and it is burdensome to visit her.
    Michelle: Isn't it a little different because you never got along with her.

Segment 3 is more paratactic than Segment 4. There is far more assumed in Segment 3. Except for a generalized "it" there are no cohesive references to the discourse. In other words, the topic and the movement of the focus are handled predominantly through mutual assumption. By contrast, in Sample 4 there are three different mechanisms by which the topicality is explicitly maintained. There is a simple repeat of noun phrases that are designed to refer to the subject at hand ("nursing homes"), an anaphoric "that" (Michelle's first utterance), and a repeat of topical noun phrase structured in a subordinate clause ("speaking of nursing homes").

The syntactic code—because it is hypotactic—makes greater use of direct semantic elaboration. The connection between ideas in Sample 3 is not very clear, regardless of a dearth of anaphoric references. One way to demonstrate this is to examine the use of conjunctives. The between-turn cohesion in Sample 3 is clearly dependent on holding the subject matter as a contextual constant. But the within-turn structure is equally paratactic. There are no conjunctions signifying a relationship between ideas in Segment 3. The "It's these schools" utterance simply appears as a response to the previous utterance and although the speaker is relating problems in the schools with the boy's behavior, the organization of this contribution is loose. The hearer is to assume that schools have something to do with the behavior of the boy. The independents in Sample 4 offer more semantic elaboration by applying language to their ideas. Ideas are coordinated via conjunctions ("and," "because") and the language connects ideas rather than relational presuppositions.

There was another very powerful predictor of syntactic and pragmatic codes in the Ellis and Hamilton data. A key feature that distinguishes the two codes is the intralinguistic organizational devices that distribute information and maintain topical focus. In the syntactic code this is achieved linguistically with various lexical devices. Information and focus are less explicit and more assumed in the pragmatic code. Pragmatic code users, then, must keep certain information foregrounded so they can use it for on-line interpretation. Chafe (1970) maintained that foregrounded items—items that are in the foreground of the mind of the participants—tend not to be stressed or linguistically expressed because they provide no new information. One aspect of a conversation that is always foregrounded is the speaker and that is why the pronoun *I* is either eliminated or unstressed, except in utterances where the *I* is contrastive or the focus of new information. Because of the increased role of shared assumptions in the pragmatic code there is the expectation of fewer personal pronouns because the speakers are foregrounded. The speakers are, of course, foregrounded for syntactic code users also, but personal pronoun usage increases when the speaker or hearer become the focus of the information in the communication. This was very apparent in the study of traditional and independent marital relationships. Various measures of pronoun usage were powerful predictors of membership in one relationship category or the other. The independents clearly communicate more personal meaning. This is essentially an egocentric phenomenon which results from highly individuated relational partners who value flexible roles, change, and novelty.

A very interesting datum component of the syntactic code is the inversion (Green, 1982). The syntactic code is much more grammaticalized than the pragmatic code. It makes heavier use of grammatical morphology and, more interestingly, uses word order to signal semantic relations. Where the pragmatic code uses immediate context and assumed presuppositional background, the syntactic code relies on lexicalization and syntacticization to establish a narrative that is internally coherent. An inversion is simply a construction where the subject follows all or part of the verb phrase. Examples 5, 6, and 7 are inversions of various types:

5. What a fuss he made.
6. Such is the state of the world.
7. At issue is Paragraph 103C of the penal code.

Each of these constructions is a syntacticized expression that alters the rhetorical and communicative function of the utterance. Inversions are an important part of the syntactic code because they are assumed to be deviations from the protosyntax of subject and verb. Givon (1979) has argued that as linguistic mechanisms developed, the basic form of language moved from a topic–comment structure to a subject–predicate structure. All communication is "about" something (topic) and "says something about" the topic (comment). This topic–comment structure has become syntacticized into what we know as the subject–predicate structure. The "I" in, "I will hit the ball," is a grammatical subject, and the "Don" in, "Don will hit the ball," is a topical subject. The grammaticalization of topic into subject means that the language has gained a syntactic coding property that incorporates the subject into the sentence. To invert the subject–predicate order requires planning in order to account for the lexical and constructive choices of a speaker.

One of the more common inversions used in the oral mode is the inversion that takes place after negative adverbs. Samples 8 and 9 are from professors in a faculty meeting talking about students:

8. Rarely have I seen such poor work.
9. Only recently have I begun to understand it.

A second very common inversion is for conditionals as in the following examples:

10. Were I to live life over again, life would be different.
11. Should you change your mind, I will be in at 9 a.m.

Inversions in the oral mode are certainly a bit formal and perhaps pretentious sounding but they are not uncommon. They are characteristic of highly considered forms of discourse in either the oral or written mode. Formal and considered speech is the result anytime that syntax and lexicalization does the "work" of communication. Just as special pragmatic codes characterize some highly group-specific communication, so does the syntactic code. Legal, administrative, bureaucratic, academic, and scientific language all rely on group-specific variations of a syntactic code.

The linguistic and communicative strategies of a specialized syntactic code are typically consistent with the features of a "frozen binding text" (Twining & Miers, 1976, p. 120) and have explicitness, precision, and endurance as their primary functions. Maley's (1987) analysis of legislative language explains how such language and communication constitutes a text of a very special nature. These texts are authorative and assumed to be fixed and canonical. Legislation is a large and important source of information in our society, which affects the life of all citizens, but it is essentially written in a mysterious code that is impenetrable to most people, except for specialized interpreters such as lawyers and public servants. Since the text, and its internal mechanisms, must do the work of meaning in the syntactic code—as opposed to presuppositional knowledge—the language and structure of a particular syntactic code can become quite ponderous. Maley (1987) described how the legislative code is driven by the two goals of explicitness and precision. A written legislative text, for example, must be exhaustive and try to achieve a degree of precision rarely achieved outside math or logic. In the following example from Maley (1987) explicitness derives from the distinctions made and the specifications of members of a class of objects. Such explicitness is more difficult to achieve in the pragmatic code because the role of language in the pragmatic code is more to stimulate extant meaning shared by the language users rather than to specify and establish meaning in an enacted text.

Whosoever—
steels, or destroys or damages with intent to steal the whole, or any part, of any tree, sapling, shrub, or plant, or any underwood, growing in any park, pleasure ground, garden, orchard, or avenue, or in any ground belonging to any dwelling house, where the value of the article, stolen, or the amount of injury done, exceeds two dollars, or steals, or destroys or damages with intent to steal, the whole, or any part, of any tree, sapling, shrub or plant, or any underwood respectively growing elsewhere than in any situation before mentioned, where the value of the article stolen, or the amount of injury done, exceeds ten dollars, shall be liable to be punished as for larceny. (p. 35)

The goal of this text is to minimize ambiguity, which is the reason that repetitive strings of possibilities are used rather than general semantic classes (e.g., "plants"). Precision is of course achieved with technical language (a semantic feature common to particular syntactic codes) but it is also achieved through extratextual means such as numbering, index, and paragraph arrangements of various sorts. Some words like "intent" are vague and cannot be too precise but have the advantage of adaptability to circumstances. Furthermore, the legislative code uses syntactical mechanisms to condense clauses and phrases into participial phrases and nominalizations. Nominalizations can be effective at achieving condensation of space and words. The syntactic code is usually wordier than the pragmatic but there are often practical reasons for condensation. Nominalization is a syntactic device for coding more information into a single word, or noun phrase that substitutes for a verbal construction or a subordinate clause. The sentence *The acceptance of this procedure is a first requirement* is more condensed than the sentence *It is first of all required that you accept the procedure that we propose here.* Nouns can also be placed in the subject position of a sentence and thereby given thematic prominence. Finally, nominalization objectifies the process and allows the legislative text to be treated as something separate from individuals, time, and place. This is an important part of a communicative strategy designed to produce an authorative text that can successfully regulate social conduct.

The legislative code is predominantly communicated in the written mode, but what about a group-specific syntactic code that is essentially orally expressed. Dubois (1985, 1987) has been investigating oral presentations of biomedical research. She has been studying the popularization of science and how information is communicated during the social production of science. Dubois demonstrated how scientists making oral presentations to colleagues use imprecision to background information from other scientists, or contradictory information, and become more precise when discussing their own data. Scientists use hedges, rounding, and numerical ranges for rhetorical effect. One pattern is for listeners to be exposed to a series of hedges and imprecise numerals followed by a clear piece of data, which essentially points to the importance of the number. It is a technique for stressing important information and establishing stress. Such a strategy is more likely in the syntactic code because it requires linguistic resources.

The Oral and Literate Tradition

The pragmatic and syntactic code developed from the oral and literate tradition respectively. This tradition began by establishing the effects of writing on cognitive and social processes and now has implications for education (Olson, 1977), interpersonal relations (Ellis & Hamilton, 1985), media images (Ellis & Armstrong, 1989), the composition process (Flower & Hayes, 1984), cultural tendencies (Havelock, 1986), coherence (Tannen, 1984), and others. The essential argument is that speech and writing have salient characteristics. Thus, speech is informal, spontaneous communication that draws on assumed contextual information and typically involves more interaction involvement on the part of the participants. Writing, on the other hand, gravitates toward explicit lexicalization and internally coherent reference that gives the message an autonomy. Writing is more orderly, explicit, and linguistically complex than speech; it suppresses personal involvement in favor of the ideas in the text. The oral tradition assumed that language and expression "contained" less meaning and were really tools used to stimulate meanings that were already shared by the speaker and hearer. Thus, language from this tradition is composed of loosely connected utterances and formulaic expressions. The oral epics of antiquity were passed on by annexing memorable and poetic phrases to a basic and familiar plot. Sayings, cliches, and proverbs were handy devices for recalling important information.

Thought in the oral tradition is delicately subjective. It uses common language and sayings to create a rhythm between communicators that increases the sense of involvement in the interaction. Truth is based on experience and is quite dependent on interpersonal behaviors. Thought in the literate tradition is analytical and sequential. Truth resides in logical and coherent argument rather than experience. Knowing is logical in the literate tradition, but an achievement through identification with a speaker in the oral tradition.

It is certainly clear from the work in this tradition (oral–literate) that the distinction between the two should not be drawn too sharply. The terms *syntactic* and *pragmatic* capture the essence of each tradition but in no way imply that speakers use one to the exclusion of the other. On the contrary, it is best to consider the oral and literate a continuum in discourse. In the broad sense the pragmatic code emphasizes shared knowledge and interpersonal relationships, while the syntactic code uses words to convey information and content. This gives rise to the "illusion" that language is autonomous—that words carry meaning separate from the people that use them—but, in fact, all language is situated in a context that includes people and relationships to some degree. Brandt (1989) argued very strongly that writing does not make personal involvement less relevant; in fact, involvement is crucial for the writer–reader-relationship or the writing becomes meaningless. Tannen (1985) has given up the terms *oral* and *literate* and replaced them with *involvement focus* and *messages focus*. Involvement focus carries a message of personal rapport and commits the speaker and hearer, or writer and reader, to a personal relationship that evokes meanings that lay in the matrix of the relationship (e.g., traditionals). Message focus emphasizes ideas and content and suppresses involvement with the other.

Oral and literate language use and processing are intertwined in most people and cultures. Just as no individual is either "oral" or "literate," no individual is either "pragmatic" or "syntactic." Rather, people use devices from both in various contexts. Lakoff (1982) and Tannen (1980) have demonstrated how linguistic features of both oral and literate traditions can be found in writing and other cultural contexts. They suggest that it is possible to make the linguistic and cognitive distinction between the two, but both are present in many modes of communication. And, moreover, there is a tendency to assume the superiority of literate forms of expression, but that this tendency is unfounded empirically. There are advantages and disadvantages of each code but no natural superiority of one or the other.

There are two continua that offer the most dramatic distinction between the pragmatic and syntactic codes: These are a *fragmentation–integration* continuum and a *involvement–detachment* continuum (Chafe, 1982). The pragmatic code is, of course, more consonant with the oral tradition and "looks" more like spoken language. The communication in the pragmatic code is produced in spurts and more fragmented because of unexpressed information available from assumptions and contexts. Communication in the pragmatic code is organized by "intonation contours" that are syntactically simple and bounded by pauses. Such contours can be considered "paratones" that are the semantic equivalent in phonology to paragraphs in writing (Brown & Yule, 1983, see chapter 6, pp. 136–137). These contours typically contain a single idea that is contingent on the previous idea. This type of fragmentation reflects the on-line processing and thinking rate of spoken language. This simple syntax is basically a topic–comment structure that finds its way into integrated language in the syntactic code through subject–predicate structures. There are conventions for repre-senting oral language use in written discourse (Lakoff, 1982). Quotation marks, italics, ellipses, and capitalization are all designed to either represent spoken language (e.g., quotation marks), or to emphasize and highlight important infor-mation (e.g., ellipses, capitalization). These are visual cues that function as a sort of suprasegmental that instructs the reader to alter his normal way of under-standing a word or phrase. Following is an example of typical fragmented speech. The example is of a student explaining why he did so poorly on an exam. Note how idea units follow one another without connectives:

12. I studied for the test.
    . . . I studied like . . . 3 or 4 hours.
    I thought I knew it.
    . . . I went home,
    I had dinner,
    . . . I sat at my desk.

The most common coordinating conjunctions are *and, but, so*, and *because*; they are four times as likely to appear in spoken discourse than written (Chafe, 1982), and are characteristic of the pragmatic code. The following example is from the same student when asked about a class he is taking:

13. A—nd it's . . . well . . . a pretty good class.
    . . . you know the the teacher,
    . . . and the other students,
    . . . and the book is okay . . . lots of . . . you know . . . interesting things,
    and you can . . . ya know . . . get extra help . . . and stuff.

Integrated language use is the hallmark of the syntactic code. Here, more information is loaded into idea units by adding additional elements and annexing grammatical morphemes onto lexical units. There are usually more participles, relative clauses, nominalizations, adjectives, and prepositional phrases that serve to integrate information. Examples 14–18 are drawn from the same data set as in Examples 12 and 13 but represent integrated language use that organizes into the syntactic code.

14. He is only concerned with *satisfying* the class requirements. (participle)
15. The book, *which has been recently revised*, is still a problem. (relative clause)
16. These handouts are for your *use*. (nominalization)
17. That *boring* class about did me in. (attributive adjective)
18. The teacher should be aware *of* the potential *of* students *in* the university. (prepositional phrase)

The involvement–detachment continuum represents the extent to which a language user is experientially involved in the communication. More precisely, it indicates the extent to which involvement with the other is communicated. Cegala (1982) and Villaume and Cegala (1988) described interaction involvement as being sensitive to the flow of the conversation and working to ensure that one's feelings and interests are expressed and appreciated. Low-involved communicators are usually unresponsive and detached from the interaction. It is important to distinguish between involvement with another person and involvement in interaction. Cegala's work is concerned with interaction involvement, or the extent to which a communicator cares about and monitors the process; Chafe's (1982) use of the term *involvement* refers to relationships with respective audiences. In this sense, face-to-face communication is far more involved because of experiential richness, and the fact that speakers are in the presence of listeners. Writing is assumed to be fundamentally different because the writer is detached from the reader. The writer is concerned with producing a consistent and understandable text. The reader is less relevant because the interpersonal channel is muted. Brandt (1989) made an insistent and interesting case against this distinction by arguing that writing requires considerable involvement. She demonstrated how written texts attend to the writer–reader relationship through vocabulary and various cohesion devices.

Brandt's argument notwithstanding, there are obvious and intuitive differences between messages that are involving and those that are more distanced. There is a correlation between involvement with others and involvement with the process of communication. A speaker who is concerned about how he or she expresses themselves, and works to guarantee that his or her attitudes are represented in the interaction, is by definition involved. We are concerned with the relationship between the pragmatic code and individuated experience. Involvement, therefore, as expressed in the pragmatic code, is primarily about personalizing, commonplaces, and familiarity. These things can be accomplished by a concern for interaction process, but that is not the fundamental nature of involvement. Oral communication is naturally more involving. Written communication can move somewhat along an involvement continuum but can never duplicate the experiential richness of face-to-face interaction. The pragmatic code contains linguistic signs that promote involvement and while they take on different values depending on mode (oral-written), they are peculiar to involvement nonetheless. Some

TABLE 8.1
Summary of syntactic and pragmatic codes

Feature	Pragmatic Code	Syntactic Code
Meaning	In person, presuppositional	In text
Comprehension	Coherence: Link language to experience, (Top Down)	Cohesion: Internal lexical ties, (Bottom up)
Reasoning	Subjective, organic	Logic
Structure	Paratactic	Hypotactic
Context	High context (Hall, 1984)	Low context (Hall, 1984)
Fragmentation-Integration	Fragmented	Integrated
Involved-Detached	Involved	Detached
Level of Planning	Unplanned	Planned
Oral-literate	Oral-like	Literate-like

of the more typical pragmatic code characteristics that communicate involvement are illustrated below. These include references to interactant's mental processes, which directly taps into participant experiences; first person references that signal individuated experience; intensifying particles that reveal enthusiasm; and attempts to monitor the interaction process such that participants track the flow of information and acknowledge the goals and patterns of the communication.

19. *I* liked it ... *I* mean *I had this feeling* that *I* was really in the story. (representative mental processes and first person references)
20. *I* didn't *think I* did that bad ... *ya know* ... *I* had no idea that *I* was on the wrong track. (first person references, and mental processes)
21. I *just* don't understand ... ya know ... I was *totally* honest. (intensifying particles)
22. Well ... I mean everyone thinks that. That's what we were talking about yesterday. (directs the meaning and flow of interaction)

The linguistic features of the syntactic code are especially useful for communicating detachment from the other. It is particularly easy to be detached in writing because the interpersonal channel is suppressed. Nevertheless, highly skilled authors can certainly succeed in involving a reader through the use of dialogue—which if done properly establishes the perception of the interpersonal channel—and features extracted from the pragmatic code. Detachment most often results from nominalization and the passive voice. Nominalization allows more information to be integrated into a sentence, and also favors more abstract conceptualization because it increases the role of nouns in idea units.

23. Cheating *was observed* on more than one occasion. (passive)

24. The instructor had to give me *authorization* to register for the class. (nominalization)

Table 8.1 summarizes the key cognitive and linguistic characteristics of each code.

Code and Comprehension

The two codes discussed here have important implications for comprehension. Comprehension is the cognitive process whereby individuals build meanings from either sounds in oral communication or visual marks in written communication. Comprehension necessarily involves a number of processes, but my concern is essentially with the construction process, or the way listeners and readers build an interpretation of a sentence or utterance from the words. The two codes as described here imply a social influence on comprehension processes. Research on comprehension concludes that listeners or readers build meanings from constituent parts of utterances or sentences, and they do this on the basis of two broad approaches: The syntactic and the semantic (see Clark & Clark, 1977, chapter 2). In the syntactic approach to constructing interpretations people are assumed to use the surface features of a sentence to identify sounds, words, and phrases and then connect them for an interpretation of the entire sentence. It is a type of bottom-up processing (see chapter 6). In the semantic approach people are assumed to begin with an interpretation (semantic script). This approach starts with the assumption that people communicate for a reason, and that what they are hearing or reading is purposeful, relevant, and appropriate to the context. They then search for sounds, words, and phrases that satisfy the assumptions. It is a type of top-down processing. The goal here is not to discuss or contrast these processes, but to suggest that code usage influences the constructive process. It is surely the case that all listeners and readers use a mixture of the syntactic and semantic approaches, but the question is how much of each do they use and what influences these usage patterns.

The comprehension of language necessarily requires a few different processes. All language, especially oral speech, relies on knowledge and information beyond what is specified in spoken or written text. Communication requires agreement among language users as to phonological, syntactic, semantic, and pragmatic conventions. But these relatively small set of linguistic structures must map onto a very broad and complex array of referential events. Ambiguity and flexibility, as I suggested in the beginning of this chapter are inevitable and organic. Oral communication and the pragmatic code have contexts and paralinguistic cues to help reduce ambiguity. Comprehension in the pragmatic code is assisted by (a) shared knowledge of events, (b) established patterns of interpretation, (c) agreed upon lexical and pragmatic conventions, and (d) shared prosodic conventions. Given the discussion of the pragmatic code in this chapter it is logical to conclude that its comprehension process is essentially semantic. Pragmatic codes that are highly group specific are laden with entering assumptions and interpretive frames. Special code users assimilate language to their knowledge base. Sentences that occur in the appropriate context cue the speaker's or writer's meaning. People are anxious to make sense of a sentence so they work to tie sentences to contexts. The Gricean cooperative principle holds that people assume that a sentence is relevant to the flow of the interaction—so cognitively readers and listeners take the subject matter of a text (typically expressed in noun phrases) and refer it to their interpretations. Consider Examples 1f and 1g (given earlier) of the tattoo enthusiasts:

1f. Jesse: Yea, I am thinkin' bout getting some new ink.
1g. Gene: Where you gonna put it?

A speaker hearing Line 1f expects the next utterance to be relevant and sensible and perhaps refer to decision making and new ink (a phrase the hearer must understand as "getting a new tattoo"). So when Jesse (or a competent bystander) hears Line 1g they look for nouns and verbs that refer to these entities and they find a "question form" (where), "put" (which implies an object, agent, and location for the decision), and "it" (which refers to the noun phrase "new ink"). They must be able to translate "new ink" into "tattoo" in order for it to be sensibly referred to as a single pronoun "it." These semantic strategies enable a listener to eliminate many alternatives and assimilate the language into their existing interpretive frame.

There are situations when semantic processing of a pragmatic code can be especially important in choosing among alternative interpretations. Consider:

25. Bob said that Roger had a keg left over from the party so happy hour is at his house.

Statement 25 is ambiguous because of simple unclear pronoun reference. There is no internal way to tell whether "his" refers to Bob's house or Roger's house. But the context or preceding utterance might make the actual interpretation quite simple. If the preceding utterance were, "I have an announcement from Bob" then the conclusion that happy hour was going to be at Bob's house would be preferred. Or, there could be some prior knowledge about Bob or Roger that would preclude one of them from having the happy hour.

Although all comprehension surely involves some syntactic and some semantic approaches there is a continuum from the general characteristics of the syntactic and pragmatic code to the more group-specified nature of codes. Particular codes such as legislative discourse constructed for specialized interpreters, medical talks, or the in-group interaction of tattoo enthusiasts results from the acquisition of similar concepts from past mutual interaction. And the participants in specialized code interaction share a perspective and a desire to participate in future interaction. This results in a strong degree of conceptual convergence between interactants and stimulates semantic or top-down processing. There is an important difference between knowledge and constructs acquired in mutual group interaction and that acquired either privately or separate from a group. In the latter case the knowledge between one communicator and another is more differentiated and not oriented toward dissipating those differences. Knowledge acquired in group interaction becomes the basis for future interpretation. Communicators are in a state of readiness to understand language in a particular way. When the gap between interactants is wide they have recourse only to the surface features of language to form an interpretation; that is, they use a syntactic or bottom-up method of constructing meaning.

The chances for misunderstanding are increased with the syntactic approach to processing. When communicators can interpret an instance of language on the basis of previous knowledge of the world, they are operating with existing knowledge. Their comprehension resembles the enthymeme process. But when there is a gap between the knowledge represented in language and the knowledge of the speaker or writer, then that person must work hard to construct meaning from text. In these cases conclusions about meaning are more logical in nature and flow more directly from sentences. This is more difficult for most people because they lack experience with situations where the text provides the full and complete information necessary for interpretation. This problem is analogous to the experimental conditions where subjects are known to confuse logical conclusions from conclusions that they simply agree with. Explicit textual meaning is typically thought of as desirable or a goal of communication. But it is desirable only in some circumstances and is often the reason for a "failure of communication."

This failure of communication was demonstrated in the medical context by Tannen and Wallat (1986). Doctors and patients have incongruent interpretive frames for medical language and this produces interaction that is erroneous and unfounded. Tannen and Wallat were surprised at how resilient patient assumptions were about medical information. Because patients do not have the proper interpretive frames for medical language they incorporate much of the information into their existing schemes for understanding. Even after important information was introduced and discussed between the doctors and patients, much of that information was condensed and lost because patients reverted to their own systems of representation. Doctors communicated in a way that required patients to syntactically process information. Doctor language was formulated into a syntactic code and patients were at a loss to construct meaning from such a code because doctors were unaware of the difficult cognitive requirements. Patients therefore reverted to a semantic processing approach, which resulted in erroneous assumptions and associations.

CONCLUSION

I began with the assumption that the human communication system is indeterminate and that individuals must construct their own internal representations of meaning. To do this individual organize cognitive categories into systems of signs called *codes*. Sign relationships are the elements of codes and they organize themselves along an iconicity continuum such that some signs are clear designates of reality and others are very symbolic. These sign relationships represent the fundamental nature of the construction of meaning because information storage, retrieval, and communication is influenced by the extent to which signs are isomorphic with experience. This led to the formulation and elaboration of two code systems termed the pragmatic code and the syntactic code. Each of these general codes can be expressed in highly group specific codes. These codes are an attempt to show that the requirements of language processing are pluralistic; the pragmatic and the syntactic codes are two different ways to structure knowledge. Although it is probably true that some individuals are more reliant on one code or the other, the codes are presented as governed essentially by social requirements. Thus, it was demonstrated that any number of social conditions (group identity, professional or educational groups, etc.) might combine with individual experiences to prompt the use of special codes of one type or the other. The ideas presented here should be helpful in future efforts to fill out the contours of the respective codes, and in the conduct of further investigations into the particular communicative conditions that prompt the development, application, and consequences of communication codes.

Significant portions of the material in this chapter will appear in Donald G. Ellis, "Syntactic and Pragmatic Codes in Communication," *Communication Theory*.

REFERENCES

Adlam D. S., Turner, G., & Lineker, L. (1977). *Code in context*. London: Routledge & Kegan Paul.

Anderson, A., Garrod, S. C., & Sanford, A. J. (1983). The accessibility of pronominal antecedents as a function of episode shifts in narrative text. *Quarterly Journal of Experimental Psychology, 35A*, 427–440.

Applegate, J. L., & Delia, J. G. (1980). Person-centered speech, psychological development, and the contexts of language use. In R. St. Clair & H. Giles (Eds.), *The social and psychological contexts of language* (pp. 245–282). Hillsdale, NJ: Lawrence Erlbaum Associates.

Atkinson, J. M., & Heritage, J. (Eds.). (1984). *Structures of social action: Studies in conversation analysis*. Cambridge: Cambridge University Press.

Austin, J. (1962). *How to do things with words*. New York: Oxford University Press.

Bach, K., & Harnish, R. M. (1979). *Linguistic communication and speech acts*. Cambridge, MA: MIT Press.

Barthes, R. (1967). *Elements of semiology*. (A. Lavers & C. Smith, Trans.). London: Cape.

Barthes, R. (1973). *Mythologies*. (A. Lavers, Trans.). London: Paladin.

Bartlett, F. C. (1932). *Remembering: A study in experimental and social psychology*. Cambridge: Cambridge University Press.

Berger, P. L., & Luckmann, T. (1966). *The social construction of reality*. New York: Doubleday.

Berlin, B. (1971). *Speculations on the growth of ethnobotanical nomenclature* (Language Behavior Research Laboratory Working Paper no. 79). Los Angeles: University of California.

Bernstein, B. (1975). *Class, codes and control* (Vol. 3). London: Routledge & Kegan Paul.

Bernstein, B. (1981). Codes, modalities, and the process of cultural reproduction: A model. *Language in Society*, 10, 327–363.

Bloom, A. H. (1981). *Language development: Form and function in emerging grammars*. Cambridge, MA: MIT Press.

Bloom, A. H. (1981). *The linguistic shaping of thought: A study in the impact on thinking in China and the West*. Hillsdale, NJ: Lawrence Erlbaum Associates.

Bloomfield, L. (1933). *Language*. New York: Henry Holt.

Blumer, H. (1969). *Symbolic interactionism*. Englewood Cliffs, NJ: Prentice-Hall.

Boas, F. (1911). Introduction. In F. Boas (Ed.), *Handbook of American Indian languages* (pp. 1–83). Washington, DC: Smithsonian Institution.

Bolinger, D. (1979). Pronouns in discourse. In T. Givon (Ed.), *Syntax and semantics: Vol. 12. Discourse and syntax* (pp. 289–309). New York: Academic Press.

Bolinger, D. (1984). The inherent iconicity of intonation. In J. Haiman (Ed.), *Iconicity and syntax*. Amsterdam: Benjamins.

Bolton, N. (1977). *Concept formation*. Oxford: Pergamon Press.

Bower, G., & Cirilo, R. K. (1985). Cognitive psychology and text processing. In T. van Dijk (Ed.), *Handbook of discourse analysis* (Vol. 1, pp. 71–105). New York: Academic Press.

Brandt, D. (1989). The message is the massage: Orality and literacy once more. *Written Communication, 6*, 31–44.

Bransford, J. D., & Johnson, M. K. (1973). Consideration of some problems of comprehension. In W. G. Chase (Ed.), *Visual information processing* (pp. 393–427). New York: Academic Press.

Bresnan, J. (1978). A realistic transformational grammar. In M. Halle, J. Bresnan, & G. A. Miller (Eds.), *Linguistic theory and psychological reality* (pp. 1–59). Cambridge, MA: MIT Press.

Brown, G. (1977). *Listening to spoken English*. London: Longman.

Brown, G., & Yule, G. (1983). *Discourse analysis*. Cambridge: Cambridge University Press.

Brown, R. (1979). Reference: In memorial tribute to Eric Lenneberg. *Cognition, 4*, 125–153.

Cappella, J. N. (1991). The biological origins of automated patterns of human interaction. *Communication Theory, 1*, 4–35.

Cassirer, E. (1944). *Essay on man. An introduction to a philosophy of human culture*. New Haven, CT: Yale University Press.

Cassirer, E. (1953–1957). *The philosophy of symbolic forms* (Vols. 1–3). New Haven, CT: Yale University Press.

Cegala, D. J. (1981). Interaction involvement: A cognitive dimension of communication competence. *Communication Education, 30*, 109–121.

Cegala, D. J. (1982). An examination of the concept of interaction involvement using phenomenological and empirical methods. In J. J. Pilotta (Ed.), *Interpersonal communication: Essays in phenomenology and hermeneutics*, Washington, DC: Center for Advanced Research in Phenomenology and University Press of America.

Chafe, W. L. (1970). *Meaning and the structure of language*. Chicago: University of Chicago Press.

Chafe, W. L. (1982). Integration and involvement in speaking, writing, and oral literature. In D. Tannen (Ed.), *Spoken and written language* (pp. 35–53). Norwood, NJ: Ablex.

Chomsky, N. (1957). *Syntactic structures*. The Hague: Mouton.

Chomsky, N. (1965). *Aspects of a theory of syntax*. Cambridge, MA: MIT Press.

Chomsky, N. (1966). *Cartesian linguistics*. New York: Harper & Row.

Chomsky, N. (1971). Deep structure, surface structure, and semantic interpretation. In D. D. Steinberg & L. A. Jakobovits (Eds.), *Semantics* (pp. 183–216). London, England: Cambridge University Press.

Chomsky, N. (1975). *Reflections on language*. New York: Pantheon.

Cicourel, A. (1973). *Cognitive sociology: Language and meaning in social interaction*. London: Cox & Wyman.

Clark, H. H. (1969). Linguistic processes in deductive reasoning. *Psychological Review, 76*, 387–404.

Clark, H. H., & Clark, E. V. (1968). Semantic distinctions and memory for complex sentences. *Quarterly Journal of Experimental Psychology, 20*, 129–138.

Clark, H. H., & Clark, E. V. (1977). *Psychology and language*. New York: Harcourt Brace & Janovich.

Clark, H. H., & French, J. W. (1981). Telephone goodbyes. *Language in Society, 10*, 1–19.

Clark, H. H., & Haviland, S. E. (1977). Comprehension and the given-new contract. In R. O. Freedle (Ed.), *Discourse production and comprehension* (pp. 1–40). Norwood, NJ: Ablex.

Collins, A. M., & Loftus, E. F. (1975). A spreading-activation theory of semantic processing. *Psychological Review, 82*, 407–428.

Collins, A. M., & Quillian, M. R. (1969). Retrieval time from semantic memory. *Journal of Verbal Learning and Verbal Behavior, 8*, 240–247.

Coulthard, M. (1985). *An introduction to discourse analysis.* New York: Longman.

Coulthard, M., & Brazil, D. (1981). Exchange structure. In R. M. Coulthard & M. M. Montgomery (Eds.), *Studies in discourse analysis.* London: Routledge & Kegan Paul.

Coulthard, R. M., & Montgomery, M. M. (Eds.). (1981). *Studies in discourse analysis.* London: Routledge & Kegan Paul.

Craig, R. T. (1986). Goals in discourse. In D. G. Ellis & W. A. Donohue (Eds.), *Contemporary issues in language and discourse processes* (pp. 257–273). Hillsdale, NJ: Lawrence Erlbaum Associates.

Danes, F. (Ed.). (1974). *Papers on functional sentence perspective.* The Hague: Mouton.

Darwin, C. (1899). *The descent of man.* New York.

de Beaugrande, R., & Dressler, W. U. (1981). *Introduction to text linguistics.* London: Longman.

de Saussure, F. (1959). *Course in general linguistics.* Trans. Wade Baskin. New York: Philosophical Library.

De Stefano, J. (1984). Learning to communicate in the classroom. In A. Pellegrini & T. Yawkey (Eds.), *Advances in discourse processes: Vol. 13. The development of oral and written language in social contexts* (pp. 137–163). Norwood, NJ: Ablex.

Delia, J. G., O'Keefe, B. J., & O'Keefe, D. J. (1982). The constructivist approach to communication. In F. E. X. Dance (Ed.), *Human communication theory: Comparative essays* (pp. 147–191). New York: Harper & Row.

Dubois, B. L. (1981). "Something on the order of around forty to forty-four": Impressive numerical expression in biomedical slide talks. *Language in Society, 16*, 527–541.

Dubois, B. L. (1985). Popularization at the highest level. Poster sessions at biomedical meetings. *International Journal of the Sociology of Language, 56*, 67–85.

Dummett, M. (1976). What is a theory of meaning? (II). In G. Evans & J. McDowell (Eds.), *Truth and meaning* (pp. 67–137). Oxford: Clarendon Press.

Duncan, S. (1973). Toward a grammar for dyadic conversation. *Semiotica, 9*, 29–46.

Duncan, S. (1974). On the structure of speaker-auditor interaction during speaking turns. *Language in Society, 3*, 161–180.

Eco, U. (1976). *A theory of semiotics.* Bloomington: Indiana University Press.

Edmondson, W. J. (1981). Illocutionary verbs, illocutionary acts, and conversational behavior. In H. Eikmeyer & H. Reiser (Eds.), *Words, worlds, and contexts* (pp. 171–186). Berlin: Walter de Gruyter.

Ellis, D. G., & Armstrong, G. B. (1989). Social class, sex, and linguistic code structure on prime-time television. *Communication Quarterly, 37*, 157–169.

Ellis, D. G., & Hamilton, M. (1985). Syntactic and pragmatic code usage in interpersonal communication. *Communication Monographs, 52*, 264–279.

Ellis, D. G., Hamilton, M., & Aho, L. (1983). Some issues in conversation coherence. *Human Communication Research, 9*, 267–282.

Fillmore, C. J. (1968). The case for case. In E. Bach & R. T. Harms (Eds.), *Universals in linguistic theory* (pp. 1–88). New York: Holt, Rinehart & Winston.

Fisher, B. A., & Hawes, L. C. (1971). An interact system model: Generating a grounded theory of small groups. *Quarterly Journal of Speech, 57*, 444–453.

Fitzpatrick, M. A., & Indvik, J. (1982). The instrumental and expressive domains of marital communication. *Human Communication Research, 8*, 195–213.

Flower, L., & Hayes, J. R. (1984). Images, plans, and prose: The representation of meaning in writing. *Written Communication, 1*, 120–160.

Fodor, J. A. (1965). Could meaning be an r_m? *Journal of Verbal Learning and Verbal Behavior, 4*, 73–81.

Fodor, J. A., & Garrett, M. F. (1966). Some reflections on competence and performance. In J. Lyons & R. J. Wales (Eds.), *Psycholinguistic papers* (pp. 135–154). Edinburgh: Edinburgh Press.

Fodor, J. A., & Garrett, M. F. (1967). Some syntactic determinants of sentential complexity. *Perception and Psychophysics, 2*, 289–296.

Fodor, J. A., Garrett, M., & Bever, T. G. (1968). Some syntactic determinants of sentential complexity. II: Verb structure. *Perception and Psychophysics, 3*, 453–461.

Fodor, J. A., Bever, T. G., & Garrett, M. F. (1974). *The psychology of language: An introduction to psycholinguistics and generative grammar.* New York: McGraw-Hill.

Fodor, J. D., Fodor, J. A., & Garrett, M. F. (1975). The psychological unreality of semantic representations. *Linguistic Inquiry, 6*, 515–531.

Forster, K. I. (1976). Accessing the mental lexicon. In R. J. Wales & E. C. T. Walker (Eds.), *New approaches to language mechanisms* (pp. 465–495). Amsterdam: North Holland.

Forster, K. I. (1979). Levels of processing and the structure of the language processor. In W. E. Cooper & E. C. T. Walker (Eds.), *Sentence processing: psycholinguistic studies presented to Merrill Garrett* (pp. 21–53). Hillsdale, NJ: Lawrence Erlbaum Associates.

Fox, A. (1983). Topic continuity in biblical Hebrew. In T. Givon (Ed.). (1983). *Topic continuity in discourse: Quantified cross-language studies.* Amsterdam: J. Benjamins.

Frazier, L., & Fodor, J. D. (1978). The sausage machine: A new two-stage parsing model. *Cognition, 6*, 291–325.

Freedle, R. O. (Ed.). (1977). *Discourse production and comprehension.* Norwood, NJ: Ablex.

Frege, G. (1972). Conceptual notation: A formula language of pure thought modelled upon the formula language of arithmetic. In T. W. Bynum (Ed. and Trans.), *Conceptual language and related articles.* Oxford: Oxford University Press. (Original work published 1879).

Fries, C. (1964). *Linguistics and reading.* New York: Holt, Rinehart & Winston.

Gardner, H. (1985). *Frames of mind.* New York: Basic Books.

Garfinkel, H. (1967). *Studies in ethnomethodology.* Englewood Cliffs, NJ: Prentice-Hall.

Garnham, A. (1983). Why psycholinguistics don't care about DTC: A reply to Berwick and Weinberg. *Cognition, 10*, 341–349.

Garnham, A., Oakhill, J. V., & Johnson-Laird, P. N. (1982). Referential continuity and the coherence of discourse. *Cognition, 11*, 29–46.

Gazdar, G. J. M. (1979). *Pragmatics: Implicature, presupposition, and logical form.* New York: Academic Press.

Gazdar, G. J. M. (1981). Speech act assignment. In A. K. Joshi, B. L. Webber, & I. A. Sag (Eds.), *Elements of discourse understanding* (pp. 21–96). Cambridge: Cambridge University Press.

Geertz, C. (1972). *The interpretation of cultures.* New York: Basic Books.

Givon, T. (1979). From discourse to syntax: Grammar as a processing strategy. In T. Givon (Ed.), *Syntax and semantics* (Vol. 12, pp. 81–112). New York: Academic Press.

Givon, T. (1989). *Mind, code and context.* Hillsdale, NJ: Lawrence Erlbaum Associates.

Goffman, E. (1971). *Relations in public.* Harmondsworth: Penguin.

Goffman, E. (1974). *Frame analysis.* New York: Harper & Row.

Gough, P. B. (1965). Grammatical transformations and speed of understanding. *Journal of Verbal Learning and Verbal Behavior, 4*, 107–111.

Green, G. M. (1982). Colloquial and literary uses of inversions. In D. Tannen (Ed.), *Spoken and written language*, Norwood, NJ: Ablex.

Greimas, A. J. (1970). *Sign, language, culture.* The Hague: Mouton.

Grice, H. P. (1975). Logic and conversation. In P. Cole & J. L. Morgan (Eds.), *Syntax and semantics 3: Speech acts* (pp. 46–58). New York: Seminar Press.

Grice, H. P. (1978). Further notes on logic and conversation. In P. Cole (Ed.), *Syntax and semantics 9: Pragmatics.* New York: Academic Press.

Gulich, E., & Quasthoff, U. M. (1985). Narrative analysis. In T. van Dijk (Ed.), *Handbook of discourse analysis* (Vol. 2, pp. 169–197). New York: Academic Press.

Hakes, D. T. (1971). Does verb structure affect sentence comprehension? *Perception and Psychophysics, 10*, 229–232.

Hall, E. T. (1984). *The dance of life*. Garden City, NY: Doubleday.

Halliday, M. A. K. (1978). *Language as social semiotic*. London: Edward Arnold Press.

Halliday, M. A. K., & Hasan, R. (1976). *Cohesion in English*. London: Longman.

Havelock, E. A. (1986). Orality, literacy, and star wars. *Written Communication, 3*, 411–420.

Henderson, L. (1982). *Orthography and word recognition in reading*. London: Academic Press.

Heritage, J. (1984). A change-of-state token and aspects of its sequential placement. In J. M. Atkinson & J. Heritage (Eds.), *Structures of social interaction* (pp. 299–345). Cambridge: Cambridge University Press.

Hirsch, E. D. (1987). *Cultural literacy*. Boston: Houghton Mifflin.

Hjelmslev, L. (1961). *Prologomena to a theory of language*. Madison, WI: University of Wisconsin Press.

Hobbs, J. R. (1982). Towards an understanding of coherence in discourse. In W. D. Lehnert & M. H. Ringle (Eds.), *Strategies for natural language processing* (pp. 171–197). Hillsdale, NJ: Lawrence Erlbaum Associates.

Holmes, V. M., & Forster, K. I. (1972). Perceptual complexity and understanding sentence structure. *Journal of Verbal Learning and Verbal Behavior, 11*, 148–156.

Hopper, R. (1989). Sequential ambiguity in telephone openings: 'What are you doin.' *Communication Monographs, 56*, 240–252.

Hymes, D. (1974). *Foundations in sociolinguistics*. Philadelphia: University of Pennsylvania Press.

Jacobs, S., & Jackson, S. (1983). Speech act structure in conversation: Rational aspects of pragmatic coherence. In R. T. Craig & K. Tracy (Eds.), *Conversational coherence: Form structure and strategy*. Beverly Hills, CA: Sage.

Jakobson, R. (1962). *Selected writings I: Phonological studies*. The Hague: Mouton.

Jefferson, G. (1972). Side sequences. In D. Sudnow (Ed.), *Studies in social interaction* (pp. 294–338). New York: The Free Press.

Jefferson, G. (1978). Sequential aspects of storytelling in conversation. In J. Schenkein (Ed.), *Studies in the organization of conversational interaction* (pp. 219–248). New York: Academic Press.

Jespersen, O. (1922). *Language: Its nature, development and origin*. London: Allen & Unwin.

Johnston, J. R. (1985). The discourse symptoms of developmental disorders. In T. van Dijk (Ed.), *Handbook of discourse analysis* (Vol. 3, pp. 79–93). New York: Academic Press.

Johnson-Laird, P. N. (1969). On understanding logically complex sentences. *Quarterly Journal of Experimental Psychology, 21*, 1–13.

Johnson-Laird, P. N. (1983). *Mental models: Towards a cognitive science of language, inference, and consciousness*. Cambridge: Cambridge University Press.

Kasher, A. (1985). Philosophy and discourse analysis. In T. van Dijk (Ed.), *Handbook of discourse analysis* (Vol. 1, pp. 231–248). New York: Academic Press.

Katz, J. J. (1977). *Propositional structure and Illocutionary force*. New York: Crowell.

Katz, J. J., & Fodor, J. A. (1963). The structure of a semantic theory. *Language, 39*, 170–210.

Kaufer, D. (1979). The competence/performance distinction in linguistic theory. *Philosophy of the Social Sciences, 9*, 257–275.

Kellermann, K., Broetzmann, S., Lim, T.-S., & Kitao, K. (1989). The conversation MOP: Scenes in the stream of discourse. *Discourse Processes, 12*, 27–61.

Kellermann, K. (1991). The conversation MOP: II. Progression through scenes in discourse. *Human Communication Research, 17*, 385–414.

Kimball, J. (1973). Seven principles of surface structure parsing in natural language. *Cognition, 2*, 15–47.

Kintsch, W. (1985). Text processing: A psychological model. In T. van Dijk (Ed.), *Handbook of discourse analysis* (Vol. 2, pp. 231–243). New York: Academic Press.

Kintsch, W., & Greene, E. (1978). The role of culture-specific schemata in the comprehension of recall of stories. *Discourse Processes, 1*, 1–13.

Kleiman, G. M. (1975). Speech recoding in reading. *Journal of Verbal Learning and Verbal Behavior, 14*, 323–339.

Knapp, M. L., Hart, R. P., Friederich, G. W., & Shulman, G. M. (1973). The rhetoric of goodbye: Verbal and nonverbal correlates of human leave-taking. *Speech Monographs, 40*, 182–198.

Kreckel, M. (1981). *Communicative acts and shared knowledge in natural discourse.* New York: Academic Press.

Kripke, S. A. (1963). Semantical considerations on modal logic. *Acta Philosophica Fennica, 16*, 323–339.

Krivonos, P. D., & Knapp, M. L. (1975). Initiating communication: What do you say when you say hello? *Central States Speech Journal, 26*, 115–125.

Labov, W., & Fanshel, D. (1977). *Therapeutic discourse.* New York: Academic Press.

Lakoff, G. (1968). Instrumental adverbs and the concept of deep structure. *Foundations of Language, 4*, 4–29.

Lakoff, G. (1971). Presupposition and relative well-formedness. In D. D. Steinberg & L. A. Jakobovits (Eds.), *Semantics* (pp. 328–340). Cambridge: Cambridge University Press.

Lakoff, G. P. (1972). Structural complexity in family tales. *The Study of Man, 1*, 128–190.

Lakoff, R. L. (1982). Some of my favorite writers are literate: The mingling of oral and literate strategies in written communication. In D. Tannen (Ed.), *Spoken and written language* (pp. 239–260). Norwook, NJ: Ablex.

Langacker, R. W. (1973). *Language and its structure: Some fundamental linguistic concepts.* New York: Harcourt, Brace & World.

Langer, S. (1942). *Philosophy in a new key: A study in the symbolism of reason, rite, and art.* Cambridge, MA: Harvord University Press.

Levinson, S. C. (1981). Some pre-observations on the modelling of dialogue. *Discourse Processes, 4*, 93–110.

Levinson, S. C. (1983). *Pragmatics.* Cambridge: Cambridge University Press.

Liles, B. L. (1971). *An introductory transformational grammar.* New York: Prentice-Hall.

Longacre, R. E. (1979). The paragraph as a grammatical unit. In T. Givon (Ed.), *Syntax and semantics volume 12: Discourse and syntax* (pp. 115–134). New York: Academic Press.

Lyons, J. (1969). *Introduction to theoretical linguistics.* Cambridge: Cambridge University Press.

Maley, Y. (1987). The language of legislation. *Language in Society, 16*, 25–48.

Manning, R. A. (1980). Notes on the visual differential theory. *Visible Language, 13*, 410–427.

Marslen-Wilson, W. D., & Tyler, L. K. (1980). The temporal structure of spoken language understanding. *Cognition, 8*, 1–71.

McCawley, J. D. (1968). The role of semantics in grammar. In E. Bach & R. T. Harms (Eds.), *Universals in linguistic theory* (pp. 124–169). New York: Holt, Rinehart & Winston.

McClelland, J. L., & Rumelhart, D. E. (1981). An interactive model of context effects in letter perception. Part 1: An account of basic findings. *Psychological Review, 88*, 375–407.

McGurk, H., & MacDonald, J. (1976). Hearing lips and seeing voices. *Nature, 264*, 746–748.

McKoon, G., & Ratcliff, R. (1980). The comprehension processes and memory structures involved in anaphoric reference. *Journal of Verbal Learning and Verbal Behavior, 19*, 668–682.

McNeill, D., & McNeill, N. B. (1968). What does a child mean when he says "no"? In E. M. Zale (Ed.), *Language and Language Behavior* (pp. 51–62). New York: Appleton-Century-Crofts.

Meyer, D. E. & Schvaneveldt, R. W. (1971). Facilitation in recognizing pairs of words: Evidence of a dependence between retrieval operations. *Journal of Experimental Psychology, 90*, 227–235.

Meyer, D. E., Schvaneveldt, R. W., & Ruddy, M. G. (1974). Functions of graphemic and phonemic codes in visual word recognition. *Memory and Cognition, 2*, 309–321.

Miller, G. A. (1953). What is information measurement? *American Psychologist, 8*, 3–11.

Miller, G. A., & McKean, K. E. (1964). A chronometric study of some relations between sentences. *Quarterly Journal of Experimental Psychology, 16*, 297–308.

Morris, C. (1938). *Foundations of the theory of signs.* Chicago, IL: Chicago University Press.

Morris, C. (1971). *Writings on the general theory of signs.* The Hague: Mouton.

Morton, J. (1970). A functional model for memory. In D. A. Norman (Ed.), *Models of human memory* (pp. 91–121). New York: Academic Press.

Mosenthal, J. M., & Tierney, R. J. (1984). Cohesion: Problems with talking about text. *Reading Research Quarterly, 19*, 240–244.

Mowrer, O. H. (1954). The psychologist looks at language. *American Psychologist, 9*, 660–694.

Murphy, G. L. (1985). Psychological explanations of deep and surface anaphora. *Journal of Pragmatics, 9*, 785–813.

Nofsinger, R. E. (1975). The demand ticket: A conversational device for getting the floor. *Speech Monographs, 42*, 1–9.

Norris, D. G. (1982). Autonomous processes in comprehension: A reply to Marslen-Wilson and Tyler. *Cognition, 11*, 97–101.

Olson, D. R. (1970a). *Cognitive development*. New York: Academic Press.

Olson, D. R. (1970b). Language and thought: Aspects of a theory of semantics. *Psychological Review, 77*, 257–273.

Olson, D. R. (1977). From utterance to text: The bias of language in speech and writing. *Harvard Educational Review, 47*, 257–281.

Osgood, C. E., Suci, G. J., & Tannenbaum, P. H. (1957). *The measurement of meaning*. Urbana, IL: University of Illinois Press.

Piaget, J. (1947). *The psychology of intelligence*. London: Routledge & Kegan Paul.

Piaget, J. (1950). *The language and thought of the child*. London: Routledge & Kegan Paul.

Planalp, S., Graham, M., & Paulson, L. (1987). Cohesive devices in conversation. *Communication Monographs, 54*, 325–343.

Planalp, S., & Tracy, K. (1980). Not to change the topic but . . . : A cognitive approach to the study of conversation. In D. Nimmo (Ed.), *Communication yearbook 4* (pp. 237–258). New Brunswick, NJ: Transaction.

Pomerantz, A. (1978). Compliment responses: Notes on the co-operation of multiple constraints. In J. Schenkein (Ed.), *Studies in the organization of conversational interaction* (pp. 79–112). New York: Academic Press.

Pomerantz, A. (1984). Agreeing and disagreeing with assessments: some features of preferred/dispreferred turn shapes. In J. M. Atkinson & J. Heritage (Eds.), *Structures of social interaction* (pp. 57–101). Cambridge: Cambridge University Press.

Posner, R. (1980). Semantics and pragmatics of sentence connectives in natural language. In J. Searle, F. Kiefer, & M. Bierwisch (Eds.), *Speech act theory and pragmatics* (pp. 169–204). Dordeecht: Reidel.

Quillian, M. R. (1968). Semantic memory. In M. Minsky (Ed.), *Semantic information processing* (pp. 115–134). Cambridge, MA: MIT Press.

Quirk, R., & Greenbaum, S. (1973). *A university grammar of English*. London: Longman.

Raskin, V. (1978). Presuppositional analysis of Russian, 1: Six essays on aspects of presupposition. In V. Raskin & D. Segal (Eds.), *Slavica hierosolymitana* (Vol. 2, pp. 51–92). Jerusalem: Magnes.

Raskin, V. (1981). Script-based lexicon. *Quaderni di Semantica, 2*, 25–34.

Raskin, V. (1985). *Semantic mechanisms of humor*. Dordrecht: Reidel.

Raskin, V. (1986). Script-based semantic theory. In D. G. Ellis & W. A. Donohue (Eds.), *Contemporary issues in language and discourse processes* (pp. 23–61). Hillsdale, NJ: Lawrence Erlbaum Associates.

Reichman, R. (1978). Conversational coherency. *Cognitive Science, 2*, 283–327.

Rips, L. J., Shoben, E. J., & Smith, E. E. (1973). Semantic distance and the verification of semantic relations. *Journal of Verbal Learning and Verbal Behavior, 12*, 1–20.

Robbins, R. H. (1967). *A short history of linguistics*. Bloomington: Indiana University Press.

Rochester, S. R., & Martin, J. R. (1979). *Crazy talk: A study of the discourse of schizophrenic speakers*. New York: Plenum Press.

Rosaldo, M. (1982). The things we do with words: Ilongot speech acts and speech act theory in philosophy. *Language in Society, 11*, 203–237.

Rosch, E. (1977). Human categorization. In N. Warren (Ed.), *Advances in cross-cultural psychology* (pp. 63–97). New York: Academic Press.

Rosch, E., Mervis, C. B., Gray, W., Johnson, D., & Boyes-Braem, P. (1976). Basic objects in natural categories. *Cognitive psychology, 8,* 382–439.

Rubenstein, H., Lewis, S. S., & Rubenstein, M. A. (1971). Evidence for phonemic recoding in visual word recognition. *Journal of Verbal Learning and Verbal Behavior, 10,* 645–657.

Rumelhart, D. (1975). Notes on a schema for stories. In D. G. Bobrow & A. Collins (Eds.), *Representation and understanding* (pp. 211–236). New York: Academic Press.

Rumelhart, D. E. (1980). Schemata: The building blocks of cognition. In R. J. Spiro, B. C. Bruce, & W. F. Brewer (Eds.), *Theoretical issues in reading comprehension: Perspectives from cognitive psychology, linguistics, artificial intelligence* (pp. 61–83). Hillsdale, NJ: Lawrence Erlbaum Associates.

Rumelhart, D. E., & McClelland, J. L. (1982). An interactive model of context effects in letter perception. Part 2: The perceptual enhancement effect and some tests and extensions of the model. *Psychological Review, 89,* 60–94.

Sachs, J. S. (1967). Recognition memory for syntactic and semantic aspects of connected discourse. *Perception and Psychophysics, 2,* 437–442.

Sacks, H. (1973). Lectures at summer linguistic institute. University of Michigan: Ann Arbor.

Sacks, H. Schegloff, E. A., & Jefferson, G. (1974). A simplest systematics for the organization of turn-taking for conversation. *Language, 50,* 696–735.

Sadock, J. (1974). *Toward a linguistic theory of speech acts.* New York: Academic Press.

Sag, I., & Hankamer, J. (1984). Toward a theory of anaphoric processing. *Linguistics and Philosophy, 7,* 325–345.

Sanders, C. R. (1988). Marks of mischief: Becoming and being tattooed. *Journal of Contemporary Ethnography, 16,* 395–432.

Sanders, R. E. (1981). The interpretation of discourse. *Communication Quarterly, 29,* 209–217.

Sanders, R. E. (1984). Style, meaning, and message effects. *Communication Monographs, 51,* 154–167.

Sanders, R. E. (1986). Tools for cohering discourse and their strategic utilization: Markers of structural connections and meaning relations. In R. T. Craig & K. Tracy (Eds.), *Conversational coherence* (pp. 67–80). Beverly Hills, CA: Sage.

Sanders, R. E. (1987). *Cognitive fundations of calculated speech.* Albany: State University of New York Press.

Sanford, A. J., & Garrod, S. C. (1981). *Understanding written language: Explorations in comprehension beyond the sentence.* Chichester: Wiley.

Sapir, E. (1921). *Language.* New York: Harcourt, Brace.

Schank, R. C. (1973). Identification of conceptualizations underlying natural language. In R. C. Schank & K. M. Colby (Eds.), *Computer models of thought and language* (pp. 16–39). San Francisco: Freeman.

Schank, R. C., & Ableson, R. (1977). *Scripts, plans, goals, and understanding.* Hillsdale, NJ: Lawrence Erlbaum Associates.

Schank, R. C., & Burstein, M. (1985). Artificial intelligence: Modeling memory for language understanding. In T. van Dijk (Ed.), *Handbook of discourse analysis* (Vol. 1, pp. 145–166). New York: Academic Press.

Schegloff, E. A. (1968). Sequencing in conversational openings. *American Anthropologist, 70,* 1075–1095.

Schegloff, E. A. (1972a). Notes on a conversational practice: Formulating place. In D. Sudnow (Ed.), *Studies in social interaction* (pp. 75–119). New York: The Free Press.

Schegloff, E. A. (1972b). Sequencing in conversational openings. In J. Gumperz & D. Hymes (Eds.), *Directions in sociolinguistics* (pp. 346–380). New York: Holt, Rinehart & Winston.

Schegloff, E. A., & Sacks, H. (1973). Opening up closings. *Semiotica, 8,* 289–327.

Schiffrin, D. (1977). Opening encounters. *American Sociological Review, 42,* 679–691.

Schneider, K. P. (1988). *Small talk: Analyzing phatic discourse.* Marburg: Hitzeroth.

Scribner, S., & Cole, M. (1981). *The psychology of literacy.* Cambridge, MA: Harvard University Press.

Searle, J. R. (1969). *Speech acts: An essay in the philosophy of language.* London: Cambridge University Press.

Searle, J. R. (1974). Chomsky's revolution in linguistics. In G. Harman (Ed.), *On Noam Chomsky: Critical essays* (pp. 2–33). New York: Anchor Books.

Searle, J. R. (1975). Indirect speech acts. In P. Cole & J. Morgan (Eds.), *Syntax and semantics 3: Speech acts* (pp. 59–82). New York: Academic Press.

Sebeok, T. A. (1969). *Approaches to semiotics.* The Hague: Mouton.

Sigman, S. (1987). *A perspective on social communication.* Lexington, MA: D.C. Heath.

Sillars, M. O. (1964). Rhetoric as act. *Quarterly Journal of Speech, 50,* 277–284.

Sinclair, J. M., & Coulthard, R. M. (1975). *Towards an analysis of discourse.* Oxford University Press.

Skinner, B. F. (1957). *Verbal behavior.* New York: Appleton-Century-Crofts.

Slobin, D. (1966). Grammatical transformations in childhood and adulthood. *Journal of Verbal Learning and Verbal Behavior, 5,* 219–227.

Slobin, D. (1971). *Psycholinguistics.* Glenview, IL: Scott Foresman.

Snider, J. G., & Osgood, C. E. (1969). *Semantic differential technique: A sourcebook.* Chicago: Aldine.

Stam, J. H. (1976). *Inquiries into the origin of language.* New York: Harper & Row.

Stanners, R. F., & Forbach, G. B. (1973). Analysis of letter strings in word recognition. *Journal of Experimental Psychology, 98,* 31–35.

Stanovich, K. E., & West, R. F. (1983). On priming by a sentence context. *Journal of Experimental Psychology: General, 112,* 1–36.

Strawson, P. F. (1950). On referring. *Mind, 59,* 320–344.

Stubbs, M. (1983). *Discourse analysis.* Chicago, IL: University of Chicago Press.

Sutherland, N. S. (1966). Discussion of 'Some reflections on competence and performance' by J. A. Fodor and M. F. Garrett. In J. Lyons & R. J. Wales (Eds.), *Psycholinguistic papers* (pp. 126–141). Edinburgh: Edinburgh University Press.

Swadesh, M. (1971). *The origin and diversification of language.* Chicago: Aldine.

Tabossi, P., & Johnson-Laird, P. N. (1980). Linguistic context and the priming of semantic information. *Quarterly Journal of Experimental Psychology, 34A,* 79–90.

Tannen, D. (1980). A comparative analysis of oral narrative strategies. Athenian Greek and American English. In W. Chafe (Ed.), *The pear stories* (pp. 51–87). Norwood, NJ: Ablex.

Tannen, D. (Ed.). (1984). *Coherence in spoken and written discourse.* Norwood, NJ: Ablex.

Tannen, D. (1985). Relative focus on involvement in oral and written discourse. In D. R. Olson, N. Torrance, & A. Hildyard (Eds.), *Literacy, language, and learning: The nature and consequences of reading and writing* (pp. 146–167). New York: Cambridge University Press.

Tannen, D., & Wallat, C. (1986). Medical professionals and parents: A linguistic analysis of communication across contexts. *Language in Society, 15,* 295–312.

Thomas, S. (1980). Some problems of the paradigm in communication theory. *Philosophy of Social Sciences, 10,* 427–444.

Thorndyke, P. W. (1977). Cognitive structures in comprehension and memory of narrative discourse. *Cognitive Psychology, 9,* 77–110.

Tracy, K. (1982). On getting the point: Distinguishing "issues" from "events," an aspect of conversational coherence. In M. Burgoon (Ed.), *Comunication yearbook 5* (pp. 279–301). New Brunswick, NJ: Transaction.

Tracy, K. (1983). The issue-event distinction: A rule of conversation and its scope condition. *Human Communication Research, 9,* 320–334.

Tracy, K. (1984). The effect of multiple goals on conversational relevance and topic shift. *Communication Monographs, 51,* 274–287.

Twining, W., & Miers, D. (1976). *How to do things with rules.* London: Weidenfeld & Nicholson.

Tyler, L. K., & Marslen-Wilson, W. D. (1982). The resolution of discourse anaphora: Some on-line studies. *Text, 2,* 263–291.

van Dijk, T. A. (1980). *Macrostructures*. Hillsdale, NJ: Lawrence Erlbaum Associates.

van Dijk, T. A. (1985). Semantic discourse analysis. In T. A. van Dijk (Ed.), *Handbook of discourse analysis* (Vol. 2, pp. 103–136). London: Academic Press.

van Dijk, T. A. (1987). *Communicating racism*. Newbury Park, CA: Sage.

van Dijk, T. A. (1988). *News as discourse*. Hillsdale, NJ: Lawrence Erlbaum Associates.

van Dijk, T. A., & Kintsch, W. (1983). *Strategies of discourse comprehension*. New York: Academic Press.

Venneman, T. (1975). Topic, sentence accent, and ellipsis: A proposal for their formal treatment. In E. L. Keenan (Ed.), *Formal semantics of natural language* (pp. 151–161). Cambridge: Cambridge University Press.

Ventola, E. (1987). *The structure of social interaction: A systematic approach to the semiotics of service encounters*. London: Francis Pinter.

Villaume, W. A., & Cegala, D. J. (1988). Interaction involvement and discourse strategies: The patterned use of cohesive devices in conversation. *Communication Monographs, 55*, 22–40.

Vygotsky, L. S. (1965). *Thought and language*. Cambridge, MA: MIT Press.

Wanner, E., & Maratsos, M. P. (1978). An ATN approach to comprehension. In M. Halle, J. W. Bresnan, & G. A. Miller (Eds.), *Linguistic Theory and Psychological Reality* (pp. 193–213). Cambridge, MA: MIT Press.

Whorf, B. L. (1956). Languages and logic. In J. B. Carroll (Ed.), *Language, thought and reality: Selected writings* (pp. 39–54). Cambridge: MIT Press.

Wilensky, R. (1981). PAM. In R. C. Schank & C. K. Reisbeck (Eds.), *Inside computer understanding: Five programs plus miniatures* (pp. 136–179). Hillsdale, NJ: Lawrence Erlbaum Associates.

Winograd, T. (1972). Understanding natural language. *Cognitive Psychology, 3*, 1–191.

Wish, M. D., D'Andrade, R. G., & Goodnow, J. E., II (1980). Dimensions of interpersonal communication: Correspondences between structures for speech acts and bipolar scales. *Journal of Personality and Social Psychology, 39*, 848–860.

Author Index

217

Subject Index

223